Foreign trade in a planned economy

# Foreign trade in a planned economy

edited by the late IMRE VAJDA
*formerly President of the Hungarian Economic Association*
and Professor MIHÁLY SIMAI
*University of Economics, Budapest*

CAMBRIDGE
at the University Press 1971

Published by the Syndics of the Cambridge University Press
Bentley House, 200 Euston Road, London NW1 2DB
American Branch: 32 East 57th Street, New York, N.Y.10022

© Cambridge University Press 1971

Library of Congress Catalogue Card Number: 74-149433

ISBN: 0 521 08153 X

Printed in Great Britain
at the University Printing House, Cambridge
(Brooke Crutchley, University Printer)

# Contents

# Note by Professor Mihály Simai

The better understanding of the planning system, management and economic problems is a key factor in international co-operation. The late Professor Imre Vajda, by initiating this book, hoped to promote not only trade flows but also the exchange of views and ideas. He wanted to encourage scholars from different countries to discuss some of the vital issues of economic relations between East and West. This volume should serve as a basis for such discussion.

# Preface

The purpose of these essays is to give the reader an opportunity to explore the scope of Hungarian economic research on the problems of foreign trade and the international division of labour. They may also contribute to other scientific and practical knowledge in a field of study which has assumed unparalleled importance in the second half of the twentieth century.

International economic co-operation is as important now as were the inflow of gold and silver from the Americas to the trading nations of Europe in the sixteenth and seventeenth centuries, the riches of overseas mining resources and food to the Atlantic countries of Europe in the nineteenth century, or as the discovery of oil and its use as a new source of power have been in the twentieth century. The increasing economic interdependence of the industrially developed areas, in particular, constitutes a fact of epoch-making importance. Our time, apart from being the age of the second industrial revolution, may be described as the beginning of a new phase in the world economy. Nevertheless, parallel with this process of increasing interdependence, the sphere of government intervention has expanded in every country, in both the internal and the international economic fields. The point has been reached where the change is qualitative, and to ignore it, or to dissociate it from the contemporary picture, is to indulge in self-deception.

Two opposing tendencies have thus gained ground in the world economy, independent of the antagonism between capitalist and socialist systems and the conflicts which arise from widely differing levels of development, and these tendencies are likely to continue for a long while. For want of more precise terms I propose to call the two tendencies on the one hand *interdependence*, which extends to all countries and areas of the globe, and on the other *monocentrism*, referring to the governmental sphere of authority.

In my view neither of these tendencies has so far reached its zenith; they are both still increasing in strength and we should not, therefore, cherish any illusions about their harmonization in the near future. An inescapable problem of global interdependence is the *de facto* dependence of certain countries and regions, and of certain branches of the economy, on others, and its strength should not be under-estimated. But at the same time there are effects also strong enough to create a state of interdependence. What I have called the monocentrism of governmental authority is constantly in conflict with interdependence, and it is by no means clear which will have the upper hand. In spite of these facts the reality forms the foundation of their co-existence.

The emergence of these two contrasting tendencies has been reflected in the heated theoretical discussions which have centred on international trade, or, in a wider sense, on the international division of labour. The narrow scope of this preface does not allow me to give here a comprehensive analysis of the two opposing schools of thought. In brief, we have on the one hand a development from neoliberalism to the positive theory of integration, with a preference for supra-national organizations, and on the other the opponents of supra-nationality, who adopt their position in defence of the classical theory of sovereignty, the national monocentrism referred to above. It should be borne in mind that supra-integration, *viz.*, the process of integrating the existing and future integrations, so far possesses no theoretical basis of its own, although for some time the operations of the economy have been pinpointing the increasing importance of the problem and drawing attention to the fact that, in a few decades or so, economic theory will not be able to avoid the challenge of real circumstances. The emergence of socialist states has deprived the capitalist system of its claim to universality. (The use of the term 'capitalism' can no longer be avoided, despite the critical flavour of the expression and the fact that it indicates a certain historical period and its ephemeral character.) It seems to me that the economic theory of capitalism possesses no comprehensive and up-to-date theoretical approach to the international division of labour.

From 1960 onwards the search for solutions to various pressing problems has been intensified and the reader will find the results of some of these efforts in the pages of our work. We can admit without shame – for a feeling of shame inevitably produces a constricting effect on the frankness of the admission – that so far socialism has found no acceptable concept of its own covering the question of foreign trade and international economic relations; still less a theoretical approach which would apply to a given historical period of some considerable length during which it has to share the world with a number of other social systems, which, like socialism itself, present a picture of steady domestic development with both positive and negative tendencies. National monocentrism, moreover, has also been a characteristic feature of the countries of the socialist sphere and has been more successful than internationalism in establishing concrete and effective institutions which conform not only to the demands of interdependence but equally to the ideology of socialism. Stalin's thesis of two parallel world markets has had to be rejected, and not only because the parallelism never materialized, although, despite the alienation of the two systems, they were never totally separated. The thesis also had to be abandoned because the socialist 'world market' revealed itself to be a fiction, with in fact hardly any of the characteristics of a real market. The principal reason for its rejection was its implicit rigidity; the mutual isolation of the two spheres could not, and certainly should not, be accepted as a political-economic end. A clear proof of the lack of any comprehensive concept of international trade on the part of the socialist countries was to be found in the name given to the organization formally incorporating the economic community of the socialist countries: the Council of Mutual Economic Assistance. *Nomina sunt odiosa*; the concept of mutual assistance recognized the existence and sovereignty of national states, but failed to acknowledge the demands of the modern international division of labour. It is impossible not to see in this choice of attitude what was unquestionably a negligent disregard of the stage of development reached by the productive forces at that time and of their future course, and – painful as it is to admit it – a missed chance. Now, in circumstances which are in some respects more complex than before, and hindered by fossilized institutions, we have to fight to remedy the failure of twenty years ago.

Macro-economic planning as the corner stone of the socialist economic system is not necessarily conceptually opposed to a constructive appraisal of the international division of labour and its inclusion in the system of planning. The techniques and organisation of planning were, to be sure, developed in the Soviet Union at a time when it stood alone as the only socialist country in existence, at a relatively low stage of economic development and surrounded by a generally hostile world. The marginal role which foreign trade came to play in the Soviet Union was to some extent due to the fact that the Soviet Union is a 'big country' where the internal division of labour is of an importance far exceeding that of its external counterpart. And it has to be admitted that we, the new-born socialist countries making common cause with the Soviet Union, accepted the pattern of planning in operation there as the ideal, not so much at the beginning, when we possessed too little information about it, but all the more later when its influence became paramount; although the size, the resources, the external and internal conditions of our economy were far different from those of the Soviet Union. As a consequence of this misconception, foreign trade was reduced in the Hungarian planning concept to exchanges of 'scarcities and surpluses', with the emphasis to this day on the scarcities – raw materials, fuel and some kinds of food. Foreign trade was consequently stigmatized as the lesser evil, a second best solution. Its recognition as a factor of growth came only after exports of manufactured goods to the Soviet Union had developed on a scale previously unknown to Hungarian industry. But, because of their small volume, and the restricted range and rigid structure of the export pattern over a number of years, these exports, on their exclusively quantitative criteria, could easily be included in the system of planning.

The conflict between effective foreign trade and the old planning techniques came to a head just as a full-scale critical attack was being launched against the quantitative concept of planning. For research had started to reveal the discrepancies between investment and its effective use, and in the course of an analysis of the structure of foreign trade the strategic concept and structure of industrial production were challenged. The fundamental theoretical issue was raised, whether there can and does exist in the socialist system, apart from the field of individual consumption, a *market* for producers. The accepted pattern of planning was best suited to *distribution*; these two concepts complemented each other. The chief difference was that the use of the concept of distribution conformed to the assiduously maintained thesis that producer goods are not commodities, but rather goods disposed of inside the socialist sphere without changing ownership. No market activity could consequently be admitted in connexion with the process of distribution. On the other hand it could not be denied that indications of market activity (though showing special features), and even a degree of competition, were emerging in the trade between socialist countries. But competition did not extend to prices, or at least not openly. This phenomenon gave a new dimension to the theorem of 'imperfect competition' so much discussed in economic text-books.

The inevitable consequences were distortions of the pattern of growth, retarding technical progress and producing a technological gap. Conclusions on the disastrous effects of this concept forced themselves on the observer who compared the concept of distribution prevailing in the planning model with the results of East–West trade, which was steadily growing in importance from the mid-fifties onwards. A number of the essays collected in this book deal with this question.

The solution reached in the reform of the Hungarian economy introduced in 1968 embraced the principle that macro-economic planning and a regulated market can and should go together. This fundamental change of concept abolishes the strait-jacket attitude that foreign trade is no more than a primitive makeweight to supply deficiencies, and frees it from the policy of import-substitution; it is now at liberty to develop into a dynamic activity, a fully-fledged partner in the international division of labour, a factor of growth in the world economy. 'We *can* talk', said the Tiger-lily to Alice, 'when there's anybody worth talking to'. Planning, in general and in depth, and the extent of central regulations and control are now devised on lines very different from the earlier mechanism. This new system which, in order to stress the dividing line between past and present, we refuse to call a 'mechanism', or even a 'new mechanism', since we are doing all in our power to turn slavery to the machine into mastery, will operate with flexibility and with sufficiently wide safety margins to allow for the vagaries of foreign trade. Dynamic foreign trade may thus become a constructive element of planning, not only as a factor of growth but also as a criterion for the economic structure to be developed.

The authors of these essays are Hungarian economists, economic historians, and statisticians; their research work has been focused on the economic and social development of Hungary, and on Hungarian foreign trade as a part of this development. Our findings consequently make no claim to be applicable to all planned economies, nor even to all socialist planned economies, so that our proposals for eventual solutions are not intended to be generally valid. We hope our critics will take notice of the warning, and will not be tempted to ignore this statement of our modest intentions. Geographical and national limitations are related to specific historical circumstances; let us once more draw our readers' attention to this fact, on the assumption that they will begin by reading the preface and then go on to the essays which form the body of this book.

The Hungarian economy had in fact very few links during the inter-war period with the process of world market integration which followed so closely the growth of the world economy, or perhaps constituted its real content. Until 1918, Hungary, as part of the Hapsburg empire, was open to foreign influences, partly through Austrian intermediaries, partly directly. Some of these influences seem to have been favourable in their effect; recent studies in economic history have revealed a relatively high rate of growth in the thirty to forty years before the First World War. Mass emigration, it is true, might have eased the internal pressures and so contributed to this result. Nevertheless Hungarian economic backwardness, due to the survival and dominant political role of feudalism, matched her social structure. In the inter-war period the economic backwardness of the country became relatively still greater; the landlords, politically predominant, succeeded in preventing the industrialisation of the country, a process which could no more be based on the latifundia in Hungary than anywhere else. The missed opportunity for industrialization could have led to a greater participation in international trade and brought about a growth-inducing influx of capital. Nothing of this sort happened. Hungary's economic structure, apart from a handful of pioneering large enterprises, provided an appalling contrast to the cultural level the country had achieved, represented by Béla Bartok, Mihály Karolyi, George Lukacs and the Nobel prize winner Albert Szentgyörgyi, as well as by a generation of immortal writers and poets. Economically, Hungary was doomed to remain on the periphery of Europe and the world. The situation led, as everyone knows, to a catastrophe: to the Second World War, to the alliance with the other fascist powers, to shame and ruin.

A satisfactory process of integration into the world market has been, as explained above, prevented from materialising over the last twenty years, despite rapid economic growth and intensive contacts with the socialist countries. The institutional framework provided by CMEA should and will in the future, by the joint efforts of us all, embody the full substance of integration.

This is the historical background constantly in the mind of all members of our informal study group, framing our thoughts and purposes. We shall, following Marx's words, not only interpret history, but change it.

In conclusion the authors wish to express their gratitude to Cambridge University Press for its generous help, by which we are able to present our work to the English-speaking world. We are indebted to various Hungarian periodicals for permission to reprint some of our essays which first appeared in their pages, and last but not least to the officers of the Cambridge University Press who took pains to arrange our texts, and to those helping hands, unknown to us, who corrected our linguistic blunders.

IMRE VAJDA

*Budapest, 18 February 1969*

# 1. The problem of Eastern European economic integration in a historical perspective

I. T. BEREND

Economic integration is a major problem of modern economic growth. The socialist countries have had to face this problem in the course of their industrialization. At the present stage of development the co-ordination of planning and production and the modern division of labour have taken on primary significance.

In order to understand and solve current economic problems of this kind it is, however, necessary to study the history of the processes involved. The present situation must be considered in relation to the economic developments from which it has arisen and to the economic relations between Eastern and Central European countries which have evolved as a result of these developments. Although it was mainly after World War II that efforts to achieve integration assumed a definite form, it is advisable in the first place to review the inter-war period and the situation in the countries of this area after World War I.

During the nineteenth century, modern economic development was initiated in the Central and Eastern European countries, but not within the framework of national states. The region contained powerful multi-national empires, in which nations of various characters and at different stages of development were artificially linked together in a single framework. Integration took place within the boundaries of each empire, fostered mainly by a system of tariffs that during the last decades of the nineteenth century brought about industrial expansion and commercial prosperity. Of course, the economic integration and division of labour within each empire resulted in differences in comparative advantage in production between the countries of the empire. On the other hand, as a result of the repression of national aspirations, and of the tendency to preserve the agricultural character of some backward regions, a special kind of national consciousness arose in the less developed countries within these empires in the decades before World War I. Any backwardness or actual disadvantage within the existing international division of labour was ascribed to the partial or total lack of national sovereignty. These countries felt that they had to fight for a solid national framework or to

*Ivan Berend*

strengthen the existing one by protecting themselves from the competition of the more advanced countries, as if only isolation could heal their wounds, which they held to be exclusively national. After World War I, the results of these nationalist endeavours were seen in a fundamentally changed political situation.

These were years of strong nationalist feeling. Fearing the unrestrained irredentism of the Hungarian leaders who had lost control over the national minority groups, the newly independent states claimed satisfaction for all their past national grievances as a part of the new deal that followed World War I. The great empires disintegrated; the political map of Central and Eastern Europe underwent a radical change: instead of the former vast areas of one colour, there appeared small patches of various colours. A number of small countries, each with a population of seven to fifteen million inhabitants, started to fight for their existence in the spirit of their nationalist traditions, now developing into political ideas which dominated economic principles.

In the chaotic economic situation following World War I, these new states in Central and Eastern Europe strove to break all their former economic ties. All the territories and countries that had formerly formed a single economic unit made it one of their chief aims to obliterate the traces of the former imperial division of labour and to gain full economic independence from the areas which had once been natural markets as well as sources of supply. Allowing for the territorial changes after World War I, the value of goods supplied by Austrian and Bohemian parts of the former Hapsburg Empire in 1924 to Hungary amounted only to 40 per cent of the total for 1913.[1]

The new states reinforced their political independence by the use of strong prohibitive measures and high protective tariffs. Everywhere on the continent, and especially in Central and Eastern Europe, the 1920s were characterized by rivalry in raising import duties to the highest possible level. In Hungary, at the turn of the century, the demand for an independent national tariff system within the Hapsburg Empire was a national slogan; now, after the realization of political independence, the creation of a separate customs area became the main concern of national economic policy. According to the Peace Treaty stipulations, Hungary was obliged to maintain the tariff which had formerly been adopted as valid for the boundaries of the Austro–Hungarian Monarchy by Act no. 53-1907. However, by Act no. 21-1920, the Hungarian

[1] W. Layton and Ch. Rist, *The Economic Situation of Austria*, Report presented to the Council of the League of Nations, Geneva, 19 August 1925, p. 27.

2

government was empowered to elaborate a new system of measures to regulate foreign trade activities as a whole. From July 1921, a series of decrees was issued according to which an embargo was laid on a number of goods, chiefly textiles, leather and machinery, which had formerly been freely imported. Whereas the tariffs of the Austro–Hungarian Empire had generally varied between ten and twenty per cent, the new tariffs rose on average to thirty per cent (and on consumers' goods to fifty per cent), thereby barring from the Hungarian market the principal items previously imported.[1]

The Central and Eastern European countries were fully protected against foreign competition, though the protective measures hit neighbouring countries hardest. As both agriculture and industry in this region were based on inefficient techniques, their costs of production were higher than in the advanced countries, so that their products could not compete on world markets. This can be seen from the following examples: Austria and Czechoslovakia had a uniform tariff on cereals and flour; yet these countries imported more American than Hungarian produce despite the high transport costs. And the increased tariff on imported machines into the Balkan countries did more harm to Austrian than to Belgian or British industry.

In fact, as a result of this protective system, the barriers between Central and Eastern European countries became higher than those between the countries of Eastern and Western Europe. It is characteristic that during the whole of the inter-war period Yugoslav foreign trade with the neighbouring Balkan countries was insignificant, fluctuating between 5 and 9 per cent. In the years immediately after World War I, about 50 per cent of Czechoslovakia's exports were directed to the Danube states, virtually in continuation of the pre-war pattern. However, by the middle of the twenties this ratio had sunk to about one third.[2]

We can illustrate the mutuality of this process thus: at the end of the twenties, while Czechoslovakia's exports to the Danube countries were declining sharply, more than half of her flour requirement was procured not from the neighbouring agricultural countries but from overseas, partly as a result of political considerations. The same holds true for Austria: about one third of her wheat supply was imported from America, while her engineering products could find no market in the Eastern European agrarian countries. The Balkan countries and Hungary purchased machine

[1] I. T. Berend and Gy. Ránki, *Magyarország gazdasága az I. világháboru után 1919–1929* [The Hungarian Economy after W.W.I, 1919–1929], Akadèmiai Kiadó, 1966, p. 175 ff.
[2] J. Tomasevich, *Foreign Economic Relations 1913–1941*, United Nations Series, Vol. 1949, p. 172; Layton and Rist, *The Economic Situation of Austria*, p. 29.

tools, textile machinery and implements in France and Great Britain, while by the mid-thirties the output of the Austrian engineering industry was hardly higher than a third of its pre-war production.[1]

Despite geographic advantages and historical traditions, the level of trade between the Central and Eastern European countries shrank to 10–15 per cent of their total foreign trade. The exclusion of the Soviet Union from economic life played no small part in this process. Although large territories of Poland had previously belonged to Russia, and provided her with natural markets, after World War I Poland transacted only about 1.5 per cent of her total foreign trade with the Soviet Union. In Czechoslovakia figures were similar, while in the other Eastern European countries they were still lower. The Central and Eastern European countries strove to carry on foreign trade with the West: before World War II the participation of Western Europe in the trade of these countries was about 70 to 80 per cent.[2]

The strong political tendency towards national seclusion was accompanied by a conception of autarky as the basis of economic expansion. For example, in Austria and Czechoslovakia great efforts were made to promote agriculture, especially to increase livestock breeding. In other words, the tendency was to produce on a large scale goods which before World War I had been imported from the Eastern agricultural regions of the former Austro–Hungarian Empire. For instance, Austria doubled her pig stock between 1920 and 1934;[3] in the early twenties she supplied domestically less than a third of her wheat requirements, but by the early thirties she was supplying more than half. In the middle of the 1920s wheat production in Czechoslovakia amounted to about 1 million metric tons; over the next ten years it increased to about 1.7 million metric tons. Thus, this country, formerly compelled to import, produced a surplus when the harvest was good and in some years it was able to hoard part of its crop.[4]

Given the tendency towards autarky, emphasized after the crisis of 1929–33, trade between the Danube states was restricted. Whereas after World War I one fifth to one sixth of Hungarian exports went to Czechoslovakia, by the mid-thirties the figure was only five per cent. Furthermore, great efforts were made in Hungary to allocate more capital to industrial development, including production of consumer goods, for many of these industries had been practically non-existent in pre-war times. Compared

[1] K. Hudaczek, *Die Österreichische Volkswirtschaft und ihr Wiederaufbau*, Wien, 1946, p. 171.
[2] N. Spulber, *The Economics of Communist Eastern Europe*, London and New York, 1957, p. 9.
[3] Hudaczek, *Österreichische Volkswirtschaft*, p. 27.
[4] H. Wanklyn, *Czechoslovakia*, London, 1954, p. 237.

to the level before World War I, textile production doubled by 1925, trebled by 1929, and by the late thirties quadrupled. Imported textile goods supplied about 70 per cent of the domestic market in 1913, but by the thirties this had fallen to 2 or 3 per cent.[1] The best example of the disruption of relations deriving from earlier division of labour is provided by the industrial independence achieved by Austria and Czechoslovakia. Owing to the peculiar division of labour in the textile industry within the Hapsburg Empire before World War I, the spinning industry had been located chiefly in Austria and the weaving industry in Bohemia. After World War I both countries hastened to make themselves independent of each other. Consequently, by 1925, 5,000 weaving machines were installed in Austria, and, correspondingly, a series of spinning mills were established in Czechoslovakia.

In the Balkan countries, where political freedom had been partly achieved some time before World War I, the tendency to establish an independent economy was especially strong. These countries wished to promote their own development. Their efforts were fruitful in so far as they succeeded in moderating the blatant discrepancies formerly prevalent in Central and Eastern Europe. So, as a result of their own efforts, the first steps were taken to promote industrialization in the Balkans.

The tendencies which became noticeable after World War I gathered considerable strength in the thirties. Economic isolation was reinforced in the Eastern European agricultural countries by the gap between the prices of agricultural and industrial products. Their terms of trade were low and this magnified the effects of the great crisis which shook most of these countries, depriving them of foreign capital. They introduced new tariffs and embargoes and established a clearing system in foreign trade. More generally, they adopted a policy of state intervention.

However, this independent path of development was not entirely efficient. Though they were small and possessed few natural resources, the Danube countries pursued nationalist, independent policies aimed at autarky. This proved to be costly, for there was much duplication of productive capacity within the region as a whole. What were the consequences of this? In Austria and Czechoslovakia, the textile industry lost most of its former markets and passed through an acute crisis when a new self-reliant textile industry was developed in Hungary. The same happened in Hungary, notably in agricultural production and the flour-

---

[1] Cf. *Magyar Statisztikai Évkönyvek* [Hungarian Statistical Yearbooks]; Berend and Ránki, *Magyarország gyáripara az II. világháboru elött és a háboru idöszakában, 1933–1944* [The Hungarian Industry before and during the Second World War, 1933–1944], Budapest, 1958, p. 216.

milling industry, when most of the former markets in Austria and Czecho-slovakia were lost in the new situation, so that chronic crisis became inevitable. The Austrian Government made great efforts to establish an independent flour-milling industry. In 1930, it created a special fund – the revenues from increased taxes on sugar and alcohol – with which to support grain production and flour milling. Again, even in the most favourable years of the inter-war period, the Hungarian milling trade, which was capable of supplying the whole Austro–Hungarian Empire, could not produce more than 75 per cent of its pre-war output. The gigantic flour mills in Hungary, which had previously engaged in a worldwide export trade, collapsed one after the other. The Steam Mill 'Hungaria' came to a standstill; the empty building of 'Erzsebet' Mill was sold to be converted into a textile factory; the Milling Trust 'Victoria', operating twelve separate mills, became bankrupt: the assets were sold off and most of the buildings were pulled down.[1]

Thus after World War I, the agrarian countries of Central and Eastern Europe found difficulties in selling their produce. Similarly, the more industrialized countries found they had surplus capacity. There was duplication of existing capacity; and some obvious investment opportunities were not taken. In many of the countries concerned these developments formed an insurmountable barrier to sound economic advancement, namely the building of plant designed to utilize the latest technical achievements, and the establishment of industries which could compete on the world market. In other words, as a result of a forced development of agriculture in countries already industrialized and of efforts to build up a new industrial autarky in primarily agricultural countries, some form of economic progress was achieved, though not without highly contradictory elements.

With the help of state subsidies and tariffs, relatively quick progress was made in consumer goods industries. In most of the Central and Eastern European countries, light industry, especially textiles, showed the quickest, most extensive development. Thus in two decades Hungarian textile production rose fourfold. Before the Second World War, domestic production completely satisfied domestic demand, whereas previously it had supplied only one third of the home market. In Yugoslavia, also, it was the textile industry which developed at the quickest pace in the inter-war period. Whereas in the early twenties imports of textiles amounted to about one third of total consumption, in the late thirties the ratio was

[1] *Magyar Nemzetgazda*, 1922, dec. 23; *Pesti Tözsde*, 1927, feb. 13; *Ungarisches Wirtschaftsjahr-buch*, 1927, p. 100.

reduced to approximately one tenth. During the same period imports of machines doubled.[1] In Rumania textile output provided over one fifth of the total of manufactured production before World War II.[2] There can be no doubt that in these decades the greatest impetus to growth came from the rapid increase of textile and other consumer goods output; but this growth was achieved with obsolete production processes. In Western Europe, during the first half of the twentieth century, textile industries in general showed a declining trend. For instance in Great Britain the share of textiles in total manufacturing production diminished from 19 per cent to 11 per cent in the inter-war period. In Western Europe, during the same period, the figure sank from 18 to 13 per cent. On the other hand, the share of metallurgy, processing of metals and chemicals increased in Great Britain from 32 per cent to 44 per cent, and in Western Europe from 41 per cent to 50 per cent.[3]

After World War I, there were major technical innovations – namely the extensive application of electricity and mass-production methods; several new sectors of the economy grew rapidly, particularly those producing labour-saving machinery. However, the majority of the countries in Central and Eastern Europe were unable to keep pace with this technical progress. A real advance was achieved only in light industry, while heavy industry, which may be considered as a suitable representative of modern technology, in general remained stagnant. In this region of Europe there was hardly any country where the engineering industry could introduce modern methods of mass production. As a result of adaptation to small markets, the engineering industry preserved its notorious character of a 'general store'. It must be emphasized here that in these countries the narrow framework of national states afforded no possibility for industrial development which would satisfy the needs of a modern economy. Attempts were continually made to stop the import of articles which had formerly been bought abroad, and to produce them at home.

The profits from some sectors of the economy were matched by losses from others; this situation was the inevitable result of the forced domestic production of certain goods. A good example in this respect is Hungary. While the production of textiles rose fourfold, heavy industry made no headway and the food industry suffered a serious setback. In summary, industry progressed slowly: in two decades production increased by only

[1] Tomasevich, *Foreign Economic Relations*, pp. 178 ff.
[2] N. Lupu-Kostaky (ed.), *Aspecte ale economiei Româneşti*, Bucarest, 1939, p. 44.
[3] After the Second World War this process becomes suddenly faster. Cf. A. Zauberman, *Industrial Progress in Poland, Czechoslovakia and East Germany, 1937–1962*, London, New York and Toronto, 1964, pp. 30–1.

30 per cent. As a result of agricultural stagnation, the rate of growth of national income was about 1.5 per cent per annum. In Austria the rate of growth was similar, while Poland, having won her long-desired independence, was unable to achieve any economic growth in the inter-war period.[1] Thus the Central and Eastern European countries were among those with the slowest rate of economic growth in Europe.

This could be partly ascribed to the low rate of accumulation. In the past each country had arranged moderate foreign loans to establish its own economic independence and had thus wasted its limited opportunities for development. Hence the efforts to industrialize were only moderately successful in the inter-war period.

In wide areas of the region unemployment presented the most difficult problem. One fifth, even one third, of the rural population could not find work in Poland, Rumania, Yugoslavia and Bulgaria, where industry was unable to absorb the surplus agrarian population.[2]

In an atmosphere of slow economic growth and serious internal contradictions, the desired economic independence could not be achieved, and, in the final analysis, little was done to eliminate backwardness: before the Second World War 75 to 80 per cent of the population of Albania, Bulgaria, Yugoslavia and Rumania earned their living on the land. The rural population of Poland was reduced from a post-war figure of 64 per cent to 61 per cent.[3] In Hungary, after a similar reduction, agricultural labour amounted to 50 per cent of the population at the end of the inter-war period.

As a general feature, the tendency towards national autarky prevailed in Central and Eastern Europe. Obviously this cannot be considered as the sole or the most important of the many interwoven factors which hampered economic growth. But this state of affairs doubtless played an important role in preserving backwardness and in the fundamental failure of economic development in the inter-war period.

In the period following World War II the political situation changed

[1] Berend and Ránki, *Magyarország gyáripara*, pp. 234 ff.; Berend and Ránki, 'Magyarország ipari szinvonala az európai összehasonlitás tükrében a II. világháboru elött' (The level of the Hungarian industry before W.W.II in comparison with European countries); *Közgazdasági Szemle*, Institute of Economics, Hungarian Academy of Sciences, Budapest, 1 Sept. 1967; *Concise Statistical Yearbook of Poland, 1939–1941*, p. 67; *Austria Public Finances, Third Report by the Financial Organisation of the League of Nations*, Geneva, 1937, p. 27.
[2] P. N. Rosenstein-Rodan, *Agricultural Surplus Population in Eastern and South Eastern Europe*, Royal Institute of International Affairs: quoted by Spulber, *Economics of Communist Eastern Europe*, p. 276.
[3] *Economic Demography of Eastern and Southern Europe*, League of Nations, Geneva, 1945, p. 26.

completely; the new circumstances, to be treated here only from the economic viewpoint, created entirely new conditions of economic co-operation. In the extremely critical economic situation, the war-torn countries of Eastern Europe were reduced to mutual support in solving the difficult tasks of reconstruction.

The consequences of the unprecedented devastation caused by World War II had to be grappled with in Hungary, Poland and Yugoslavia. But these countries could expect no aid from their former commercial and financial connections. They were compelled to establish new relations overnight.

Although considerable economic and other UNRRA aid was made available to Poland and Yugoslavia, English and American creditors in general assumed an expectant attitude. In 1946 one of the directors of the Hungarian General Credit Bank went to London in order to try to resume former contacts with the house of Rothschild, but had to return home empty-handed. After some fairly promising preliminary talks, Anthony Rothschild declared that according to the opinion of competent authorities the time had not yet come to grant credits to Hungary.[1] The situation was similar in commercial relations. Most of the Western countries showed no inclination to do business with the Eastern European countries until their immense pre-war liabilities were settled, and as long as the political situa-tion in these countries was felt to be uncertain. And when there was no real obstacle to hamper the renewal of financial and commercial relations, the political situation changed. The atmosphere of the cold war dominated international relations. In this situation it was natural that the Central and Eastern European countries, having come to political agreement, soon recognized their economic interdependence. Whereas in the period before World War II mutual transactions amounted to only 10 or 15 per cent of total foreign trade, and the aim was to trade with the Western countries in the first place, in the years following World War II trade with the West dwindled to insignificance and the bulk of foreign trade was transacted within the region on a barter basis. The most striking change took place in the relationship with the USSR, the country which had formerly been practically excluded from all kinds of trade. Previously, the countries of the Danube had conducted about 1 per cent of their foreign trade with the Soviet Union; now they suddenly found themselves in a position to trade with the USSR. Approximately 92 per cent of Hungarian foreign trade was transacted with the USSR (in 1946 the figure for imports was about

[1] *Magyar Országos Levéltár* (Central Archive of Hungary), *Gazdasági Osztály*, Hitelbank D. no. 239.

9

70 per cent).[1] By the end of the reconstruction period trade connections with other countries were gradually normalized; in the spring of 1946 the first trade agreement with a Western country was signed between Hungary and Switzerland. Poland established similar relations with the Scandinavian countries. The new trend of economic relations was taking shape. In 1948, each of the Eastern and Central European countries conducted between 10 and 20 per cent of its foreign trade with the Soviet Union. Roughly one third of Hungarian foreign trade was directed to the Central and Eastern European countries. For the Balkan countries this trend was still more evident: for instance, Rumania transacted 25 per cent of her foreign trade with the USSR and nearly 50 per cent with Eastern Europe, while 75 per cent of the foreign trade of Bulgaria was transacted with Central and Eastern Europe.

The reconstruction of destroyed and damaged productive capacity was carried out astonishingly quickly and successfully in Poland and Hungary, as well as in other countries of this region. By about 1947–8 they were able to look ahead and to seek new objectives for progress. At this stage reconstruction of ruined economies ceased to be the main task, for more complicated problems had to be faced, namely economic backwardness, a low rate of saving and a slow rate of growth. The whole future of economic development became the question of the day, and so did the ways and means of economic policy. After the Second World War the Danube countries also investigated entirely new methods of economic co-operation.

In the late forties completely new programmes of economic advancement were drawn up. A policy of rapid industrialization, on the Soviet line, was adopted by the Danube countries as the best to overcome economic backwardness. The impressive example of Soviet economic progress and military success in the war played a role in this decision, as did the dogmatic conception of the methods of Soviet economic development as the only permanently valid model of socialist progress. In connection with our theme it is important to draw attention to the new tendencies which demonstrated that these countries, having drawn a lesson from the bitter experience of the inter-war years, wished to follow the Soviet model of economic development in a form adapted to the new political situation and not within the narrow limits of separate national economies. Profiting from the similarity of their economic objectives and their common principles and views, as well as from the political solidarity which

[1] *Magyar Nemzeti Bank gazdasági jelentése a bankvezetöség részére* (Hungarian National Bank, Report on economics for the administrative board); 1946 June 1, *Wiadomošči Statystyczne*, Special Volume 1, 1947, p. 5.

they had finally achieved, they sought common roads of economic advancement. A programme for the integrated industrialization of Central and Eastern Europe assumed a steadily increasing role in the development plans for 1947-9 as well as in their practical realization.

From this time most of the European socialist countries considered economic integration as inevitable. From 1947, when most Danube countries drew up two-to-five-year plans, economic integration and a course of systematic economic collaboration became possible. As the opening step, on 4 July 1947, Czechoslovakia and Poland signed an agreement providing for economic co-operation in commerce, transport, and in the special development and planning of certain economic sectors. The aim was 'to promote industrial development and progress in both countries and to avoid unnecessary investments'. In order to carry out this project, a permanent Polish–Czechoslovak Economic Committee was set up, with a secretariat employing a large staff, and eight permanent industrial or sectoral co-ordinating committees. Co-operation had already started in 1947, as indicated by the drafting of agreements concerning production in several industries. In these agreements, the parties endeavoured to specialize in those industries in which they had a comparative cost advantage, so that they could supply each other's markets with goods produced at lower costs; they also agreed to standardize engineering products. The co-operative projects included the construction of a common generating plant with a capacity of 150 MW at Nowy Dwory.[1]

The above-mentioned Polish–Czechoslovak agreement formed part of a multilateral network of common planning and mutual understanding in a great many problems and tasks of development among the Central and Eastern European countries. For example the Hungarian–Yugoslav bauxite–aluminium agreement was concluded in May 1947. This very important development programme obliged Yugoslavia to purchase certain quantities of alumina from, and to supply caustic soda to, Hungary, while Hungary was to construct and install aluminium plants in Yugoslavia to the value of 32 million dollars.[2]

The most comprehensive and promising projects for economic integration emerged from co-operation among the Balkan countries. In

[1] H. Wencel, *Wspolpraca Polsko–Czechoslowacka, Zycie Gospodarcze*, 16–31 Dec. 1948; *Sprawy Miedzynarodowe* I, no. 1, Oct.–Dec. 1948; D. Warriner, *Reveolution in Eastern Europe*, London, 1950.

[2] *Megállapodás a Jugoszláv Szövetségi Népköztársaság és a Magyar Köztársaság között az aluminiumipar terén való gazdasági együttmüködésre vonatkozólag, 1947, május 14* (Agreement between Yugoslavia and the Hungarian Republic concerning the economic co-operation in relation to the aluminium industry, 14 May 1947. Párttörténeti Intézet (Institute of History of Party) Archivuma 2 (9–18.00242).

December 1946, as the first step, a thirty-year agreement was signed between Yugoslavia and Albania providing for 'a wide co-ordination of economic plans, union of customs' areas, and standardization of currency'.[1]

Attention must be drawn in this connection to some more facts: in July and November 1947 negotiations took place in Bled and Varna between Yugoslav and Bulgarian Government Committees, headed by Tito and Dimitrov respectively, to find new means of economic co-operation. A pact of friendship and mutual assistance was concluded. As emphasized in the protocol, the contracting parties resolved 'to enhance economic co-operation, to strengthen and widen mutual trade activity, to co-ordinate economic planning, to accelerate the realization of a customs union'.[2]

The co-ordinated economic development of the Central and Eastern European countries was a common aspiration, figuring as a permanent item on the agenda of the frequent inter-government conferences. Integration was to be realized by the far-reaching adjustment of planning and promoted by a gradually established customs union. In December 1947, at the press conference held at the Yugoslav Embassy in Budapest after the signing of the Hungarian–Yugoslav agreement, Tito declared: 'The present pact will greatly influence economic relations. The friendly people, so also the peoples of Hungary and Yugoslavia, are going to co-ordinate their constructive plans, the three year plan of Hungary and the five year plan of Yugoslavia.'[3] In the same period, the President of the Hungarian Central Planning Office announced in a statement he made in Prague: 'The project of an agreement providing for long-term economic co-operation between Czechoslovakia and Hungary was also discussed. Recently similar agreements have been concluded between Czechoslovakia and Poland, Yugoslavia and Hungary. These conventions are intended not only to regulate the exchange of goods, but also to adjust the development of certain industrial branches. The idea is that step by step, by way of economic treaties, a more or less coherent economic system should be evolved by the Eastern European People's Democracies.'[4]

In January 1948, Rumanian–Bulgarian negotiations took place which represented a new stage on the road to an economic integration on the above-mentioned scale. The protocol that was signed and the declaration that was made by Dimitrov in Bucharest contained the following statement: 'We shall co-ordinate our economic plans, widen commercial

[1] Tomasevich, *Foreign Economic Relations*, pp. 412–13.
[2] *Magyar Szó*, 29 Nov. 1947.
[3] *Szabad Nép*, 10 Dec. 1947.          [4] *Népszava*, 29 Nov. 1947.

relations, prepare and realize the union of customs areas.' Talking to journalists after the conference, Dimitrov emphasized that a customs union was an inevitable step in furthering development. He added: 'Therefore the planned customs union is openly discussed with the allied states and it will certainly be realized!'[1] Obviously, realization would not have been easy, and it would have taken many years of hard work to overcome the increasing economic and political difficulties. Moreover, a system of economic integration based on uniform plans could have been achieved only after the solution of innumerable technical problems.

However, there can be no doubt that in the years following World War II significant economic and political initiatives were taken. Newly conceived projects, discussed at preparatory negotiations and carried to the initial stage of agreement, promised a radical change from the trend towards autarky which prevailed in the inter-war period. These negotiations held out bright prospects of sound economic growth to those countries of the region which had limited resources. These projects offered possibilities for avoiding the inevitable waste involved by parallel development. They encouraged the hope that, with the help of integration, each country would be able to concentrate on developing those sectors best suited to existing conditions and to attain in those sectors the highest technical competence, while relying on extensive markets in several countries.

However, these far-reaching ideas and projects were doomed to quick frustration, and they soon ceased to be issues of general interest. Evidently, the Central and Eastern European countries which started on the road of socialist development around the years 1947–8 had not yet risen to the level of economic maturity at which circumstances would force them towards a new form of co-operation.[2] From the years 1949–50, the system of planning based on compulsory directives created a special institutional framework, an 'international mechanism' which became a positive obstacle to a new type of integration.

Even taking into account the difficulties which existed, it would be wrong to indulge in unscientific speculation about what might have been the outcome of the widely publicized plans for integration, had they been realized. On the other hand, although these concepts, as quoted here, show some naïveté in their political and economic aspects, they were products of a given historical situation. They were not simply the expression of

[1] *Pravda*, 23 Jan. 1948.
[2] An interesting opinion to be found on the criterion of 'maturity for integration' in the paper by I. Vajda, 'The Role of Foreign Trade in a Socialist Economy', Corvina Press, 1963, pp. 222–3.

over-hasty illusions; they expressed the will to co-ordinate economic progress from the initial stage of industrialization in these countries, which, in the process of post-war recovery, were gathering the strength to shake off their historical inheritance of backwardness. Such integration might have opened up less expensive paths of development and made it possible to avoid costly investments, while attaining a technical level that was inconceivable on a purely national basis. These progressive ideas anticipated a later stage of industrial production, when actual processes would spontaneously and decisively create the need for broader international co-operation.

These plans for extensive economic integration failed in a few short months in the late forties not because they proved to be too complicated, premature, or impracticable. The idea of rapid economic integration was dismissed because another programme of development was adopted and put into effect, primarily for political reasons. On the available, evidence it seems that the projects of economic integration among socialist countries were strongly opposed from an autarchic point of view. In fact, Dimitrov's talks in Bucharest about economic integration and a customs union, as well as his views expounded at his press conference, were severely criticized by Stalin in the press. After Dimitrov's press conference had been published without comment, a concise editorial in *Pravda*, on 28 January 1948, declared that the publication of Dimitrov's views did not imply that the Editorial Board approved of his ideas. 'On the contrary,' the editorial said, 'in these countries the problem to be solved is to protect and to strengthen their sovereignty and independence by organizing and mobilizing internal democratic forces and not to think out some federation or confederation, or a union of customs.'[1]

It would be wrong to ignore the difference between the two concepts of economic integration expressed by the idea of a customs union and the above-quoted conception of autarky. The conflict with Yugoslavia which broke out a few months later put an end to all the initial plans and endeavours for economic co-operation; its indirect effect was to foster adherence to autarkic principles. After the summer of 1948 nothing was said about co-ordination of planning or mutual adaptation of industrial development. During the first months of the existence of the Council of Mutual Economic Aid (CMEA) in 1949, in the preparatory period, some feeble hopes for integration may have existed.[2] But when the activities of CMEA

---

[1] *Pravda*, 30 Jan. 1948.
[2] This appears to be verified by written and spoken declarations of the first Hungarian delegate to the CMEA. Cf. I. Friss, 'Berend T. Iván könyvéröl' (On the book of T. I. Berend), *Közgazdasági Szemle*, 1 Sept. 1966, p. 104.

started, no such schemes were mentioned in its published programmes and documents, nor did it advocate them in its advisory dealings.

Of course, during its early years, the activities of CMEA reflected the economic ideas which prevailed in the socialist countries at that time. Therefore the period from January 1949 to 1954 is a distinct section in its history. What was the characteristic feature of this period, and what were the inducements that led to the organization of the Council of Mutual Economic Aid?

It seems justified to refer to two factors of almost equal importance. First we have to emphasize the political significance of establishing such an organization, particularly as at the time of its inception this seems to have been the chief consideration of the initiators of CMEA. It was politically necessary to demonstrate the unity of all socialist states in this manner and at the same time to provide an answer to the Western attitude of cold war and the resulting extensive embargoes. The organization of close economic co-operation among the socialist countries was a move in opposition to the Marshall Programme, which openly served political aims. This political motivation is clearly recognized by both Marxist and non-Marxist experts in the field.[1] However, mention should also be made of another political factor, whose importance, in our opinion, has been unduly disregarded, namely the Yugoslav affair. In 1949 a grave problem arose within the group of socialist states from the Yugoslav conflict, which deeply affected internal, external, and economic policy alike. On Stalin's initiative, CMEA was to be the appropriate answer not only to the Western world but also to Yugoslavia. Several declarations by Stalin on these matters leave no doubt in this respect. In view of existing bilateral and extensive long-term agreements between Yugoslavia and the neighbouring socialist countries, it was only natural that the organization intended to represent socialist co-operation without Yugoslavia could not be treated as a sideline.

Political motives and economic incentives may be said to have been factors of equal weight. CMEA could be an effective political answer only if it was not to play a purely political role, but was also expected to have an economic effect. It was evident that in those countries where planning had just started and industrialization was imminent, foreign trade requirements would rapidly increase. In this period of intensified cold war, when the Western powers pursued a policy of boycott, the fulfilment of the

---

[1] Cf. the paper by N. Silujanov in *Voprosi Ekonomiki*, 1959, no. 3; paper by F. L. Pryor in *Soviet Studies*, 1959–1960, no. 2, and M. Kaser, *Comecon. Integration Problems of the Planned Economies*, London, New York and Toronto, 1965.

development projects called for the greatest co-operation among the socialist countries. A favourable opportunity presented itself to profit from mutual assistance in techniques, by exchanging documents on objectives of investments and on technological processes, that could serve as valuable means of accelerating progress on a larger scale. Starting at the Moscow meeting of CMEA in January 1949, and continuing at both the April session in Moscow and the August session in Sofia, negotiations were conducted on various proposals for mutual adaptation in the field of foreign trade and technical collaboration. Long-term commercial agreements were also prepared at these meetings.[1] The importance of these negotiations was shown by the steady growth in foreign trade between the socialist countries. From 1950 to 1955, Hungarian and Bulgarian trade with the Soviet Union increased by a half, and Czechoslovak trade doubled. The foreign trade of Hungary with Bulgaria increased by 50 per cent, with Czechoslovakia doubled and with the German Democratic Republic more than trebled.

A new trend was initiated by the free exchange of information on large investments and engineering. The importance of these activities may be estimated by the assistance coming from the Soviet Union, which passed on more than 20,000 documents on science and techniques to the Eastern European countries in ten years. Extensive exchange of such documents also took place between the other socialist countries.[2]

These activities had a great influence: they accelerated economic growth and promoted economic integration among the socialist countries. Foreign trade transactions, in particular, had a definite bearing on the integration of some economic sectors of the partners. The manufacturing sectors of one of the countries became interconnected with the processing sectors in another. Some sectors in different countries tried to complement each other's activities. But these trade relations, based on spontaneous import demands on the one side and on the volume of exports on the other, were not the realization of integration. When production is not controlled by a consistent domestic and international economic policy simple co-operation through foreign trade cannot lead to true integration: such connections contain only elements of integration and a partial realization of a little-understood integrating process. If the notion of integration – which is open to more than one interpretation – is not understood as full state control over economic relations along with co-ordination of the economic

---

[1] *Zehn Jahre Rat für Gegenseitge Wirtschaftshilfe*, Berlin, 1960.
[2] Cf. *Voprosi Ekonomiki*, 1955, no. 2. Paper of V. Gorelov on the role of the scientific and technical co-operation among the socialist countries; *Voprosi Ekonomiki*, 1961, no. 5. Paper of I. Oleynik on the forms of the international division of labour in the socialist world.

16

activities and development of the co-operating countries going far beyond foreign trade, it is really nothing more than foreign trade and the term becomes a stylistic formula. Integration should be interpreted as a system of more extensive demands than foreign trade relations: hence the substantially widened commercial activities carried out within the framework of CMEA cannot properly be regarded as a considerable advance in integration, although they do constitute a part of the integration process. And if the level of development in international trade cannot be accepted as the measure of integration, we have to consider the co-operation achieved in the first period of CMEA as a limited success.

As a matter of fact, commercial and technical collaboration, important in its own right, reflected not only the recognition of the necessity to co-operate, but also the belief that economic advancement had to be organized only within rather narrow national limits, without undertaking international co-ordination of development, investments, planning, and industrialization. Thus the commercial and technical collaboration was a rejection of broader possibilities, even of earlier initiatives, for it brought a restriction and reduction of real co-operation.

Consequently, commercial co-ordination could not get further than bilateral agreements. Of course, this system exerted a restraining influence on the activity of CMEA. After the launching sessions in 1949, the next session was held in November 1950, mainly to deal in a more positive way with the principles laid down in Sofia. In 1951 and 1952 the programme of CMEA consisted only of the elaboration of standard forms of commercial contracts and of a uniform classification and nomenclature for commercial purposes. Then followed a long pause until the next meeting in 1954.[1]

In the late forties and early fifties the international situation grew more and more unfavourable; in the cold-war era the socialist countries adopted the autarkic methods of development that had been applied in the Soviet Union under the conditions prevailing in the late twenties, without considering the obvious differences in circumstances.

The Soviet economic model was formed in circumstances when quite probably only autarky could be counted on to ensure independence and self-defence. The Soviet economic system was conceived and developed as a self-contained unit: the extraordinary size and natural resources of the Soviet Union afforded possibilities for such a course. However, in the years after World War II, the smaller states which took the road to socialism

---

[1] The year 1952 was the first in which the commercial interrelations among socialist countries were characterized by long-term agreements.

were in a totally different situation. Several countries embarked almost simultaneously upon the introduction of new methods of economic development, whereas none of them possessed the resources to achieve autarky. In other words, the Central and Eastern European countries which started simultaneously a new system of economic expansion neglected all the favourable opportunities offered by integration and failed to profit from the bitter experiences of the inter-war period; they chose again the policy of autarky. Although it certainly brought rapid, significant progress in industrialization, this economic policy inevitably brought about the emergence of grave contradictions, while curbing the full exploitation of realizable possibilities.

It is worth while examining this issue. We can assume at the outset that the countries in question faced similar problems; the low rate of net saving and investment had to be raised to complete the process of industrialization. Despite the important differences between the Central and Eastern European countries, e.g. between the German Democratic Republic and Czechoslovakia, or Bulgaria and Rumania, all the socialist countries followed similar economic policies. This can be clearly seen from the new schedules of planning drawn up almost synchronously, in 1949 and 1950, after the conclusion of post-war reconstruction. Thus, a programme of development was envisaged which was a duplication of the development work carried out by the Soviet Union since the twenties. This happened in countries with such dissimilar endowments and characters as Czechoslovakia, Hungary and Bulgaria. The programmes prepared in the socialist countries in the early fifties were all very similar, with only very small differences in magnitudes; in these countries, the development indices for a five-year plan were generally as in the accompanying scheme.

| Planned increase of: | |
|---|---|
| industrial production | 2–3 fold |
| heavy industry | 3–4 fold |
| metal industry | 3–5 fold |
| mechanical engineering | 3–6 fold |
| consumer goods industries | 2 fold |

In the stepped-up industrialization programme each country was treated as a self-contained unit. It was necessary to develop every sphere of industry and especially to provide for supplies of primary materials from domestic sources.

In a strained international situation, preparing for an imminent, apparently unavoidable, war, every country strove rapidly to enlarge its industrial basis and to raise its production of coal, steel and electricity.

During the five-year plan, coal production was to increase threefold in Rumania, Bulgaria and Yugoslavia. Steel production was to increase fourfold in Hungary, fivefold in Rumania. At the end of the five-year plan, Poland was to generate five times as much electricity as she had generated in 1938, Hungary six times as much and Czechoslovakia three times as much. However, the planned development of agricultural output was moderate; on average cereal production was to be ten per cent above pre-war levels. The planned increases in livestock varied more from country to country.[1] The economic policy of the Central and Eastern European countries was dominated to an unprecedented degree by the central idea of autarky.

Everywhere in the Danube valley great efforts were made to achieve the approved targets as quickly as possible. In the countries where during the inter-war years annual accumulation amounted to an average of 5 to 8 per cent of the national income, in this period of centrally planned production the rate of accumulation rose to 25 to 35 per cent of the national income or even higher – accurate estimates of the value are impossible because of the influence exerted by the change in the price system.[2]

This was a considerable achievement, which reflected the transition from a period of rather slow evolution to one of dynamic advance in accordance with the principle of autarky. This central idea of self-sufficiency was manifested especially in two main directions. The development of autarky requires immense investments, because it demands the simultaneous growth of most sectors of the economy. Moreover, the consequences of this autarkic policy were also felt in connection with other investment problems: self-sufficiency was to be achieved by the utilization of domestic resources. This principle of self-sufficiency was entirely unknown in the Soviet Union in the first decade of its existence; nor was such a tendency observable in the policy of the other socialist states at the beginning. But from the autumn of 1947 this idea became an inviolable principle. In the inter-war period foreign capital played a prominent role in most of East and South East Europe where the rate of net saving was low. In the period after World War II investments on an extraordinarily large scale had to be realized in quick succession without foreign capital. A high rate of growth was achieved through a high rate of investment – the result of planning. During the first five-year plan, industrial production

[1] Planning principles are summarized: Spulber, *Economics of Communist Eastern Europe*, pp. 288 ff., pp. 294–6.
[2] Cf. 'Adatok ès adalékok a népgazdaság fejlödésének tanulmányozásához 1949–1955' (Data and contribution for studying the development of national economy 1949–1955), *Központi Statisztikoi, Hiratal*.

approximately doubled in most socialist countries, and national income showed a corresponding increase. As a result of the investment policy adopted, the whole economic structure changed radically. The share of industry in national income was almost as large as that of agriculture had been formerly. The Central and Eastern European countries became industrial or mixed industrial and agricultural regions. In industry particularly rapid growth was observed in the production of capital equipment.

At this point it seems apposite to examine the consequences of the policy of autarky and of the decision not to pursue the idea of the economic integration of the Central and Eastern European countries.

The matter is by no means simple. First of all, autarky could not be built up to the desired level. Countries which, because of their natural endowments, could not attain a state of self-sufficiency, soon found themselves in an awkward situation: as a result of the forced growth of heavy industries, the demand for raw materials and investment goods could be satisfied only by imports. Instead of self-sufficiency, they established steadily widening foreign trade connections. But the process of rapid industrialization brought with it further problems. The ratio of industrial investment to national income became so large that agriculture did not develop. For instance, Polish agricultural production fell 10 per cent below the pre-war level. By 1953, Czechoslovak industrial production was double the pre-war level, while agricultural output was lower than before the war.[1]

In general, the situation was similar in Hungary. The rigorous principle of self-sufficiency proved too burdensome and, because of the excessively fast rate of industrialization, the standard of living deteriorated. From 1949 to 1953, real wages fell by nearly 20 per cent.[2] And wages fell at a similar rate in Czechoslovakia and Poland.[3]

Thus rapid industrialization brought with it the decline of agriculture, sectoral imbalance, foreign trade difficulties, a falling standard of living and a low efficiency of investment, due to bad management. The tendency to a self-sufficient economy undoubtedly exerted a strong influence in the same direction. Again, when in the early fifties the standard of living stagnated or fell considerably, the cause could be traced to too high a rate of accumulation as well as to the priority given to the development of the

[1] *Economic Survey of Europe Since the War*, United Nations, Geneva, 1953, p. 24; *Economic Survey of Europe in 1965*, United Nations, Geneva, p. 191; *Tartós békéért, népi demokráciáért*, 18 Sept. 1953.
[2] 'Adatok és adalékok...' (cf. p. 19 n 2), pp. 361–2.
[3] Zauberman, *Industrial Progress*, p. 95.

mining industry and the production of basic materials, branches which demanded the largest investments.

Because of the adherence to autarky, the prevailing economic attitude ignored such decisive factors as national resources and trading opportunities. Frequently plans were dominated by targets far beyond practical possibilities. In Hungary this is illustrated by the preposterous decision to develop the iron, steel, and mill plate industries most quickly, to make Hungary 'the country of iron and steel',[1] despite the fact that the necessary raw materials were not available in the country. This created contradictory conditions. The outcome was that rapid industrialization came too heavy a burden for the population; moreover, the results failed to justify the sacrifices which it had demanded. For the time being this did not cause any slowing in the rapid rate of growth. However, productive capacity was engaged in less profitable activities and there were few opportunities to apply modern techniques. Production was inefficient and this contributed to serious imbalance and the tendency of undulatory growth.

It must be emphasized that in countries where the preconditions of a self-sufficient economy were not fulfilled, this irrational endeavour to achieve autarky led to a quite paradoxical result: the consequences were contrary to the original objectives. Launched as it was to counter aspirations towards a new type of integration, this policy of self-sufficiency did not truly promote the realization of economic independence. Autarky and independence, integration and defencelessness, when viewed in the light of modern economic realism, are not correlated notions, unless approached by formal logic. Forced industrialization, the alleged basis of autarky, in reality involved the need for large supplies of raw materials which did not conduce to the economic independence of these countries: instead of strengthening their economic independence, they experienced an uneasy position of increased economic instability, while suffering from import difficulties and currency problems. The economic processes of the fifties underlined this experience. It is possible for vertical and horizontal integration in certain sectors to make a small country so competitive that it can hold its own in international markets; such a position brings economic reciprocity and its impact is instrumental in strengthening the country's sovereignty. Undoubtedly, the non-realization of integration

---

[1] '...the basic problem of our Five Years' Plan is the development of our iron- and steel-production at a rapid pace unheard-of in the history of the Hungarian industry'. Ernö Gerö, *Harcban a szocialista népgazdaságért* (The fight for a socialist national economy), Szikra, 1950, pp. 529–30, and *idem*, *A vas, acél és gépek országáért* (For a state of iron, steel and machines), Szikra, 1952.

contributed to the intensification of internal economic difficulties: political conditions had changed by the end of the first five-year plans and so economic policy had to be modified in nearly all the socialist countries.

During 1953–4 careful examination of the economic development carried out in the preceding years led to the recognition of the grave contradictions inherent in the concept of autarky. Besides the revision of economic policy a new conception of mutual collaboration became indispensable. In spring 1954, after a long pause, the fourth session of the Council of Mutual Economic Aid was convened.

This date may be considered as the beginning of a new period in the history of the economic co-operation of the socialist countries.[1] Three sessions followed in quick succession; three months after the fourth session, held in Moscow in December 1955, came the fifth and the sixth sessions were organized in Budapest. These meetings opened the road to new modes of co-operation in several spheres of economic activity. The third session was conducted along the earlier lines of preparing and co-ordinating long-term commercial agreements. At the same time new ideas emerged, one of the most important of which was the project for a unified electric power network which was launched in the summer of 1954. The first steps towards the realization of co-ordinated planning and development were immediately made, mainly on the basis of bilateral negotiations. In 1954 Hungary, Rumania and Czechoslovakia drew up contracts for the construction of aluminium and chemical plants. Hungary reached further agreements with Czechoslovakia and Poland concerning the manufacture of rolled steel products and with Rumania and Poland concerning specialization in the tractor industry. In 1955 similar agreements were concluded between the German Democratic Republic and Poland and between Rumania, Czechoslovakia, and Bulgaria.

The most important event of the CMEA meeting held at the end of December 1955, in Budapest, was the recognition and the discussion of the urgent need to co-ordinate planning and production in general[2] and to specialize in engineering. These developments point to a gradual change in the interpretation of the possibilities and the role of CMEA. For the Conference not only settled questions of principle, but also, for the first time, adopted practical resolutions and initiated a

[1] The suitability of this date as a point of division between periods is agreed by all experts on the problem. Cf. 'Mirovaya Ekonomika i Mezhdunarodnye Otnoshenyia', 1963, no. 3, editorial study on the 'Present situation of the CMEA'.
(In this paper, the period from 1954 to 1962 is considered as a uniform cycle, but this opinion cannot be considered as a generally adopted one.)
[2] *Társadalmi Szemle*, 11 Sept. 1958, p. 84.

thorough specialization of the manufacture of automobiles, tractors, railway rolling stock and some agricultural machines.

It cannot be said that in these years the whole structure of economic co-operation changed completely. International collaboration continued to rest mainly on bilateral trading relations. What was of decisive significance in 1954 and 1955 was a recognition of the existing possibilities and requirements. This period of transition reached the stage of consummation at the seventh session held in Berlin in May 1956, which ended another chapter in the history of the Council of Mutual Economic Aid.

The list of the subjects put on the agenda of the meeting will suffice to confirm what has been said: the possibilities of finding a common solution to the raw material and fuel problems were dealt with; another discussion took place on the probabilities of co-ordination within the engineering industries. Suggestions were made for the specialization in the manufacture of more than 600 groups and articles of machinery, implements, and accessories. Twelve permanent consultative committees were established, with the aim of promoting better collaboration.[1]

This was the opening of an extremely dynamic period in the life of CMEA. From June 1957 to the summer of 1963 eleven sessions were held, the schedules becoming more crowded and better adapted to practical purposes. In this instance it is unnecessary to go into a detailed analysis of the themes discussed at the sessions (from the eighth to the eighteenth); it is the general tendency which deserves notice. At these talks attention was concentrated throughout on a single issue, notably the co-ordination of development projects, mutual specialization of production and expansion, and all-round co-operation. At the 1957 meeting in Warsaw, a detailed discussion also raised the question of how the other socialist countries could contribute by investment goods to the advancement of the Polish coal and sulphur industries, because the processes were most efficient in Poland and investments could be recovered in a short time. In 1958, in Prague, the crucial points of the talks were the building of a common pipeline and further specialization in the production of equipment. In the spring of 1959, at the Conference held in Sofia, co-ordination was extended to the sugar and paper industries and meat products. The next year, at the Budapest meeting, specialization in agricultural products was among the questions of the day.

After so many errors and centuries of unfortunate historical experiences, the Central and Eastern European countries finally discovered the route to

[1] W. Mosterty: *Spezialisierung und Kooperation im Maschinenbau zwischen den sozialistischen Ländern*, Wirtschaftswissenschaft, 1958, no. 5, pp. 659, 671.

an integration which would liberate them from the narrow national frames of development. Growth was stimulated by new ideas and perceptions. A number of studies demonstrated the economies of large-scale production.[1] Today extensive literature is available on the new co-ordination and partial specialization carried out by the early sixties, mainly in the generation of energy, the production of raw materials and the manufacture of machinery and chemicals.

But all these measures should be regarded only as first steps, for specialization in industry applied only to products that had already been manufactured. The spectrum of products was not reduced, although further increase in numbers was prevented by the new arrangements.

The ratio of machinery production based on CMEA agreements did not surpass 2 to 6 per cent of total output, not taking into account the spontaneous effect of actual business transactions. For instance in Poland this ratio amounted to 6 per cent as late as 1964.[2] According to the pertinent comment of a Soviet scientist published in 1962 'the most efficient division of labour among the socialist countries has been reached in the production of primary and raw materials, that is to say in a domain where the division of labour is the simplest and is determined chiefly by natural circumstances'.[3]

As a matter of fact, multilateral investments were made in many industries, in order to exploit sources of raw materials. Iron ore mining in Czechoslovakia and the Soviet Union, coal mining in the German Democratic Republic, Poland and Czechoslovakia, common enterprises set up by Poland and the Soviet Union, by Hungary, Bulgaria, the German Democratic Republic and Czechoslovakia, were all conducted in the new spirit of collaboration. The Polish–Hungarian enterprise Haldex may be mentioned as a striking example of a jointly operated establishment.

The developments also indicate the important change that ensued in the activities of the Council of Mutual Economic Aid: the socialist countries were gradually freed from the restricting conditions accompanying bilateral agreements and the first important signs of multilateral co-operation appeared. Of these the most significant was the first multilateral agreement, which was concluded in 1957 and deserves special mention: it created a system of international clearing of the balance of payments among the socialist countries. Another example is the pipeline 'Friendship', the

[1] Cf. the paper by Dudynskiy in *Mirovaya Ekonomika i Mezhdunarodniye Otnosheniya*, 1962, no. 12, and the Editorial as quoted under n. 1 on p. 22.

[2] O. Bogomolov, *Economic Cooperation between the countries of CMEA*, Planovoye Hozyaystwo, 1964, no. 4.

[3] Dudynskiy, paper in *Mirovaya Ekonomika*, 1962, no. 12.

building of which was decided upon in 1958. In 1964 the first oil supplies were sent by the Soviet Union along this pipeline to Poland, the German Democratic Republic, Hungary and Czechoslovakia.

The long-distance electric transmission line which connects the national networks of the Central and Eastern European countries became operative in 1962. The foundation of a Common Bank of the socialist countries under the auspices of the Council of Mutual Economic Aid was intended to promote multilateral economic relations. As a completion of this process, a new project was conceived in November 1962, namely the foundation of a common Central Planning Office. A high-level meeting was announced at which the principal objective was to promote integration.[1]

Thus, at the beginning of the present decade the Central and Eastern European countries adopted an economic policy favouring rapid advancement of integration.

In this connection it is only natural to wonder what forces were at work in bringing about such a quick acceptance of the new positive attitude to integration. There were various inducements. In the first place we have to point to a factor which has been mentioned before, namely the adverse influence of the trend of autarky in the early fifties. The general recognition of the contradictions made it a common concern to abandon former mistakes, thereby clearing the ground for the acceptance of integration. This awareness of the reasons for failure was a fundamental element, yet it cannot be assumed to have played a decisive role in the case of the Soviet Union, which now showed the strongest initiative. As a matter of fact the Soviet Union did not suffer from the development of autarky, and integration, even when achieved, was likely to exert only a relatively marginal influence.

In the late fifties and early sixties, the leading advocates of integration in the Soviet Union argued in favour of competing with the capitalist countries and achieving their economic level, with the fastest rate of growth of the socialist countries. This initiative was supported by the highly industrialized socialist countries, chiefly by Czechoslovakia and the German Democratic Republic, as well as by countries with inadequate sources of raw materials, for instance Hungary, which regarded integration as a matter of vital importance.

However, reception was by no means uniform, and the problems presented by the realization of these ambitious projects soon became evident. Integrated planning was frowned upon because of traditional attitudes, and socialist economic expansion was acceptable only within a national

[1] *Pravda*, 20 Nov. 1962.

framework. This attitude, resulting from historical–political traits, still has to be taken into account when planning new projects.

There were certain economic realities which were not conducive to the development of integration. It is beyond the scope of the present study to deal with the probable effect of a centralized planning system on the realization of integration. As pointed out before, the planning system based on compulsory directives which was in force until recently exerted a strongly restraining influence.[1] Efforts at integration proposed by politicians and leading economists frequently foundered as a result of the indifference, clumsiness, or resistance shown by the managers of the firms in question.

The former system of planning was an impediment to progress in more than one respect. Being anachronistic, it had a complicated bearing on international relations and a peculiar national impact. This finally resulted in the frustration of any suggestion for an extension of the centralized planning system to an international scale, even when a new type of integration was proposed. Also, conflicting interests and varied conditions prevented integration in the socialist countries.

This method of integration based on the centralized planning system in an international form as proclaimed in the early sixties, proved to be impractical. Formerly, hostility to any integration beyond simple commercial interconnections was regarded as wrong. Now the idea of integration on a large scale was condemned because it went beyond the given possibilities and existing economic requirements. Despite its unequivocal objectives, the project elicited contrary reactions and considerably hindered the development of sound economic integration among the socialist countries.

In fact an extensive economic integration of the socialist countries was tackled soon after World War II but, handicapped by numerous obstacles, it progressed only in the field of foreign trade. The fact that integration, so important and advantageous for the Central and Eastern European countries, advanced only by very slow degrees over two decades was evidently due to the enormous obstacles inherent in economic conditions. The present study was not intended to investigate these aspects of economic relations. However, an analysis of the economic policy of the age suggests the conclusion that it was the grave mistakes in this field which hampered the progress of integration: in the late forties and the early fifties the rejection of integration on a large scale; in the late fifties and the early sixties the insistence on unrealistic objectives. In the two periods in

[1] Cf. S. Ausch, 'A KGST országok együttmüködésének fej lesztése' [Development of the co-operation between the countries of CMEA]. *Közgazdasági Szemle*, 1966, no. 3.

question, policy concerning economic integration assumed completely contrary characteristics, and, strangely enough, set up contradictory targets with varying effect and in varying form; they all barred steady growth.

Once these mistakes of economic policy are recognized, the views expressed by several experts on the subject have to be rejected as erroneous. These authors are inclined to think that the history of CMEA from the years 1963–4 reveals a tendency for the socialist countries to increase their economic independence, to loosen their mutual relationships, and to make an approach to economic relations with the West.[1]

Of course, the events of the last few years are too close to be evaluated reasonably. In fact significant advances in co-operation have been achieved in recent years, but contradictory steps and failures have also been recorded. In some instances true (or apparent) national interests have clashed with the principle of integration, while trade with the Western countries has increased. However, it would be wrong to conceive of the advancement of trade with the Western countries as a factor which acts against systematic co-operation within the framework of CMEA. As has been proved in ingenious and convincing ways,[2] Western commercial relations are apt to, and should, become complementary and supporting forces in the countries of CMEA, since division of labour among the socialist countries could be realized to the best advantage in a European, rather than an Eastern European, context. At all events, even relatively short experience has shown that it was not integration itself that failed but certain methods and forms of the process.

The problem is not that integration is impracticable, but that inadequate and unrealistic methods, which are obsolete even by national standards, have been used. It is also certain that the great majority of the countries which set up the Council of Mutual Economic Aid have no wish to emancipate themselves from co-operation. However, they do seek for suitable practical means, which truly promote progress and correspond to the new stages of socialist economic development, the changing system of planning and control.

It would be easy to quote here the true but rather weak explanation that the road to integration is rough, and this should be regarded as natural. However, it is more important to notice the real roads to progress, and not to be led astray in the apparent labyrinth of occasional success and numerous set-backs or recurring deadlock.

---

[1] Ausch, 'A KGST országok', p. 354.
[2] E.g. W. Gumpel, 'Fortschritte und Grenzen der Zusammenarbeit im Rat für Gegenseitige Wirtschaftshilfe', *Osteuropäische Wirtschaft*, 1967, no. 3.

*Ivan Berend*

Of course, an analysis of the present in relation to the future is the domain of the economist rather than that of the economic historian. When the present problems, possibilities, and obstacles of economic integration are estimated, the inheritance of the past century and its influence on the present have to be taken into consideration. Besides political and economic necessities, the path of economic integration in the socialist countries is equally affected by differences in the levels of development in Central and Eastern European countries, that were influenced by past trends.

The traditions of distrustful national isolation and the self-sufficient national economy are still a heavy burden. The advance of integration demands tough, persevering efforts and is gradual rather than precipitate. These facts may also be ascribed to the same influences, to which due heed should therefore be paid in economic policy.

Despite the contradictions of the last decade there can be no doubt that something new is about to emerge. Yet the inheritance of the past is still alive, loaded with mistrust, with adverse experiences and prejudices, and with forces striving for undeserved advantages. It would be childish to hope that all this might be wiped out by the enlightening dictates of pure reason. Contradictory tendencies fight against each other: there are claims for increased co-operation and there are indifferent, even inimical, elements, appearing as the outcome of differences of economic and social levels.

Progress will be realized by the ever-increasing tendency to conclude bilateral and multilateral agreements in every field in which opportunities arise, and by founding common enterprises in certain sectors of the economy. This is the practical path to a more complete co-operation among the socialist countries.

## 2. Integration, economic union and the national state

IMRE VAJDA

Even among the many paradoxes of the modern world, the contradictions inherent in the situation of the nation-state are conspicuous. As the colonial system disintegrates, the process by which new nations and states are created roars over our heads like a historic tempest, and its storm-like character is intensified by the fact that we have not been sufficiently prepared for it. Neither those who have already passed through the principal stages of national evolution (including ourselves, although the process is not long behind us), nor those who initiated the process, foresaw the complications and inevitable internal struggles attendant on the birth of nations. Yet we should have been able to predict that after the disappearance of foreign oppressive empires, the nations, which in their conscious strata had seemed more or less united, would experience the upheaval of class-conflict, and of struggles for positions in the hierarchy of power. We should have been forewarned by our own history and by the ample experience of peoples in Europe and elsewhere. We have not learned our lesson well enough from this experience.

In addition to these storm-centres, although not quite independently of them, we are experiencing in some places the appearance of a striking degree of national consciousness in peoples which have long enjoyed independence. I might call this phenomenon neo-nationalism, if this word did not have a somewhat simplifying and derogatory ring, and if I did not wish to refrain from over-simplification in an area where earlier sympathies and antipathies could play a role. I might mention here the France of General de Gaulle, the vocation of the French nation, which has been passionately proclaimed, but (except for the praiseworthy rejection of American supremacy) hardly defined, or the slogan of 'Europe des patries' – beautifully sounding, but again not clarified. I might mention the convulsions in Britain, one focus of which is the concern whether the new orientation of economic policy – which has been recognized as imperative – will bring Britain into Europe, and if so, what will become of the British nation which has been accustomed to the idea of 'splendid isolation'. We have to think of German nationalism, the rejection of which is justified not only by our antipathy for its past manifestations, but also by its concrete, continuously voiced objectives: the re-expansion of German frontiers (i.e. those of the Federal Republic); and by its means: intensive political and economic pressure, intended to overcome all resistance. But in addition there are the problems of multi-national countries, whether they are capitalist or socialist states; for instance, the Walloon–Flemish problem of Belgium, and the recently rekindled hostility between English-speaking and French-speaking Canadians. I mention only countries whose social system is very different from our own, out of consideration for our neighbours and in the knowledge that it is by historical accident, and not by our own virtue, that we have avoided the aggressive features of nationalism. We Hungarians hardly have the right to consider ourselves better or more moderate than others.

National consciousness has not weakened; its institutional framework, sovereignty, which is in part a concept and in part a phenomenon, will be dealt with later. The nation which exists for its own sake and values its existence does not find itself on the horns of a dilemma simply because international political interdependence places the newborn nation in a course of events which inevitably determine its future. This course is frequently set without consulting the nation concerned, although some pretence of international equality is usual. At the same time, international political interdependence also confines the independent, self-centred actions of older, stronger nations within narrow limits, and renders independence an illusion. If we attempted to weigh our opportunities for really sovereign action against those actions which are controlled by inter-dependence, how many cases can we imagine in which the former would outweigh the latter? And how often would this balance not threaten us with disaster?

A particularly close network of interdependence has developed in the domain of international economic activity, and it is no exaggeration to say that unless some catastrophe obliterates human culture, the mutual econo-mic interdependence of peoples and of continents will become permanent and develop even further. It is in these new forms of integration that the tension between the independence of the national state and the economic interdependence of the integrated area is most apparent. This is the focus of the political crises of the European Economic Community. Does the Treaty of Rome lead through the Common Market customs union to economic union, and through the latter to political union? Is this in fact the feasible and realizable historic sequence? Is it economic union, the unification of economic and legal institutions and systems, and of objec-tives of economic policy, in the countries belonging to the union, that brings about political union? Explaining the crux of the matter with less restraint than is usual, this means the merging of several, previously independent, sovereign national states into a single multi-national state, for supra-nationality is only a station on the road leading to multi-nationality, and who knows what will be the step beyond that? Or is this supposed sequence misleading, does political union in fact not grow out of economic union, are the paths to the former still uncertain and unfathomable? The experience we have already gained of the process of integration certainly bears witness to the fact that the national state is strong and cannot be easily liquidated by integration. It is not the absence of economic union that blocks the path to political union, but rather the contradiction between the national state, representing a social and historical entity, and the economic union.

I should emphasize that, in examining the creation of the Common Market, political motivation cannot be neglected. The endeavours to put an end to German–French rivalry, with its long history and its burden of recent unpleasant memories, played an important role. The extent to which the creation of the European Economic Community was a result of the political attitude of the United States is well known, and the latter was at that time dominated by the cold war (centred on Europe) and by the establishment of NATO. Let me quote here the Swedish Professor Gunnar Myrdal: '...this was the period of the intense cold war, when West European economic integration appeared as a means of building up the anti-Communist front. For the United States, that gave its strong support to the establishment of EEC – in spite of the strong discrimination created against its exports as well as the exports from other outside countries – the last political motive was the main one.'[1] But in the course of the ten years of its existence, the Common Market, despite the changing political climate and the frequent disharmony of intentions and consequences, has gained an independent existence, and this is what primarily interests us in our further investigations.

The applicability of the term 'integration' to CMEA (Comecon) is often doubted, because the latter is considered as a regional grouping or as the economic gathering of the socialist countries. However, I believe that the obvious affinity of problems does not permit us to retreat into formalism. We shall see that many of its features differ from the integration of the Western European capitalist countries; most conspicuously, it is not built on the integration of the market, but on the coordination of plans. Further,

[1] Myrdal: 'The Effects toward Integration in Rich and Poor Countries', a lecture given in Mexico City, 3 Oct. 1966.

with the exception of the short period of common planning, the institutional requirements of supranationality have not found a place in Comecon – and, of course, the social system of the countries united in it is socialist, while that of the EEC countries is capitalist. But if we wish to define the concept of integration by its economic content and its attainable objectives, we have to realize that the purpose of Comecon is the furthering of the economic integration of its member states and that therefore a parallel between the EEC and the Comecon is not unjustified. Another justification is provided by the fact that in both cases we are faced with the unsolved problem of the national state and economic union, and that in neither case did or could the community take over the tasks of the national state.

THE CONCEPT AND ECONOMIC CONTENT OF INTEGRATION

The clarification of the concept and the economic content of integration should be our next step. Economic literature offers us little assistance in this. B. Balassa called economic integration both a process and a situation. According to him, considered as a process it means the introduction of measures which aim at the elimination of discrimination between economic units belonging to different national states, and as a situation it means the absence of discrimination between national economies.[1] The study of integration by the Swiss authors Sannwald and Stohler offers essentially the same definition,[2] while Jean Weiller, supported by other French scholars, appears to reject the narrow confines of these definitions and tries to expand them polemically. 'Integration does not mean simple addition, but in a given area the increase of the compatibility of the plans of decision-making centres with the objective of forming of them a single economic system. To study integration means accordingly to rise above the level of the market and turn our attention towards decision, anticipations and intentions.'[3]

The 'decision-making centres' which are to be integrated are here obviously the authorities of the various national states; they cannot mean companies, for the definition refers to Europe. Thinking at the market-level has to be rejected because of the need to differentiate between integration and the free-trade area (EFTA). This is understandable, since we have quoted a French author.

Balassa's definition restricts integration entirely to the market level, and

[1] B. Balassa, *The theory of integration*, Irwin, Homewood, 1961.
[2] Rolf Sannwald–Jacques Stohler, *Wirtschaftliche Integration*, Kyklos-Verlag, Basel, 1961.
[3] Jean Weiller, *L'économie internationale depuis 1950*, Presses Universitaires de France, Paris, 1965, p. 97.

32

as such is the child of neo-classical bourgeois theory; he recognizes the facts of modern economy, which are prying apart the limitations of this theory, only insofar as in addition to the *surmised* free trade he also recognizes the *existing* protectionism. According to him, the task of integration is to extend the area protected to the external boundaries of the integrated countries – for the free competition of the microeconomic units. I call this form *market integration*, and wish to express by this term the fact that it by no means exhausts all the objective functions of integration. However, it is incontestable that, in spite of its limitations, market integration has contributed considerably to the expansion of world trade, the rationalization of production, and the raising of the standard of living in the countries where it has been applied consistently. The acceleration of economic growth and the elimination of cycles, which earlier used to develop into crises, are to a great extent the result of integration alone. Western European capitalist integration also played a positive role in raising the real income of the working class, by widening the boundaries for competition, by creating opportunities for the application of new technologies through mass production, by assuring that competition made it impossible for the weaker and less efficient to shelter behind narrow tariff walls and also created a wide market.

But it should be noted that market integration had unexpected consequences too. The gradual elimination of discrimination opened up earlier jealously guarded gates, not only for the companies of countries participating in the integration, but also for companies in 'third countries', if they had associated companies in one of the integrated countries. In theory the role of a 'third country' may be filled by any state – India as well as the United States. In practice, the United States could be and has been the only third country; its companies have made ample use of the vacuum created for them by anti-discriminatory policy. According to Western sources American companies control the following share of the production of the electronics industry in Western Europe:

15 per cent of consumer goods: radio and TV sets, recording equipment;

50 per cent of semi-conductors;

80 per cent of computers and control equipment;

95 per cent of integrated circuits, ballistic missiles and the new generation of computers.[1]

American firms were not disturbed by the institutional weakness of European supra-nationalism; as American companies, they have enjoyed in Europe all the advantages of extra-nationality without its disadvantages,

[1] Jean-Jacques Servan–Schreiber, *Le défi americain*, Dencel, Paris, 1967, pp. 25–6.

since their headquarters are in the United States. The situation is made even more paradoxical by the fact that 'fourth countries' are unable to trade through the common customs frontiers without losses, and thus the trade-restricting and production-distorting effects of regional protection are increased. While those who profit from the integration – including the American enterprises which have worked their way in – obtain all the advantages of the economies of scale, the economic units of the excluded countries cannot obtain these economies because major markets (the integrated one and the traditionally protectionist United States) are closed to them, and hence losses arise from their inability to develop their production to an optimum scale on account of the lack of a large enough market.

The conceptual looseness of the term 'integration' – the above-mentioned French approach is not precise either – has recently induced the English author John Pinder to contest the attempts of his predecessors and to suggest the following definition: 'I will therefore define economic integration as both the removal of discrimination as between the economic agents of the member countries, and the formation and application of coordinated and common policies on a sufficient scale to ensure that major economic and welfare objectives are fulfilled. It follows that economic union is a state in which discrimination has been largely removed, and coordinated and common policies have been and are being applied on a sufficient scale.'[1]

This definition obviously extends but also circumscribes the conceptual limits of integration. It includes market integration, in which it sees the elimination of discrimination (Jan Tinbergen's 'negative integration'), but beyond this it operates in the domain of economic policy with its hazy perspectives and does not attempt any sharper definition of the limits of integration. The boundary between economic union and integration is almost entirely obliterated, and the former is at most clothed with a small quantitative surplus.

## THE POSITIVE CONTENT OF INTEGRATION – SELECTIVE INTEGRATION

In any view, integration is not a spontaneous process, but an institutionalized system of state economic policies. In certain sectors of the economy these policies are intended to maintain the political sovereignty of the state, and, in other sectors, its economic sovereignty as well. The basic

[1] John Pinder, 'Problems of economic integration', Paper prepared for the Bailey Conference, 1968, London (multigraphed).

forms of international integration, which will be discussed here, assume a level of economic development in which the modern forces of production have already reached a thorough integration within the domestic economy – in the capitalist system the existence of a united market, in the socialist system the existence of an economy united on the basis of state ownership of the means of production and state organization of productive activity. Our attention is directed towards the phenomenon of international integration growing out of domestic integration. In my view the range of tasks of the former is as follows:

(*a*) Market integration; the guarantee of unhindered sale of each other's products within the framework of the social system of participating countries, as long as this is not obstructed by social–political interests or excluded by common production agreements. I consider that this concept should include financial integration. One decisive element in this respect is the creation of a transferable currency which circulates unobstructed in the international sphere and has the same purchasing power throughout. Further, credits and the transfer of capital must be possible on an international scale, for which an international currency is a precondition.

(*b*) Production and development integration: raising to an international level and programming the production of those branches of industry which, in view of their technological development, vertical integration, the size of their investments, and the shorter-than-average life of their capital equipment, cannot be developed to an optimum size within national boundaries without upsetting the internal equilibrium of the national economy. I do not believe that production integration is mandatory in all branches of processing activity; many sectors of industrial production have reached or can reach an optimum size within the boundaries of many of the Western European capitalist or of the socialist countries. In the capital-intensive sectors, the optimum input–output ratios and unit costs are substantially reduced, mainly because of automation and managerial mobility. In other sectors, the economies of scale are insignificant or even negative beyond a certain limit. The former branches of industry include electronics, computers, vehicle-building, many branches of plastics and engineering, power and metallurgy; the latter include almost all branches of light industry and the food industry, nearly all tertiary industries, and agriculture.

Integration and the modernization of the structure of production are necessarily interrelated. The greater the ambition to modernize the structure of production, the greater the need for international integration, and the more consistent the programme of integration, the faster the process of modernization may proceed. In Western Europe, this most important task has been mainly fulfilled by the network of European companies financed by American capital – with American development and producing centres behind them – and this is now the most integrated sector of the Western European economy. The European Economic Community, because of its almost exclusive market-orientation, has practically no results to show in the field of production integration. At the end of 1967, John Pinder, who as a supporter of Britain's entry took account of the achievements of the European Community, enumerated the following:

(1) The establishment of the customs union.

(2) The creation of the agricultural common market...Notable though the achievement was, however, its importance as a contribution to positive integration should not be exaggerated. In effect the 'policy' at present is almost entirely centred on the fixing of a common price (and an uneconomically high one at that), which is the only way of removing discrimination between the member states.

(3) The successful negotiation of the Kennedy round.

(4) The cartel policy – yet another aspect of negative integration.

(5) The fifth major achievement in the Community is the agreement to adopt a uniform value added tax (TVA)...the TVA is designed to remove competitive distortions and, when the rate is made uniform in each country, to enable the member countries to abolish fiscal frontiers between them. There is so far no element of positive integration: of the use of tax policy or tax revenue for ends other than the removal of discrimination and of economic frontiers between the member states.

Production and developmental integration (Tinbergen's positive integration) were entirely subordinated by the Treaty of Rome to the microeconomic level:[1] the spontaneity of the market, the force of competition. The first decade of the EEC is evidence that this policy, based on neoclassical ideas, a misunderstanding of the trends of industrial development, the primacy of capitalist private property and the underestimation or outright denial of the economic role of the state, has been insufficient and inadequate for modern requirements.

[1] Weiller, *L'économie international*, p. 101. Jean Weiller enumerates the following points of the Treaty of Rome: (*a*) application of a cyclical policy in the case of 'questions of common interest'; (*b*) determination of a common financial policy, which extends to exchange rates, in the case of difficulties or grave dangers; defensive measure to overcome balance of payments crises; (*c*) determination of a common agricultural policy; (*d*) search for a common trade policy; (*e*) harmonization of social security legislation; (*f*) establishment of a European Investment Bank; (*g*) agreements of association with overseas countries which have special links (*sic!*) with member countries.

But can we be satisfied with revealing the theoretical and practical shortcomings and omissions of integration so far, without seeking its deeper causes? Can the Marxist observer stop short at such surface phenomena as the oft-repeated opposition of General De Gaulle to the supranationality of the Common Market authorities? I see the deeper-lying causes of the negative features in the following:

(1) At its present stage, of which agreements between government bodies are in essence characteristic, integration should demand the international use of that part of national income which is to be redistributed for development purposes. Today, all development policy is carried out by substantial state means. Integration cannot be effective as long as it does not dispose of an adequate part of the financial means that are redistributed through the state budgets for its objectives. The centres of integration have thus far operated without any of the substantial funds available for development; consequently, their development programmes were unable to unfold, or were limited to the elaboration of programmes recommended but not executed.

(2) The appropriation and redistribution of part of the national income is one of the most important manifestations of state sovereignty, but the state can exercise permanent sovereignty only through democratic institutions. The internal sovereignty of the national state grows in step with the increase in the proportion of income which is redistributed; with this increase the importance of democratic control and of participation in decision-making grows. True, the actual role of democratic control in no way corresponds to its growing importance. One of the characteristics and serious problems of our era is the preponderance of the apparatus – the state bureaucracy and the large corporate hierachy, which is closely linked with the former – over the democratic institutions. The most striking examples of this are presented by advanced capitalist countries, such as the United States and West Germany, but this problem is present in the socialist state too, and our economic reforms, even if they do not solve this problem entirely, are directed towards its mitigation. In the organs of integration this situation implies even graver dangers in view of the complete absence of democratic control, i.e. the apparatus becomes completely independent.

I wish to emphasize that optimum integration would not use the majority of the funds which are available to the state for distribution, as there are many sectors where little or no advantage can be gained from integration. Although defence and security are important areas of redistribution, they are peripheral to our study, so we shall refrain from evaluating them.

4-2

*Imre Vajda*

Just as in the case of integration, it is important to define 'sovereignty' at the outset.

The legal definition of sovereignty: 'Sovereignty; in the internal aspect, the unrestricted and undivided supreme power of the state, and towards foreign powers its independence. A state may be considered sovereign if in all domains of its activity, in all aspects of its decisions it is independent',[1] is not satisfactory for our purpose.

We do not wish to remove sovereignty from the sphere of international law; yet is not 'independence in all aspects' an unrealistic requirement? The acceptance of this definition would only prove to us that actual sovereignty does not exist. In its internal aspect, 'supreme power' does not appear satisfactory either, because it is not clear over whom or what supreme power is wielded, nor is it made clear in what way this supreme power is being exercised. Personal power, Machiavelli's *Il Principe*, the 'l'état c'est moi' declaration of Louis XIV, needed the symbol of sovereignty just as little as did later dictators. In modern times, sovereignty is a popular revolutionary aim. In its content, even though not etymologically, it is a political–ethical concept; to me it says: this state is my state, the people's state, with defined, though continuously changing, social and humanitarian goals. It is made sovereign by my will, by the will of the people, the power with which the people have endowed it for the realization of their accepted goals through accepted means, not the power which it exercises over the people. Engels in his *Anti-Dühring* speaks highly of Saint-Simon, who had clearly foreseen the transformation of political government over people into the administration of goods and the management of production processes. The socialist state, in this interpretation and in its full development, is more sovereign because its people put the means of production and the results of their labour at the disposal of the state to a greater extent than is the case in capitalist society. The socialist state is entrusted with greater tasks, 'with the administration of goods, the management of production processes'. The economic activity of the capitalist state is continually limited by the demand for sovereignty of private monopoly capital, disguised as freedom and clothed in the mantle of neo-classical theory. Its most consistent and most docrinaire representatives claim the restriction or extension of the sovereignty of the state, to be a sort of 'Ordnungspolitische Grundentscheinung' – a basic decision defining the system, in the spirit of which they condemn all intervention by

---

[1] *International Diplomatic and Legal Encyclopedia.*

the state, and see the state's internal sovereignty as supreme power over people rather than over processes. Yet in the last fifty years the capitalist states have been unable to prevent the extension of power over the processes as well, which has increased the attraction of socialism. They prefer to describe this as 'Keynesianism' rather than in Marxian terms, but it is the essence and not the disguise that counts. The national state – the capitalist state too – is more sovereign today than it was in the inter-war period, although it is less independent in its decisions.

It has obtained this increased sovereignty, which exists in its most complete form under socialism, through the increased importance of its role in the redistribution of the social product and national income.

The economic basis of the national state is the high proportion of the national income which is redistributed. The Welfare State and the development of culture depend on the redistributed portion of national income, as does the complicated network of research and development programmes connected with production, including regional and urbanization plans. It is from the reservoirs of redistribution that such 're-structuring' investments are financed. But numerous vested interests, representing companies or social strata, also demand a share of the income redistributed, with or without justification.

ECONOMIC UNION

I believe the most problematic part of the development of integration to be its concluding stage – economic union. It is a fact that economic union is an essential part of the concept of the European Economic Community. Its Western critics emphasize primarily the slowness of its progress towards union or its obstruction by French policy. The Treaty of Rome created institutions at the very beginning of the process of integration. Within these institutions, despite the fact that officeholders are delegated by the national states and represent the interests of the latter, a new kind of internal loyalty and cohesion has developed. This indicates that economic union, its future bureaucracy already in existence, was considered a realistic perspective. The apparatus so created has often come into conflict with the stand taken by the governments of some of the member states; for instance, the debate concerning the common agricultural market which caused the first serious crisis in the Community, and the question of the concentration of the West German metallurgical concerns within the ECSC. On a broader plane there was conflict over the question of common planning, or more recently concerning the legal status of the 'European'

39

*Imre Vajda*

(not national) companies.[1] The West German government opposed supranationalism in the question of common planning, partly because it rejected any kind of state planning. As far as European companies are concerned, it is the French government that refuses the claim of the Brussels institution to regulate and to interpret this legislation. In all these cases the sovereignty of the national state was opposed to the apparatus of integration, which is not a state or an institution that stands above the states, but one which should look after technical tasks and prepare resolutions. But can it be more? Is it possible to imagine the economic union of several states occurring through the voluntary limitation, rather than abandonment, of sovereignty, without a political union? Is the divorce of the economic functions of the state from its political functions conceivable today? Or to put the question more forcefully: is it possible to leave the political functions formally intact without the right of disposition over all material resources that are needed to carry them out? Or to continue this train of thought: are political functions| secondary among the tasks of today's state? Even if there should be proof – of which I have seen no trace so far – that economic union (i.e. total integration) could achieve considerably better results, spread evenly throughout the community, than the selective integration which I consider the ideal, would that in itself mean the end of the national state?

Without attributing decisive importance to historical examples – after all, not all events have a precedent – it is noteworthy that in the two most important creations of states of the modern age, that of the United States in the eighteenth century and of the German Empire a century later, political motives of power were predominant, although economic factors also played a considerable part. The revolt of the thirteen North American colonies began as a protest against the tyranny which hurt the interests of the local merchants, but the Declaration of Independence appealed to human and civil rights and declared that the attitude of the British Parliament and Government, which legislated over the heads of the colonists and denied their right to representation, was the real cause of the rupture. Although the Zollverein preceded it by half a century, the Reichsgrundung of 1871 was brought about by Prussian supremacy and the integration of an enlarged Prussian Germany, yet was not completed by the end of the Weimar period. At the same time, the extensive and multi-national monarchies, although forming a single customs area, were not at all integrated economically.

[1] Jan Tinbergen, *International economic integration*, Elsevier, Amsterdam, 1965, p. 77.

40

I shall only risk tentative answers to the questions raised above, in the hope of starting a discussion that might help to clarify them.

My tentative answers concerning the problem of economic union are:

(1) Economic union is not a stage on the path leading towards political union, but a possible and desirable consequence of the latter. An economic union may be brought about by an already achieved political union, but the existing states are at present far from the required level of internationalism. The division of Germany presents a special problem, but, in this case too political union appears to be a more likely possibility than economic union.

(2) A political union is the creation of a new state, with all the imponderables well known from history. It requires further research in a field still hardly explored to discover what transitional forms may be feasible between the national state and the political union which represents the creation of a new state; forms of integration on the basis of increasingly extensive common interests, with institutions in which the participating states voluntarily limit their sovereignty in some areas, while maintaining their independence in others.

(3) Although political institutions are determined by the mode of production and by social conditions, economic interest in itself is, according to historical experience, not a force which brings new states into existence.

(4) On account of the above, I maintain that the concept of economic union is unrealistic.

THE SOCIALIST INTERNATIONAL DIVISION OF LABOUR

The description and evaluation of the European development of the socialist division of labour would be beyond the scope of this study. It is remarkable what a short time it has taken to unite, and in some ways integrate, an area so heterogeneous as the socialist bloc. This has been achieved by the correct recognition of the socialist system, by an international approach and by the direction of the development of production. It is also true that this process has resulted in a preponderance of industrial production, through which it has been possible to overcome the backwardness inherited from the former capitalist-feudal system. We do not wish to engage here in a critical evaluation of this process, which has been partly undertaken elsewhere, but which to a large extent requires further research into economic history. Let us now concentrate on the conclusions which may be drawn from our earlier discussion. I do not conceal that in investigating the problems of integration, even when analysing the institutions of the Common Market, I had the development of CMEA continuously in mind, since *tua res agitur*. The main conclusions may be summarized as follows:

(1) In the socialist international division of labour both forms of integration have to be applied: market integration and production development integration in its selective framework; at present neither basic form can be considered to be achieved to a sufficient extent;

(2) The socialist international division of labour need not necessarily be directed towards total integration; it is more important that in the sectors which determine technical progress and are important in increasing the productivity of labour a more planned and institutionalized co-operation should be achieved than has been attained so far;

(3) The fulfilment of integrated development plans requires in CMEA or in the framework of multilateral agreements the internationalization of part of the national funds that are to be redistributed;

(4) The authority, capacity for action and competence of CMEA would be greatly enhanced if an organization endowed with representative, consultative, controlling and initiating powers were constituted in addition to the executive committee. By this means, CMEA could be fitted into the democratic system of the socialist countries with more authority over international organizations;

(5) CMEA should also gradually loosen its closed economic character, both towards the advanced industrial and the developing countries. It is very important to stress this, since it is possible that the efforts directed towards the improvement of the functioning of CMEA and the development of its institutions could lead to the strengthening of its 'closedness'; although autarky has not been found (and could not be found) to be a successful way of developing the socialist economies. The abandonment of the trend towards 'closedness' and its replacement by a wider, continental and eventually global attitude does not imply the elimination of regional advantages, but eliminates exclusive and self-centred characteristics. These should not be asserted through protection but through development.

The closed model – or its less emphatic version, which still persists in many places – cannot be maintained from a political point of view either. 'Closedness' may lead to contradictory interests and even bring about an intensified nationalism, in which the differing characteristics of the various countries are either hidden or expressed openly. Among the movements and arguments working against 'closedness', an important role is played by different degrees and forms of interest in foreign trade. At the same time it is necessary – but not in a spirit of 'closedness' – to co-ordinate intelligently the activities directed towards the other spheres of the world market.

Being shut off is contrary to the international policy of socialism; it strengthens imperialism, and weakens the social and national forces opposed to imperialism; it is contrary to the endeavours directed towards peaceful coexistence.

(6) I hold that today the development of the Council of Mutual Economic Assistance into an economic union would be a no more realistic aim than in the case of the European Economic Community.

I began my investigations by showing the paradox presented by international independence and mutual international interdependence, the contradictory situation of the national state. Now in conclusion, I have to confess that I have arrived at a slightly different position than I intended. I confess without embarrassment that I did not grow up with a respect for nationalism, national sentiment, the national state and national traditions. Socialists and Communists have rejected all these as alien to their creed, and have condemned them in the name of the general solidarity of workers, in the name of international revolution. I had ample opportunity to experience the reactionary character of nationalism both in Hungary and in neighbouring countries. I lived in the belief that the days, or at least the years, of the national state were numbered, and that I myself would be able to live the better years of my life as a member of a society which rejected this unloved and unrespected adjective. The confrontation of the two world systems, socialism and capitalism (or imperialism), also directed my attitude toward the denial, or at least the underestimation of national separateness. It was through an agonizing reappraisal that I arrived at a rejection of this fatal over-simplification. I had to see, in spite of my wishes, expectations and theories, that the nations were living, were productive, their culture was flourishing, and that they had not yet reached the end of their historic course, which was not even in view. Having progressed this far, I could not be satisfied with taking note only of the psychological, sociological, historic and linguistic elements of the continued existence and even the strengthening of the various nations; I considered it to be the task of a Marxist economist to explore the social–economic basis of the national-state superstructure, the structure which holds the national state together in spite of all contrary trends. I saw as the most important of the contrary, state-destroying trends the endeavours towards integration, and my task was again made more difficult by the fact that I recognized in integration an effective, even indispensable, means for the assertion

43

of the modern forces of production, given socialist principles of distribution and effective means for assuring general material welfare.

I have presented two results of my thinking: one is the separate economic basis of the national state, its growing role in the redistribution of national income, which becomes complete in the socialist state, although no capitalist or socialist state has yet arrived at this level; the other is that integration as the international organization of the productive processes does not necessarily encompass the whole of economic activity, does not require the liquidation of the national state, and is not the motive force of such destruction. Integration is not the antithesis of the national state; integration and the national state go well together; the former may be built into the latter and this is even desirable, for the latter does not lose its identity in the integration.

And yet the national state is a historic formation, a stage in the development of the forces of production and of social consciousness. Its rigidity and isolation will disappear in the melting-pot of socialist humanism, of internationalism – when, and in what circumstances, and under the influence of what forces, this will happen, remains to be decided by the future.

# 3. External equilibrium, and economic reform

IMRE VAJDA

The new approach to Hungarian economic reform stems largely from experience and lengthy discussion. Though such discussion has clarified the guiding principles, the organizational measures are still being worked out. So it will be hardly surprising that on many questions opinions clash and reservations and qualifications are made. In other words, the debate is still in full swing, although within the limits of already accepted principles.

In this paper I intend to analyse the necessity of the reforms from the viewpoint of balance-of-payments equilibrium and of the effects of technical progress on the world market. The two are closely related and both have bearings on the future of Hungarian foreign trade. I will not review the general principles of reform, which I assume are known. However, I hope that my analysis will contribute to these general principles.

I am fully aware that these two aspects of the problem are not independent, nor can they be entirely isolated from other factors. But the same may be said of any problem of economics.

There are, at the moment, no analytical tools at the disposal of economic science with which to assess in an unequivocal manner the mutual effects and intensity of partial problems, and to put them beyond dispute. The limited character of the analytical possibilities is reflected in the extensive discussions going on throughout the world over the most important subjects of economic policy, discussions which do not stop at the frontiers of different economic systems.

Only a decade ago, the desirability of rapid development of the underdeveloped countries seemed to present almost the only insuperable problem in economic discussions (although for truth's sake it must be admitted that a decade ago we felt nearer the solution than today). Official wisdom was apt to consider the economic development of both the industrially advanced capitalist countries and the socialist countries as a more or less settled matter. Of course there were differences in opinion and approach. In the West, neo-liberalism offered consistent opposition to Keynes' theories. Similarly, criticism of Stalin's theses began to be voiced in the socialist countries, where doubts arose about the validity of earlier established priorities such as industry versus agriculture, heavy industry versus consumer-good industries, centralization versus decentralization, or autarky versus international division of labour. But none of the doubts went so far on either side as to touch upon the fundamental structure of the system itself or to question its suitability for the task of further development.

In recent years, however, much more forcefully formulated doubts have arisen in several fields. Heated debates are going on all over the world about the inadequate degree of international liquidity and methods of improving it, about the gold standard and about the price of gold. Some well-known and influential experts, such as Professor Rueff, conjure up the shadows of the crisis of the thirties, to make us aware of the dangers this situation involves. The question, what measures of economic policy should be proposed to fight inflation and to ensure price stability without putting a brake on economic development, is still unsettled. To escape this dilemma, several representatives of bourgeois economics have chosen to discard the centennial dogma of price stability and to accept the slow but steady process of inflation as not detrimental to dynamic development, rather than facing the consequences of deflation, of the unemployment which, spreading over the economy, would replace the one-sided 'imported inflation', bad in itself, by a still worse 'exported deflation' expanding in every direction.[1] Sir Roy Harrod gives expression to his doubts when writing:

There are certain views widely, but not universally, held about maxims of behaviour for countries for their securing external equilibrium in their balances of payments. The doctrine of free trade has had some reinforcement since the war, although compliance has by no means been perfect, and there is a growing recognition, granted only grudgingly at first, that the maxims flowing from it may not always be applicable to the less developed countries. But if equilibrium does not come about automatically in consequence of free trade or such partially free trade as may prevail, the question arises what the economic authorities ought to do about it. Even when we are on the very threshold of the subject, it is not clear that doctrines currently prevailing give a precise answer. The great majority of economists would readily concede that there are many cases when this would be an inappropriate remedy. What then, is the appropriate remedy? I have the idea that the consequence of the inadequacy of prevailing maxims is that disorder in the world is increasing, and may even lead to a critical situation.[2]

Referring back to the words of Keynes, Harrod goes so far in his doubts as to say that, under the pressure of menacing 'disorder', he would accept

[1] In an 'imported inflation' domestic prices rise sharply under the pressure of rapidly growing foreign demand, whereas in the case of an 'exported deflation' the deflationary curbing of domestic purchasing power may release crisis waves in the related external markets.
[2] R. Harrod, 'Methods of securing equilibrium', *Kyklos*, Vol. 20, 1967, Fasc. 1, pp. 24–33.

protection of the domestic market, a 'little preference' to be given to the 'homespun', though he adds with unconcealed disillusion: 'It is rather sad to be driven back towards protection, after all the brave hopes of 1944.'[1]

It is by some curious play of history that at a time when protection is being invoked in the citadels of free trade, the socialist planned economies should be becoming increasingly conscious of the fact that the current techniques of planning tend to preserve an atmosphere of protection in production. Criticism of and opposition to this situation are now growing strongly and ways are increasingly sought to give a greater importance to the international division of labour and to co-operation. Protection of the domestic producer by means of customs duties may be considered as outdated in this era of state intervention. Modern methods are more sophisticated, many-sided – and often concealed. However, protection exercised in a system of central planning – where imports can be effectively restricted through the control of foreign trade, production and investments – is of an entirely different nature. The realization that the possibility of absolute protection had brought about considerable negative features in our economic development has given rise to doubts concerning the efficiency of the planning techniques and the methods of economic management hitherto applied. These may be considered analagous to those voiced by Harrod, although they have arisen in a context and on the basis of experiences which were fundamentally different from those he was considering. In Hungary, import substitution was an aim of policy and the question was never raised whether efforts in this direction would pay off in due time, or whether similar efforts would not pay off more quickly and with better results in other sectors – nor were the proper means available to measure these effects.

These doubts were strengthened particularly by the trends in the country's foreign trade; the securing of external equilibrium brought about increasingly growing problems, in spite of the undeniable efforts at import substitution. To put it more precisely: the policy, which was aimed at import substitution as an element of centralized planning, instead of doing away with or at least mitigating the equilibrium disturbances, rather tended to increase the difficulties. But this situation does not lead us to the conclusion that protection should be strengthened; on the contrary, we are of the opinion that the economic policy measures needed to secure equilibrium must be sought in new ways and at a higher level. As a matter of fact, the opinion is now generally accepted all over the world that lasting external disequilibrium can be eliminated only by measures of

[1] *Ibid.*

macroeconomic policy, and that the market mechanism is inadequate for that purpose. Now, it should be obvious that the measures needed in the industrially developed countries (and even here the problem will vary from country to country, as e.g. the balance-of-payments deficit of the United States is due to factors other than an adverse trade balance) differ from those needed in the countries only recently liberated from colonial oppression and struggling with the heritage of the past, or in the moderately developed countries, or in those which have only recently reached the level of the latter. We propose to examine this special and generally neglected problem later on.

TENDENCIES IN THE EXTERNAL TRADE OF HUNGARY

In the period from 1961 to 1965 the foreign trade of this country nearly doubled in volume compared with the preceding five-year period. Imports were up by 82 per cent and exports by 88 per cent. The foreign trade turnover of the OECD countries showed a less marked increase with imports growing by 45 per cent and exports by 44 per cent in the same period.[1] In spite of this considerable growth, the lack of external equilibrium in Hungarian foreign trade was more marked than before.

TABLE I. *Summary figures of Hungarian foreign trade* (million foreign exchange forints)*

| Year | Imports | Exports | Turnover, total | Balance† |
|---|---|---|---|---|
| 1956–60 | 8366.2 | 7752.8 | 16119.0 | – 613.4 |
| 1961 | 12039.6 | 12079.6 | 24119.2 | + 40.0 |
| 1962 | 13485.2 | 12905.5 | 26390.7 | – 579.7 |
| 1963 | 15326.7 | 14155.5 | 29482.2 | – 1171.2 |
| 1964 | 17546.0 | 15869.8 | 33415.8 | – 1676.2 |
| 1965 | 17848.5 | 17721.3 | 35569.8 | – 127.2 |
| 1966 | 18378.5 | 18705.1 | 37083.6 | – 326.6 |

* Foreign exchange forint: 1 US $ = 11,72 Ft.
† Deficit ( – ) and surplus ( + ).

As can be seen from Table 1, the average yearly trade deficit was higher in 1961–5 than in the preceding five-year period, with peaks in 1963 and 1964. In 1965 it was reduced by means of vigorous import restrictions, but this highly aggregated picture does not reveal the essential elements of the problem and requires further analysis. Breaking down the turnover by groups of countries, balances are obtained for the last four years as in Table 2.

[1] *Board of Trade Journal*, 26 August 1966.

TABLE 2. *Hungarian trade balances according to groups of countries* (million foreign exchange forints)

|  | 1963 | 1964 | 1965 | 1966 |
|---|---|---|---|---|
| CMEA /Comecon/ | − 577.6 | − 488.3 | + 299.7 | + 739.9 |
| Western industrial countries | − 542.9 | − 1040.3 | − 633.5 | − 282.2 |
| Others | − 50.7 | − 147.6 | + 205.6 | − 131.1 |
| TOTAL | − 1171.2 | − 1676.2 | − 127.2 | + 326.6 |

In respect of the CMEA countries, the unfavourable tendency was reversed by 1965 and the favourable trend continued in 1966; in the trade with the advanced capitalist countries, on the other hand, there was a deficit in all four years, although it somewhat decreased in the years 1965 and 1966.

Thus with one group (which for the sake of convenience may be called that of the convertible-currency countries) the deficit persisted in spite of the fact that it was always one of the objectives to abolish this deficit. However, this objective could not be attained and the dual trend in foreign trade – equilibrium and often trade surplus with CMEA countries and an enduring deficit with respect to convertible-currency markets – proved to be irreversible for the time being.

The tendency towards equilibrium with the CMEA countries is due to the bilateral character of trade and to the lack of convertibility. All countries were aiming at balancing their trade with each of the CMEA partners bilaterally and, if possible, in every year – even if these efforts led to a restriction of external trade. The volume of trade was determined by the country with the lower export potential or, more exactly, with the lower potential supply of 'hard' commodities. In the course of the years 1961 to 1965, the yearly deficit of surplus was usually between one and three per cent of the total trade volume. It surpassed 10 per cent rarely and only transitorily, and in such cases the balance was quickly restored to equilibrium.

One of the harmful effects of these efforts at yearly equilibrium and of the concomitant exaggeration of the importance of the end-year trade position manifested itself in the disproportionate volume of deliveries in the last quarter, and even in the last weeks of the year. This strange seasonal character of trade is quite independent of the seasonal fluctuations in production or consumption. It is due exclusively to the techniques of planning and accounting and is entirely unjustified from the economic point of view. Its harmful effect cannot be questioned, since the sudden increase in shipping towards the end of the year necessarily led to an undesirable accumulation of stocks and to warehousing shortages, and the stocks thus accumulated were absorbed only in later periods of the following year. However, these automatic results of efforts at obtaining equilibrium could not be eliminated without a fundamental change in the system. The same applies to the chronic disequilibrium with the group of convertible-currency countries.

However, the analysis cannot stop at this point. The same duplicity characterizes the commodity pattern of foreign trade and there is no sign of a change for the better in this respect either. First, let us investigate the pattern of exports (Table 3).

TABLE 3. *Pattern of Hungarian foreign trade by commodities and groups of countries, 1965*

| SITC | Groups of commodities | Exports (in percentages) | | | |
|------|----------------------|-------|------|----------------------------------|--------|
| | | Total | CMEA | Western industrial countries | Others |
| 0 | Food and live animals | 18.1 | 12.0 | 42.7 | 4.2 |
| 1 | Beverages and tobacco | 2.6 | 3.1 | 1.6 | 0.6 |
| 2 | Crude materials excl. fuels | 3.3 | 2.2 | 8.2 | 0.1 |
| 3 | Mineral fuels, etc. | 1.5 | 1.1 | 2.9 | 0.2 |
| 4 | Animal and vegetable oils and fats | 0.5 | 0.3 | 1.4 | • |
| 5 | Chemicals | 6.7 | 7.3 | 4.7 | 6.7 |
| 6 | Basic manufactures | 18.4 | 15.7 | 21.5 | 41.8 |
| 7 | Machinery and transport equipment | 34.7 | 43.5 | 4.5 | 35.6 |
| 8 | Misc. manufactured goods | 14.2 | 14.8 | 12.5 | 10.8 |
| | | 100.0 | 100.0 | 100.0 | 100.0 |
| | (Groups 5–8) | 74.0 | 81.3 | 43.2 | 94.9 |

\* Classification according to Standard International Trade Classification used in U.N. publications.

The pattern of exports in 1965 invariably reflected the relative state of industrial development and its qualitative limitations. More than two-thirds of Hungarian exports consisted of manufactures, a fact that shows a high level of industrial development; but this high share of manufactured products may be attributed mainly to the success achieved in CMEA markets. Hungarian industrial products were not so successful in convertible-currency markets. This is especially true of engineering products.

The share of machinery and transport equipment in exports to this group in 1965 was only one tenth of their share in CMEA exports – nor was there any improvement in the situation over the five-year period 1961–5. In our Western markets, which means in effect Western Europe, we sell mainly agricultural and food products and raw materials; the second place is occupied by manufactures belonging to group 6 of SITC and representing low value added, and the share of groups 7–8 (machinery, vehicles, instruments, clothing, furniture, etc.), which represent the most valuable part of exports and incorporate the highest amount of domestic value, is the lowest. These last are the groups in which the volume of trade could be expected to grow most quickly.

However, this sectoral imbalance in the development of exports is not the only problematic feature which provides food for thought. The share of machinery and vehicles has tended to decrease even in the exports to socialist countries. In 1960 engineering products still amounted to 50 per cent of our total exports to these countries, while in 1962 their share diminished to 46 per cent and in 1965 to 43.5 per cent. This decreasing demand for Hungarian engineering products in the CMEA markets is due mainly to the low degree of co-ordination in production, to the existence of parallel and unsynchronized production programmes, and to the lack of international vertical integration – in other words, to the efforts at import substitution in the individual CMEA countries. This tendency, which is in contradiction to the avowed objectives as well as to the planned specialization, will, in my opinion, remain effective as long as the production programmes are fixed by the state instead of by the productive enterprises concerned, and as long as the enterprises are only mildly interested in the implementation of the agreements. Another cause of the relatively diminishing demand is the slow progress in engineering technology, a problem to which we shall return later.

To ascertain the validity of the hypothesis according to which the disequilibrium is primarily due to the existing institution of central planning, I have employed a further form of export analysis.

One of the most important advantages to be derived from central planning is the ability to channel investments and to ensure the priorities of concentration, which have been analysed innumerable times from the economic point of view and stressed in the literature for decades. Though Western authors often accuse us of operating a 'priority economy' – and we agree with them as far as their criticism is aimed at exaggerated preferences – it must be emphasized that no economic policy is conceivable without priorities. Both the mercantilist and physiocrat schools established their own systems of priorities, and in the two centuries since, the realization of the theoretical and practical importance of a 'priority economy' has only increased. The priority policy to be actually enforced in the Hungarian economy should aim at a higher degree of concentration in the commodity pattern of exports.

I showed in an earlier study that the degree of commodity concentration of Hungarian exports in 1961–2 fell far below that of both Austria and Italy, was similar to that of Holland, but greater than that of France. For the purpose of comparison I intentionally chose some smaller countries, while Italy and France were chosen because their exports, with their multi-sectoral – industrial *and* agricultural – pattern cannot be too highly concentrated. At the time, the conclusions I drew from the unfavourable comparisons were as follows: '...the enduring low degree of concentration in the export pattern over the past years and its unchanged level are also signs of a retardation in the necessary process of specialization and of a certain fragmentation in the pattern of production and exports'.[1]

No international data are available for 1965; but as far as the statistical data series allowed, I worked out the Hungarian figures. These prove that in four commodity groups – pharmaceuticals, clothing, telecommunication equipment and instruments – we have succeeded in attaining a more highly concentrated export pattern than earlier. (However, a more detailed analysis may easily reveal that as far as individual products are concerned not even this degree of export concentration existed.) It is, however, beyond dispute that for exports as a whole the degree of concentration has further diminished. Thus, as regards the economy as a whole, the principles of a 'priority economy' were not enforced.

In the pattern of imports (see Table 4) there are two mutually contradictory features which deserve attention. While about 60 per cent of our imports from CMEA countries are composed of products belonging to SITC groups 5–8 (manufactures), the corresponding imports from capitalist countries amount to 70 per cent of the total. These proportions could not be deemed unrealistic in themselves, were it not for the fact that the bulk of industrial products imported from the West consisted not of machinery and vehicles representing the most advanced techniques, but of semi-finished, intermediary products. Together with chemical products, the share of these two groups is twice that of machines, while with the CMEA countries the situation is almost the reverse: imports of intermediary goods do not reach even half the volume of machinery imports. Here we have touched on the main cause of the disequilibrium with

[1] I. Vajda, *Hungary and World Trade*, Budapest, 1966, Corvina.

TABLE 4. *Pattern of Hungarian foreign trade by commodities and groups of countries, 1965*

| | | Imports (in percentages) | | | |
|---|---|---|---|---|---|
| SITC* | Groups of commodities | Total | CMEA countries | Western industrial countries | Others |
| 0 | Food and live animals | 8.2 | 4.8 | 11.9 | 42.7 |
| 1 | Beverages and tobacco | 0.3 | 0.3 | 0.3 | 0.2 |
| 2 | Crude materials excl. fuels | 18.0 | 16.6 | 15.8 | 50.0 |
| 3 | Mineral fuels, etc. | 12.1 | 17.0 | 0.4 | 0.2 |
| 4 | Animal and vegetable oils and fats | 0.5 | 0.2 | 1.0 | 1.1 |
| 5 | Chemicals | 8.4 | 5.7 | 17.9 | 1.5 |
| 6 | Basic manufactures | 18.4 | 16.4 | 27.1 | 3.9 |
| 7 | Machinery and transport equipment | 29.0 | 33.8 | 20.8 | . |
| 8 | Misc. manufactured goods | 5.1 | 5.2 | 4.8 | 0.4 |
| | | 100.0 | 100.0 | 100.0 | 100.0 |
| | (Groups 5–8) | 60.9 | 61.1 | 70.6 | 5.8 |

* Classification according to Standard International Trade Classification used in U.N. publications.

respect to convertible-currency markets and, at the same time, on the Achilles heel of quantitative planning without market orientation. The intermediary goods imported from the West are absorbed in the production of finished goods which are not sufficiently competitive in Western markets. The major reasons for the lack of competitiveness are the unfavourable ratio between new rapidly growing and old slowly expanding products, limited marketing activity and publicity and poor design; that is, primarily factors other than prices.[1]

Hungarian foreign trade bears the imprints of a dual market structure. The dichotomy is between rapid development on the one hand, and slower adaptation to the requirements of the international division of labour on the other. Further, the requirements of equilibrium with CMEA countries and the lasting disequilibrium with convertible currency countries complicate the issue. This dual character was brought about by the duality of the institutions: planning and the lack of competition in the domestic economy contrasted with the lack of planning and the existence of competition in export markets; the seller's market at home with the buyer's market

---

[1] The concepts of design and marketing are used in a broad sense. That of design includes performance, reliability and appearance; marketing involves packing, delivery and credit terms, assembling facilities, after-sale services, advertising – and selling itself.

abroad. From this there followed automatically – and contrary to the intentions of the planners – the conservative anti-innovation tendencies at home, while abroad a marathon race of innovations was taking place.

In spite of its numerical importance and economic weight, Hungarian foreign trade could not cope with this dualism, although it was realized some time ago that success in foreign markets required genuine, unlimited and competition-orientated marketing activities. Foreign trade executives have realized that quite different attitudes are justified beyond the country's frontiers than within. However, as long as the dualism survived and an antagonism existed between the internal mechanism and the orientation demanded by external markets, the internal system and institutions proved stronger. It was impracticable to maintain the one and conform to the other at the same time. Meanwhile it also became evident that the problems which arose in the field of foreign trade were not marginal in character and could not be neglected. Although it cannot be claimed that these problems were the only forces that brought about the pressure for economic reform, it is undeniable that they played a substantial part in the process of reappraisal that could not be put off any longer.

## THE RESTORATION OF EXTERNAL EQUILIBRIUM

It is usually suggested that developing countries should apply for financial assistance to the countries with ample capital resources in order to restore their external balances to equilibrium. In some situations, such as fighting famine in India, this becomes unavoidable and may temporarily alleviate the situation. However, no lasting equilibrium can be achieved in this way. It is for this reason that international agencies such as UNCTAD are seeking long-term solutions. In these endeavours they will repeatedly come up against certain world-market problems which seem to be insoluble for the time being.

Whenever external equilibrium is disturbed, traditional economic theory suggests two sets of measures, apart from administrative control of imports and a possible transitory raising of tariffs. One is deflation of domestic demand, the raising of interest rates and direct taxes, and possibly also restriction of capital exports, with the ensuing shrinking of investment activity and a rise in unemployment. From the example of the United Kingdom one is inclined to draw the conclusion that these measures defeat their own purposes; the policy of 'stop-go' has no 'sex-appeal' elsewhere. True, one must not forget that the issue is greatly complicated here by the special position of sterling as an international reserve currency. In fact, no analytical method exists as yet to separate the consequences of the role of a reserve currency from the effects of internal economic developments or their world interrelations.

The other measure – one of which the International Monetary Fund would consent only with reservations – is currency devaluation. This method has been resorted to lately by India, Yugoslavia and Argentina.[1]

The first method is meant to restrict by deflationary measures the volume of domestic consumption and consequently that of imports, while the second acts as an incentive to exports by offering a higher counter value in foreign exchange. The underlying assumption here is that in the devaluing country there are goods available for export, but as long as the currency is overvalued domestic sales are more attractive than exports. The assumption is undoubtedly justified in some cases, and if the countries which play an important role in the world economy but struggle with equilibrium difficulties do not easily resort to devaluation, this is not so much due to the strict rules of the IMF, nor to the danger of a loss of prestige, but rather to the anxiety that their rivals would immediately follow suit and thus the market advantages derived from devaluation would soon be lost.

In the case of a moderately developed economy – such as Hungary – neither method promises any results, and neither can be used to restore external equilibrium. Deflation cannot be resorted to, because the disequilibrium is not due to a high consumption level. This is also shown by the commodity pattern of imports from convertible-currency countries where consumer goods play but a moderate role. Deflation may affect investments which are highly import-intensive. Curtailing investments today may impair the export potential of tomorrow.[2] And devaluation will not lead to the desired goal because it was not poor economic achievement that put a brake on exports – under the Hungarian economic mechanism, this did not affect producers – but the lack of exportable and saleable goods, the deficiencies of the economic structure and of the technical level of production. This is a typical feature of moderately developed economies and not specific to Hungary. Undoubtedly, one of the most important measures of the Hungarian reform now under preparation, the changing of the conversion rate of the foreign exchange Forint, will have effects

---

[1] This article was written before the devaluation of sterling.

[2] To quote Professor Gottfried Bombach of Basel University: 'Und wenn wir über Wachstumspolitik auch noch wenig wissen, so zeigt die Nachkriegserfahrung zumindest eines, nämlich dass es ungleich leichter ist, sich von einem Zustand raschen Wachstums auf niedrigere Wachstumsraten herunterzumanövrieren als das Gegenteil zu erreichen. G. Bombach, 'Taktik und Strategie in der Wirschaftspolitik', *Kyklos*, Vol. 20, 1967, Fasc. 1, p. 117.

similar to that of devaluation. In the short run it will, however, hardly increase the amount of goods saleable in convertible-currency markets. Its stimulating effects will make themselves felt only if economic policy – that of a reasonable 'priority economy' aimed at structural changes – creates the necessary conditions. Formal devaluation will not suffice to change the relative proportions of domestic and foreign sales, nor will it increase substantially the volume of exports, mainly because the institutional duality referred to above has brought about a dualistic division in the quality of goods; to the inconvertibility of the currencies was added the inconvertibility of products and productive capacities. Now, this situation can be changed only at the cost of great efforts, for it is useless to expect any automatic effects. Furthermore, devaluation coupled with a pricing system without subsidies would stimulate exports in some sectors, but restrict them in others.

In my opinion, the specific problems of a moderate growth rate – which have found their most marked expression in Hungary in a partial external disequilibrium – are rooted in the great differences in the growth rates which have emerged in the world economy in recent decades. It seems that the distance between the rates can be reduced only by a highly deliberate 'priority economy', by entrepreneurial microeconomy, and by the resulting international integration – in a world less torn by political tensions than at present. To bring about such a synthesis will be the most important economic and political task of the years to come, a task to which all domestic forces should be devoted. The realization of the objectives of international integration does not depend entirely on us. The immense difficulties involved in the process of transforming and integrating the national economies have been recognized in capitalist and socialist, advanced and developing countries alike, but it has been realized at the same time that integration is necessary and inevitable for Great Britain in the same way as for Hungary and – according to Aleksei Kosygin – for Europe as well.

Our era is one of technical changes, as Lewis Mumford has pointed out, and this statement is borne out in all fields. For instance it is supported by the powerless anxiety with which the penetration of American capital, the backwardness in research and development, the brain drain, the heavy deficit in the patents balance are viewed in Western Europe – phenomena that inevitably lead to the delicate question: who is still using outdated techniques and who not?

Under the conditions prevailing in Hungary – and this is a result of a moderate rate of growth – economic policy need not fear the spread of foreign processes and patents in the country but should rather promote the process. We need not defend ourselves against foreign influences in industry, research and development, but should rather explore them and promote their application wherever possible, provided that they are compatible with our socialist ideology. We have to live in a world of modern techniques and this implies thinking internationally in almost all fields of the economy. It appears to be a modern tendency for all activities within a society, including those beyond the bounds of traditional international trade theory, to have international repercussions. Foreign trade itself becomes a secondary concept, that part of the iceberg which – though conspicuous because rising above the sea level – is but a fraction of the huge mass of international interaction floating under water.

What we call a 'priority economy' (at the risk of incurring criticism because of the word's bad reputation) can be nothing else than a realization of this tendency and a deliberate conforming to it. This does not mean fatalistic acquiescence in something that cannot be changed; neither nature nor society will accept anything as unchangeable. Or putting this idea in a more modest way: we, the men standing on the threshold of the last third of the twentieth century, do not yet know the automatism of nature, and within it, that of society. The maxim of La Rochefoucauld is profoundly true: 'L'homme arrive novice à tous les ages'. But in the knowledge of being a novice he should reflect, deliberate and act – this is how the priorities of his actions are established at the level of society.

The world-market aspects of technical progress are closely connected with the ideas expounded above. Formerly, it was possible in a small country, in a small-scale enterprise laboratory centred round some outstanding researcher or organizer, to develop industries on the basis of individual inventions and innovations. Several cases in point could be cited from the history of Hungarian industry in the 19th and the early 20th centuries. But this belongs to history and not the age of modern techniques.

Those familiar with the problems of Hungarian industry are all aware of its autarkic features and of the consequent technical backwardness. It is also known that the present bureaucratic organization of CMEA, as well as the tendencies inherent in centralized planning, which would hinder even a bilateral integration, have been partly responsible for this situation. But similar criticism has also been voiced in Western Europe in connection with the operation of the Common Market. Research and development have not been integrated and thus a door was unintentionally opened to American superiority and penetration. As we have read:

*Imre Vajda*

As a matter of fact, policies and the axes of research have not been integrated on a European scale; it is at best in a fraction of certain sectors of activity that some kind of co-operation can be found and even such efforts will, in concrete individual cases, owing to the lack of a common policy, come to a deadlock before reaching the threshold of economic efficiency. It is not for the sake of a paradox that I say that this co-operation operates in a dispersed manner.[1]

The same applies, in our view, to the situation in this country and it is for this reason that we are pressing for world market orientation and co-operation, for the demolition of the barriers of backwardness and for organization on an international scale.

### ENTREPRENEURIAL MICROECONOMICS

To avoid any misunderstanding, let it be stated unequivocally that a consistent economic policy, aimed at securing external equilibrium together with internal equilibrium and self-sustained growth, can be successful only in a climate of entrepreneurial initiative. Initiative involves independent decisions and the choice between alternatives as well as an adjustment to the ever changing conditions of competition. Economic theory has disclosed that in the domestic market, both under capitalism and socialism, imperfect competition prevails. Under capitalism, this imperfect competition is brought about to a large extent by capital accumulation, open or concealed cartel agreements, measures of state intervention which frequently express the interests of pressure groups and by the quasi-monopolistic organization of the money-market. In the socialist economy, on the other hand, the limitations to competition are of an inherent character and only the future can show to what extent it will be possible to expand the scope of competition and achieve an optimum intensity; for the time being, not even the marginal values of that optimum are precisely known. But imperfect competition in the domestic market will certainly put the outsider at a disadvantage and weaken his competitive position. In the external markets, Darwin's rule of 'survival of the fittest' unquestionably prevails. Competitiveness and competition-mindedness are fundamental requirements and only the enterprise which meets them to the maximum extent can be successful.

The question now is, whether under the Hungarian economic reform

[1] A. Silj, *L'industrie européenne face à la concurrence internationale*, Centre de recherches européennes, Lausanne, 1966 (Translation supplied).

While I am writing these lines, news is coming in of the collapse of Krupp – which is, of course, no bankruptcy at all, as we are dealing with Krupp, but the modern variety of collapse: a merger. Still it is a symptomatic phenomenon: from *Rheingold* the way has led to *Götterdämmerung*.

this type of enterprise is envisaged and whether it will be possible to bring it about.

Undoubtedly, the reform envisages a type of enterprise which is essentially independent in its decisions, striving to show a profit in its balance-sheet, able to provide from its own funds for the renewal, modernization and expansion of its productive equipment as well as the modernization and mechanization of its management and marketing and, should these funds prove insufficient, able to raise bank credits for any purpose, provided that its business projects are sound and well-founded. The enterprise should have a free hand in drawing up its production programme (there will be no compulsory production targets for enterprises) and in the flexible adjustment of the range of products to market conditions. It should not be limited by rigid rules in its calculation, pricing and terms of contract, nor in choosing the best form of relations with other enterprises. In foreign trade the highly important principle has been adopted by government resolution that the basic consideration must be to bring about an economic unity of production and foreign trade activity. This should be achieved primarily by economic measures aimed at making the foreign trade and productive enterprises equally interested in economic results. It has also been decided that the productive enterprises which carry out a trading activity based on international co-operation may be granted the right of exporting. This right may also be granted to enterprises which will thereby be able to enter into more favourable direct specialization contracts and co-operation agreements with foreign enterprises.

These resolutions already take it for granted that the enterprise knows that it must do all in its power to ensure a competitive position – and that it will be able to do what should reasonably be done. It is an important novel feature that specialization contracts and co-operation with foreign enterprises are given preference in an organized and institutional manner. As a consequence, these hitherto rather neglected activities take on an important role.

Nevertheless, we are not sure whether the measures, designed at the moment in the context of a transitory situation rather than with a vision of the final picture, will prove satisfactory. Still, they bear the imprint of the spirit of the reform, follow its logic and lead to a greater freedom of action and to a gradual abolition of bureaucratic institutions. Therefore, we do not think it expedient to argue now about details even if we should not approve of them.

It is, however, obvious that in addition to creating a suitable type of enterprise and the proper political and economic atmosphere, as well as an interrelated and flexible system of incentives, the success of the reform will rely to a large extent on the initiative and inventive power of management and its readiness to take risks – in other words, a subjective market orientation. It cannot be denied that up to now these abilities have played no decisive role in the choice of executives, nor – and this is particularly painful to admit for the author of this paper, a university professor – in their vocational training at the institutions of higher education.

Thus, the new system to emerge from the reform will not inherit an 'entrepreneurial' type trained to think for himself, take care of costs, and make efforts to turn out new products, or particularly concerned with the financial liquidity and solvency of the enterprise. Nor have our executives much experience in selling in a world market dominated by competition. It may also be assumed that they would rather prefer a short-term maximization of profits and are less concerned with the more difficult problems of a longer time horizon.

But the practice of recent years, with its bolder experiments, the closer and more direct contacts with foreign partners, and the climate of the impending economic reform, which made all ambitious managers and success-minded excutives realize that the boast of formal 'plan fulfilment' will not be appreciated any longer – all this paved the way for new entrepreneurial concepts. The hour of the enterprise has come. The executive agents of the past will become independent in the world market, and it will be their turn to awake the slumbering capacities of creative people and let them assert themselves. Venturesome spirit and the drive to change are ancient characteristics of *homo sapiens*. Of course, under capitalism these characteristics were institutionalized and rewarded, and those endowed with them were raised to the status of heroes. However, capitalism has not created a new man; the creative capacities of man live in man himself. And now, collective and individual creation become united, as under our system they can become united on an equal footing.

# 4. Problems of bilateralism and multilateralism in the external trade and payments system of the CMEA countries

SÁNDOR AUSCH

The general lesson that can be drawn from the post-war development of international trade in the capitalist world is that even the most advanced capitalist countries needed several years to pass from a bilateral trading and payments system to multilateralism, and that, notwithstanding the considerable external help they received, it took them some fifteen years to achieve convertibility.

This fact, and the difference in the level of development between the advanced capitalist and socialist countries, should be sufficient to explain why the attempts made by the CMEA countries in 1957 and 1963 to advance towards multilateralism have so far shown little result. The parallel is, however, misleading. It will be shown below that the bilateral clearing system of the socialist countries is of a special type, the main features of which are determined by the commodity relations of the socialist countries and by the characteristics of their system of production relations based on export and import directives. These would make it impossible to switch over to full convertibility even if adequate gold and foreign-exchange reserves were available; they even stand in the way of regional multilateralism and transferability. We will try to prove in what follows that switching over from bilateralism to a system of multilateral trade and payments requires fundamental qualitative changes in the domestic economies of the CMEA countries as well as in their external relations.

There can be no doubt that, in the initial stage of co-operation, the peculiar system of bilateralism that emerged in the CMEA countries from the economies based on plan directives had its positive traits, especially from the point of view of the less-developed countries, creating as it did, with the rapid pace of industrialization based primarily on the mobilization of external resources, secure external markets.

However, the system of plan directives sooner or later put a brake on efficient growth in each country, and the system of so-called international co-operation which was based on it, in the absence of a market mechanism,

# Sándor Ausch

in fact became an obstacle to international co-operation. The lack of the operation of the market finds its summary expression in the impossibility of creating a socialist world currency suited to fulfil all the functions of money – a precondition of multilateralism, transferability and convertibility. The drawbacks of this system make themselves felt in every domain of co-operation and international division of labour, resulting in difficulties of specialization and in launching joint ventures, in a lack of capital flows, in the difficulty of co-ordinating economic policies and plans on an international level and in the impossibility or complexity of compensation, etc. The creation of a transferable currency and the achievement of multilateralism is thus not an end in itself but a necessary precondition of the market-type co-operation.

## BILATERALISM, MULTILATERALISM, AND THE VOLUME OF EXTERNAL TRADE

The various drawbacks of bilateralism in general and of the type of bilateralism existing between the CMEA countries in particular, will not be analysed here.[1] It will, however, be useful to demonstrate its effects on the trends in the volume of foreign trade (on the basis of quite arbitrarily chosen figures), particularly as the demonstration will also throw light on certain characteristic features and requirements of multilateralism.[2]

Let us assume that between countries A, B and C, trade and the settlement of accounts are taking place on a bilateral basis. In Fig. 1 the arrows indicate the direction of trade and the debts and claims arising therefrom within a certain period of time, e.g. one year, while the figures express the amounts involved.

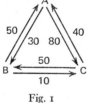
Fig. 1

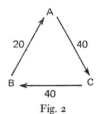
Fig. 2

[1] These questions, which require extensive analysis, are dealt with in the author's papers 'Nemzetközi munkamegosztás és gazdasági mechanizmus' (International division of labour and the economic mechanism), *Közgazdasagi Szemle*, Institute of Economics, Hungarian Academy of Sciences, Budapest, 1965, No. 7–8, and 'The possibilities of developing market relations in the co-operation of the CMEA countries', Akadémiai Kiadó and A. W. Sijthoff-Leyden, Budapest, 1969.

[2] In the analysis, use has been made of the relevant diagrams of A. Kruse, *Aussenwirtschaft* (International Economics), Berlin and München, 1965, with the conclusions adapted to the special conditions of the CMEA countries.

As a result of one year's deliveries, country A claims 80 units from country C, while the latter claims 40 units from the former. Country A has thus a net credit balance of 40 units on its account with country C, which in turn claims the same amount from country B, and country B claims 30 units from country A (Fig. 2).

In the case of bilateral clearing it will not be possible to settle these claims and debts. They will, therefore, in actual fact either not arise at all, or will diminish the volume of trade in the next, or some subsequent year (depending on the terms of credit) to the level of the trading partner with the lower export potential. In the case of bilateral clearing the volume of trade actually taking place cannot exceed 80 units (40 units between countries A and C, 10 units between countries B and C, and 30 units between countries B and A). In other words, trade is bound to diminish by 60 units in the next year if there is no granting of bilateral credits. However, unless the potential of the partner with the lower export potential increases in the meantime, bilateral credits will provide only a temporary solution.

If, however, there is a 'compensation of balances' (which is an institutional arrangement for partial mutual cancellation of debts, as will become clear from the discussion below) between the three countries, then country B will cancel its claim of 20 units from country A, country C will cancel the same amount from its account with country B, and country A from its account with country C. Accordingly, there remains an unsettled debt of 40 units (Fig. 3).

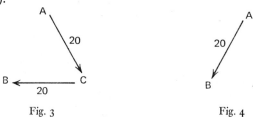

Fig. 3                     Fig. 4

With 3 times 20 units of claim mutually settled, turnover will – without any credit being granted – increase by 60 units, to 140 units as against the 80 units afforded by bilateral trading. If, however 'compensation of balances' is replaced by a system where debts and claims are settled not between the individual countries but through a central clearing account (i.e. settlements are not built into bilateral accounts), then a further increase in turnover will become possible. In the above example, after the settlement of debts country C still claimed 20 units from country B and owed the same amount to country A. These claims could not be settled because there were no unsettled amounts in the bilateral relations between countries A and B. With a clearing centre acting as a creditor or debtor to each country, the settlement becomes possible (Fig. 4).

Country A grants the clearing centre a credit of 20 units while country B owes the centre the same amount. Turnover increases, accordingly, by a further 40 units (by 20 units between countries B and C, and by another 20 units between countries C and A) to a total of 180 units, as against the 80 units which can be achieved in bilateral trade, by means of credits amounting to a mere 20 units which must be granted to the clearing centre by somebody.

The above theoretical example shows that in the case of bilateral settlements the volume of foreign trade remains limited to 80 units; by means of 'compensation of balances' this can be increased to 140 units; while settlement through a clearing centre and the granting of 20 units credit makes it possible to transact 180 units of foreign trade, by allowing the financial settlement of deficits arising from differences between the export and import potentials of the individual countries. However, between this and the 'compensation of balances' there is – and must, indeed, be – a qualitative difference which should be clear from the above schematic example. The 'compensation of balances' rests on the requirement that claims must and can be settled by debts arising from deliveries of goods within the circle of the countries concerned, i.e. that there is a global equilibrium of claims and debts. Should any country be unable to supply the goods required by the other countries, this global equilibrium cannot be brought about. The claims of the creditors must then be met out of the reserves of the centre, or the debtor countries will have to draw on resources outside the circle in order to meet their liabilities.

However, in fact the system of 'compensation of balances' will increase the volume of trade only insignificantly, because it does not alter the basic position; there remains the characteristic feature of bilateralism, that the countries participating in trade are divided into those with 'hard' and those with 'soft' currencies. As long as bilateralism is replaced only by a simple system based on the 'compensation of balances' the creditor countries will often be reluctant to accept the payment of debts in 'softer' rather than 'harder' currencies, which can be sold in the free market at a discount.[1]

[1] In the years 1948–50 the West European countries were able to eliminate only 3 to 4 per cent of their mutual deficits by means of the 'balance compensation' method. The conditional aid made available within the framework of Marshall Aid was necessary to enable the settlement of 32 per cent of these deficits. The conditional aid was granted by the USA on condition that the beneficiary country made the equivalent available in domestic currency to a third debtor country to enable it to bring its balance of payments into equilibrium.

On the other hand, the establishment of a clearing centre for all credit and debit items necessitates that all payments flow through one 'channel' and that no difference is made between the currencies concerned as regards their 'hardness' or 'softness'. This again calls for a common currency, which fulfils the functions of money in international payments.

In what follows, we shall try to prove theoretically the thesis that a currency of this kind must be *convertible* into any commodity in any country or, at least, *transferable*, i.e. convertible into any commodity, or domestic currency, of the countries participating in the regional grouping, subject only to a minimum of foreign-trade regulation, and must be freely utilizable for purchases within that region. In this case, however, it must be recognized that, with the gradual elimination of bilateral trade, the structural tensions concealed by bilateralism will come to the fore: some countries become lasting debtors (their currency becomes 'soft') and others steady creditors (their currency becoming 'hard').

In the course of transition from bilateralism to multilateralism, to a system of mutual transferability and later on to convertibility, the unification ('hardening') of the currencies will be achieved by means of settling the deficits which cannot be eliminated by trade (or, at least, part of such deficits) in gold or hard currency. This is the method that was applied in Western Europe within the framework of EPU.

It is generally known that in 1964 the CMEA countries passed over to a system of multilateral settlement through a centre. Under this system each creditor or debtor country will settle its account with the Bank for International Economic Co-operation (BIEC). Section II, paragraph (d) of the agreement which brought BIEC into being stipulated that within one year of the foundation of the Bank, the Board would investigate ways of introducing in its operations carried out in convertible roubles the possibility of conversion into gold or freely convertible currencies.

This possibility of conversion has not yet been realized, a fact that affects the situation in two respects:

(1) Under the existing conditions, the introduction of the 'transferable' rouble in the trade between CMEA countries did not change the bilateral character of that trade (i.e. the member countries continue to strive at an annually – and strictly bilaterally – balanced trade).

(2) The 'transferable' rouble cannot be converted into any currency outside the CMEA clearing system. In other words: as regards the foreign-trade aspects of the question, the net creditor country cannot use its balances outside the CMEA if the goods available in the countries of the system fail to meet its requirements either absolutely or in respect of choice,

quality, price etc. From the financial point of view, the 'transferable' rouble has thus not affected the existing degree of regional autarky and protectionism.

It may be concluded that the phenomena outlined above are due to the lack of convertibility into gold or convertible currency. Clearly, if any country outside CMEA could claim payment in gold for its holdings of 'transferable' roubles, or if central banks abroad could ask for the settlement in gold of balances‾arising within the CMEA clearing system, then the 'transferable' rouble would become suitable for operations in both directions inside and outside that system, and endeavours to balance the trade turnover bilaterally would cease (the 'transferable' rouble would become the reserve currency of the system).

The obvious solution to the problem of multilateral payments within CMEA would appear to be to set up a gold or convertible currency fund to the value of several hundred million dollars. Such proposals have been put forward in the past,[1] and the simple answer frequently voiced, regardless of the real reasons, is that there are no such reserves available.[2]

In the following we will endeavour to prove that:

(1) The convertibility of the 'transferable' rouble into gold or convertible currency is not simply a question of the availability or lack of reserves, and the lack of liquidity (gold, convertible currency, or commodity reserves) is not even the primary obstacle to convertibility.

(2) The linking up of the regional multilateral system to the convertible currencies outside the system is in the present situation not primarily a question of the availability or lack of gold or convertible currency reserves either. The establishment of such links would require a continuous flow of large amounts of gold or convertible currency into the multilateral system.

## MONEY FUNCTIONS – THREE TYPES OF BILATERALISM

It is only a currency with internal and external convertibility that can completely fulfil the functions of a world money.

International payments take place usually by means of bills and cheques, less frequently by the direct use of gold or convertible currency (convertible in the present-day sense of the word). Any restriction of convertibility (with regard to current payments) represents at the same time the restriction of some monetary function in the international exchanges from the point of view of either or both money and commodity holders.

[1] See, e.g., the Polish proposals at the CMEA Standing Committee for Financial and Currency Matters.
[2] E.g. K. Larionov in his paper delivered at the scientific conference 'The Great October Socialist Revolution‾and the socialist world system',‾Moscow, 1967.

Should convertibility apply only to aliens under the Foreign Exchange Act of some country (as e.g. at present in Greece), this means that foreigners are in a position to exchange their holdings of the domestic currency (in this case, their drachmas) into world money but the domestic importer is not; that the domestic currency is a general means of payment and purchase for the alien subject but not for the subject of the country concerned.

However, for money to function as a means of payment it is necessary to develop the storage function of social wealth, whereby the role of money as a universal equivalent is secured in the case of deferred payment.

If the currency has neither internal nor external convertibility, this means that it will be accepted as money only in the domestic market. In this case the debtor will not be able to effect payments directly to the foreign creditor in the domestic currency of his own country. He will pay the amounts due in domestic currency into an account kept with the central bank of his country. In the case of bilateral clearing the two central banks will notify each other, indicating the names of the creditor and debtor, and the central bank of the creditor country will effect the order of payment received from the central bank of the debtor country up to the amount paid in the account concerned. This type of clearing money will not be able to fulfil the international functions of money in a direct way. It can do so only indirectly on the basis of the guarantee of two banks (usually two central banks), with entries carried out in a domain and under conditions (trade and payments restrictions) defined in advance.

Bilateral clearing systems of this type and the corresponding clearing currencies are called into being by extensive government restrictions of external trade and payments, or at periods when international liquidity suffers a general decrease (as during the 1929–33 world depression, or during and after World War II), or when some individual countries are compelled to introduce extensive external trade and payments restrictions because of liquidity problems.

The limited character of clearing currencies refers not only to their function as a general means of payment and purchase, and of hoarding – which is restricted because they can be used as money in a definite way and at a definite time only – but also to their function as a measure of value.

Due to foreign trading and payments restrictions, the clearing currency will express the international value of the exported commodity not in terms of world money but only in terms of the mutual accounting unit of the two markets concerned, i.e. its value in definite markets, and generally in such a way that the accounting unit is differently valued for exports and imports, and usually even according to the use value of commodity groups.

However, the limitations of the money functions of clearing currencies, and thus their differences from convertible currencies, will vary both in degree and in character according to which type of clearing currency we are dealing with.[1]

(1) The clearing agreements and quota systems which came into being in the wake of the 1929–33 world depression had the common characteristic that the only limits set in advance were on the value of exports and imports by commodity groups. An equilibrium balance was ensured by a system of export and import licences, by the application of ever-changing restrictions in one relation or another, and by the related measures of foreign-exchange policy. The buyer and seller had thus, as far as the individual deal was concerned, a more or less free choice as regards the market of purchase or sale, and complete freedom in the question of price. Converted at some rate of exchange, the price achieved abroad represented the returns of the seller and the outlays of the buyer. The deal could be concluded only if the price that could be achieved abroad still left some profit margin for the seller over and above the domestic cost, and in the case of the buyer if the purchasing price paid abroad still enabled the realization of some profit in the domestic selling price (taking into account, of course, the systems of subsidies and import levies which became extensive at the time). Were the exporter unable to sell his product in the other country at an adequate profit, he still had the choice of looking for a more profitable outlet in a third or fourth country, within the limits and under the conditions of the existing restrictions.

In this manner, the domestic currency and the accounting (clearing) currency served also – if only in a limited and imperfect way – as a measure of the international value of domestic goods. The credit balances arising were suited, though in a limited manner (by means of 'balance compensation' and with the necessary discounts) to fulfil the functions of an international means of payments and purchase.

(2) Another type of bilateral clearing emerged from the war economy, primarily between Germany and its trading partners, but also between other countries.

In the case of Germany these clearing agreements were characterized by the fact that they constituted a suitable way of exploiting the satellite

---

[1] There is an enormous variety of clearing systems, including barter agreements on individual deals as well as clearing agreements concluded between one country with convertible currency and another with non-convertible currency.

countries; in respect of other countries and in general, their form and pattern was determined by the rules of the war economy (fixed domestic prices, the control and allocation of materials, fixed wages, etc.). Under these clearing agreements, the quotas not only fixed the upper limits of exports and imports but represented also guaranteed deliveries by commodity groups on the inter-state level.

The 'compulsory quotas' also contained inter-state price agreements fixed in some form. In the trade between Germany and Hungary, these already covered 50 per cent of turnover by 1944. Tying clauses were increasingly introduced in respect of both the type and quantity of goods to be delivered, and their prices. This clearing system thus represented a further qualitative restriction of the functions of the clearing currency as against the earlier types of clearing.

Under the earlier clearing systems, although the government restrictions limited the complete assertion of the functions of money, the principles of the national and international comparability of values and of profit maximization on the basis of comparative advantages could assert themselves only in a limited and narrow manner in the international trade of a world market divided into 'imperfect' bilateral markets. It was these that formed, though in a limited and distorted manner, the prices in external trade (affecting also the domestic prices) as well as the direction and volume of trade.

Under the clearing system described here, these principles were replaced by government instructions in respect of a considerable part of trade, instructions which determined the direction and volume of trade as well as the profit margin that could be realized, or the loss that was to be compensated for by subsidies paid to the firms concerned. In a market thus distorted, the clearing currency became more or less an accounting unit for barter trade, with the existing functions of money appearing only in the domains where the government did not or could not intervene.

Bilateral clearing systems similar to those described under (1) and (2) were – with varying degrees of difference by countries, and, naturally, with basically opposite political purposes and contents – operated in the period following World War II in the trade between the countries which were later to form the CMEA.

The destruction of the war and the concomitant general impoverishment, together with the exhaustion of gold and convertible currency reserves, made bilateralism unavoidable in this region just as in other parts of Europe. In most countries, either in continuation of the war economy or within the framework of a newly established system of planned state intervention, the domestic price level was fixed, although in a narrower domain and by less rigid methods than the price regulations that were to come later on, and material and foreign-exchange control was introduced. Foreign trade was subjected to quotas and licences. Prices in external trade were, however, left to be agreed upon by the firms concerned. Thus, the pattern of exports and imports developed basically in accordance with the profit motive. As a result of rapid reconstruction and improvement in the economic situation, by 1947-8 the restrictions on foreign trade were considerably eased in most countries, though exchange control remained in force. Under suitable conditions this initial position could have led in the more distant future to multilateralism and to the convertibility of currencies. The economies of the Eastern European countries were at that time fundamentally similar to the type of economy emerging at present in Hungary.[1]

In the post-war years the share of the USSR in the external trade of every Eastern European country increased at a rapid pace. It is a well-known fact that in accordance with the principles of the planned economy and the foreign-trade and foreign-exchange monopoly, strict bilateralism prevailed in the external trade of the USSR. There was a centralized system of export and import instructions and the rouble was non-convertible. The bilateral trade carried out with the Eastern European countries differed, however, in its forms both from the trade of the USSR with the capitalist countries at that time, and from that carried out with the socialist countries later on. The foreign-trade agreements were concluded for a term of one year, but by 1947 contracts came into being between individual enterprises which foresaw the deliveries of goods over a longer period. The pattern of exports and imports evolved in the Eastern European countries partly on the basis of compulsory quotas (e.g. deliveries under reparations agreements), partly on that of domestic market forecasts and offers submitted by individual firms, but in both cases prompted by the profit motive. Prices were fixed generally for one year, but in the case of long-term contracts for several years. The system corresponded largely to that which we are now trying to introduce in trade between the socialist countries with a controlled market economy on the one hand

[1] See S. Ausch, 'A stabilizáció 20. évfordulójára' (At the 20th anniversary of stabilization), *Népszabadság*, 1 August 1966. It is not our task to examine here the question whether in the given economic, historical, political and ideological conditions the introduction of the system of direct plan instructions was inevitably necessary or not. Most certainly, it was. However, as will be shown, this system made it impossible to switch over to multilateralism.

The possibility of transition to multilateralism and transferability in a controlled and organized market economy will be discussed in a second article, starting from the present situation.

and those with a system based on directive plan instructions on the other.

In principle – as regards the limitations on the money functions – all that has been said in connection with the bilateral clearing systems of types (1) and (2) is largely valid also for these bilateral clearings as they functioned at that time.

(3) In the bilateral relations of the planned economies based on directive plan instructions, a special type of bilateral clearing has emerged.

The limitations on the money functions existing under the bilateral clearing relations which emerged from the capitalist war economy are also asserting themselves in the special bilateral clearing systems based on directive plan instructions. This is a consequence of the fact that here the mechanism involves a complete centralization of the control of the means of production. It follows that when examining the functions of this 'clearing currency' we are compelled to survey briefly – leaving aside both the details and the arguments – certain questions which have already been treated in detail in another article.[1]

(*a*) The separation of the domestic from the external price level, the formation of foreign trade prices and the function of the clearing rouble as a measure of value

In the socialist planned economies functioning on the basis of directive plan instructions, domestic prices are institutionally completely separated from external prices. The economic units are paid for the exported goods at fixed domestic prices, and pay for their imports likewise at fixed domestic prices.

From the point of view of the present subject, this has two significant consequences:

(i) There does not and cannot exist any rate of exchange that would select the exchange of goods on the basis of comparative advantage.

(ii) In the reciprocal trade of two or more countries whose economies are based on this system, no objective value limit exists either upwards or downwards for the prices of the individual goods entering into trade. These prices necessarily become separated from international prices as well as from the relations of supply and demand.

The thesis is easy to prove. Let us start from the simple case of foreign trade carried out on the basis of comparative advantage.

In country A, product $x$ is produced in 10 hours, in country B in 12

---

[1] Ausch and Barta, 'Socialist world market price', Akadémiai Kiadó and A. W. Sijthoff-Leyden, Budapest, 1969.

hours. In country A the production of product $y$ will require 20 hours, in country B 30 hours.

Although in country B it costs more to produce product $x$ than in country A, it will pay the former to export this product to the latter and to import product $y$ from there, because in country B the production of $y$ is comparatively less efficient than in country A.

However, the exchange of goods can take place only within definite limits. Country A must receive for one unit of product $y$ at least two units of product $x$, and country B can offer for one unit of product $y$ at the most 2.5 units of product $x$.

In the world market the exchange ratios are, however, expressed not in terms of hours but in terms of money. If domestic prices are proportionate to the labour input ratios, then one unit of product $x$ will in country A be worth two units of product $y$ and in country B 2.5 units of product $y$. Supposing that both countries have the same money standard and that their balance of payments is in equilibrium, then the above ratios will also correspond to those expressed in foreign currency and the possible exchange ratios will not change in terms of the latter either. If only these two countries took part in the formation of the world-market price of the two products, then the ratio of the world-market prices would by necessity fall between the two domestic price ratios, because otherwise the exchange of goods would not pay either partner. Under the bilateral clearing systems of type (1), where domestic prices are not separated from the prices abroad, the foreign-trade price will in any case fall between the two limits. Moreover, due to the profit motive and to the quota system which sets only the upper limits, there will be a possibility of exchange also with countries C, D etc. Accordingly, the domestic price ratios of these countries will also affect the foreign-trade price, in the manner described above. This will tend to narrow the limits within which the price moves. If countries A and B are the marginal producers (i.e. those producing at the highest cost) and the high costs are not compensated for by subsidies, then the exchange of goods will take place not between the two countries, but with country C or D, etc. The world-market prices of the two products are thus set *objective* limits, determined by their domestic prices. The greater the number of the countries participating in the exchange of goods on the world market, the greater the possibility that the world-market price will emerge as an *objective* category, independent of the given exchange transaction.

It follows from the above that, under a system of bilateral clearing based on directive plan instructions, where the domestic price level is by necessity separated from the external one, foreign-trade prices have no economic limits even in the bilateral markets. The national markets of the CMEA countries do not in principle enter into the formation of (CMEA-level) value as the preconditions and results of the value formation process. As a result, the foreign-trade prices cannot express the (regional) world market value of the goods.

This finds its expression partly in the following.

Differences between the prices of the same product of a country as quoted in the different markets (the price in the highest-priced market expressed as a percentage of that in the lowest-priced market) were nowhere else as wide as in the reciprocal trade of the socialist countries.

The prices of raw materials and agricultural products (which are in short supply in the socialist world market) are less in excess of world market prices than those of machinery and other manufactures (of which there is a surplus).

Nor are the price proportions within the main price groups, especially in the case of final products, in proportion with the relations of supply and demand.

It follows from the above that as long as the internal and external mechanism by necessity brings about a foreign-trade price system of this character, it will not be possible to establish any type of multilateral trade and convertible currency.

(*b*) Means of payment and purchase, wealth-forming function

An accounting unit (the clearing rouble) which is not suited to fulfil the function of a universal equivalent, must be also unsuited to serve as a general means of international purchases, payments (credit), and hoarding (wealth-forming). For this reason – or, conversely, in order to replace the foreign-trade transactions emerging as a result of the effects of inter-national price differences, the relations of demand and supply, and the profit motive – the system of directive plan instructions regulates in an adminis-trative way, by means of compulsory export and import instructions ('compulsory quotas'), the type and quantity of the goods which the economic units can purchase from each other as well as the place and time of the transaction.

In these transactions money can thus fulfil its functions only formally. As a consequence, without qualitative changes in the basic conditions of its creation it cannot be made either transferable or convertible. It will turn out daily in actual practice that this money does not constitute a general equivalent even within one bilateral relationship; nor can it be considered a means of either long or short-term credit, but a measure of the volume of use values of a definite pattern; it is neither wealth, nor capital (nobody would pay anything for the 'capital' of the BIEC). And when money is not really money, nor capital really capital, interest, too, can be only formal – as borne out by actual practice – and not real interest fulfilling its proper functions.

### CREDIT AND INTEREST – PRESENT-DAY MULTILATERALISM AND THE BANK FOR INTERNATIONAL ECONOMIC CO-OPERATION

Money which, for the reasons outlined above, cannot be termed real money, can naturally not be lent out as real money (as a commodity defined also in other than use value).

The accounting and credit system now in force between the CMEA countries is built on the assumption that the flow of money and credit between the countries concerned will develop automatically in accordance with the fulfilment of the foreign-trade plans. Short- and medium-term credits are not 'granted' but 'purchased' as a result of the foreign trading position. The participating countries are not interested in accumulating claims and granting credits. Nor is it possible to accumulate any claim deliberately, as under the established system disequilibrium can come about only up to the degree of difference between the compulsory export and import targets on the one hand and the actually achieved turnover on the other, with credit movements released automatically. (Later on, we shall revert in greater detail to the present BIEC credit system.)

The long-term credits granted on the government level are (except, of course, those granted in convertible currency) in each case defined in physical terms and – except in the case of investment contributions – generally without particular regard to motives.

In the special bilateral clearing, interest too can fulfil only limited functions. As there is no international money to fulfil the functions of money, interest as the price of capital borrowed can also play only a subordinate role. But the links are also lacking which could transmit the effects of the international interest rate to the national economy. Credit transactions between individual enterprises do not exist under CMEA, and interest charges originating abroad appear only at the central authority in charge of foreign-exchange control. Furthermore, in an economy where there exists no discount rate, no rate of foreign exchange and no flow of capital, there can be no operation of the mechanism, of the interaction which influences loan capital, the balance of payments, the rate of foreign exchange and the direction and volume of exports and imports in the same way as the interest rate. Nor is there any short- and medium-term credit-granting independent of trade, operating under the effect of international differences in interest rates.

In a planned economy the rate of interest prevailing in the international markets can have no effect either on the flow of capital, which does not even exist there, or on the expansion, contraction and direction of trade.

The 'interest' to be paid on credits granted in international trade is, as a matter of fact, at least as much isolated from the earnings and profits of the economic units as the prices abroad of the export and import goods are indifferent to them. It is only to the finance ministries that interest means an additional income or additional liability, however, not in 'money' but in commodity deliveries of a definite pattern and in definite relations, which, in turn, are decided upon by other organs of state administration (planning offices, ministries of foreign trade, etc.). And as this pattern is determined in advance and balanced in a special manner ('hard' commodity for 'hard' commodity, and 'soft' commodity for 'soft' commodity), a higher rate of interest instead of a lower one (e.g. the now accepted 4 per cent) will not provide in itself a sufficient incentive either to the exporter to grant credit or to the debtor to effect his payments earlier.

In such conditions an increase in the rate of interest would be ineffective from the point of view of the expansion of trade. As mentioned above, the short- and medium-term 'credits' of the present practice emerge automatically as a result of surplus deliveries or delays in shipment. Now, if some country becomes, or expects to become, against its own will, the creditor of the other countries, it will change its 'ideology' – its opinion on the desirable rate of interest it wishes to enforce – and it will ask for a higher rate of interest on credits granted in excess of the overdraft.

This demand for a higher rate of interest is thus rather a *post hoc* or 'anticipated' consequence of spontaneous trends in the trade balance, and its realization would by no means lead to interest payment playing a more active role in the expansion or contraction of credit and trade.

By way of summing up, it may be said of the characteristic features of the 'multilateral clearing system' actually in operation that this system has created only the formal requirements of multilateral settlement. As regards real multilateralism, it has not and, indeed, could not have brought any progress. In the course of foreign trade negotiations it is still strict bilateralism that is being striven for.

It is true that settlements are effected through the BIEC as a clearing house. BIEC does not, however, dispose of 'funds', and the central accounting does not affect trade either in an expansive or a restrictive manner.[1] All that happens is that the formerly two-sided accounts are now kept in a central clearing house.

Under the present-day settlement and 'credit' system of the BIEC the central banks may draw on credits in accordance with the necessities of the planned development of trade. Credits have been classed, similarly to the domestic credit system of the economies based on directive plan instructions, according to the objectives related to the fulfilment of the plans (e.g. credits for trade expansion, settlement credits etc.). These credit types will not be analysed here. What is important is that as a consequence of splitting up the credit types without adequate economic reason the introduction of central account keeping has at the beginning tended to give rise to bureaucratic difficulties, as against the former situation where fewer restrictions were bilaterally applied in respect of the 'credits' automatically required in the course of trade. It was only after lengthy negotiations that conditions similar to those prevailing formerly could be brought about.

The multilateral clearing centre has, for formal reasons, hampered for some years even the operations of 'balance compensation' which had formerly occasionally occurred. It was only in recent years that a legal title could be found for such operations. The limited possibilities remaining for balance compensation after the bilateral balancing of trade (even if the viewpoints of natural, structural 'hardness' and 'softness' were disregarded) will be clear to anyone who has one of the CMEA foreign trade year-books at hand.

What has been said up to now goes to prove that the theoretical requirements of the realization of multilateral trade and a regionally transferable currency in the reciprocal trade of the economies based on directives cannot be reconciled with the basic characteristics of these economies.[2]

---

[1] So called multilateral talks take place at the end of each year, with the purpose of finding a purchaser for the (usually 'softest') goods which cannot be bilaterally sold. The trade involved is insignificant and does not exceed 1 per cent of the total turnover. The 'multilateral agreement' of 1957 was of a similar character. In its framework, the 'softest' commodities unsaleable in bilateral trade were again offered for sale. The trade transacted on this basis has never exceeded 2 to 3 per pent of total trade. Formally, this agreement was more perfect than the one in force at present, because it also called for the settlement of balances in gold or convertible currency. This was, however, never carried into effect.

[2] A country of such immense dimensions as the USSR, whose external trade amounts to a mere 5 to 6 per cent of the national income and which disposes of considerable gold reserves, could bring about by the use of the latter and by means of certain foreign trade measures the *external* convertibility of its currency in its relations with the other CMEA countries, both with those whose economy is based on directive plan instructions and with those with a market-type economy. This would enable the introduction of transferability also in the trade between the other CMEA countries – regardless of their type of economic system – and even the *external* convertibility of the currencies of the latter within the regional group. However this

From the viewpoint of the economic mechanism the basic practical requirements of multilateralism are obvious.

(1) The rate of exchange establishes an unequivocal link between the domestic and foreign prices, whereby the foreign price determines the earnings of the enterprises producing for export or utilizing the imported goods (taking always into consideration a wider or smaller range and a higher or lower degree of export subsidies and customs duties).

The enterprises and governments should be interested in the production and export of goods of a suitable quality, representing a higher technical level, and in demand abroad; in the socialist world market the prices of these goods should, in accordance with the conditions of supply and demand, be higher than those of goods of a lower quality or for which there is no actual demand; under the effect of prices and other instruments of financial policy, such as credits or capital exports, on production, the categories of 'hard' and 'soft' commodities should either disappear or be reduced to a minimum.

(2) Within the limits of government regulation, the enterprises will thus themselves determine the volume and direction of their exports and imports, giving preference to the agreements which ensure a stable volume of exports and imports over longer periods, at prices, fixed for the whole period or changing depending on certain conditions, which secure the highest profit.[1]

In Hungary, with the experience gained in the seventeen years of the operation of a system based on directive plan orders as well as in the course of the preparations for economic reform, it will hardly need detailed proof that the objectives outlined above cannot be achieved under the system of directive plan instructions.[2]

solution cannot be envisaged as a practicable alternative because, as will be demonstrated below, it implies that the USSR should be willing to carry on its trade with the other CMEA countries without regard to its own interests and to pay out continuously such amounts of gold and convertible currency, which exceed the possibilities even of a country like the USSR.

[1] This does not, of course, exclude the possibility of long-range co-operation agreements between governments. With our present level of development of technology such agreements are a frequent occurrence under not only socialism but also state monopoly capitalism. From amongst numerous possible examples, let us mention only the Franco–British 'Concorde' aircraft project, Euratom, The European Coal and Steel Community, etc. But even in such cases, the profits or losses of the company or companies concerned will provide indispensible information to the central government organs. Should the individual company show a loss, with the inter-governmental agreement being nevertheless profitable, it will be both possible and necessary to balance the losses with subsidies.

[2] However, thinking in the categories of the former system still persists and the assumption is still frequently voiced that the mechanism of the directive plan orders could have been further 'improved' and 'transformed' until it assumed certain properties which are alien to its basic principles. From the papers delivered at the symposium organised by the CMEA Standing

As regards the international mechanism, no further arguments beyond those already presented by this author and others will be needed to prove that no international market can be established unless there exists a real market within the individual national economies.

Accordingly, in order to introduce multilateralism and regionally transferable currency in the trade between CMEA countries (or, at least, in the reciprocal trade between three countries), it will be necessary to do away with two properties of the directive plan instructions system which are essential from this point of view, namely (1) the isolation of the domestic price level from international prices, and (2) the system of directive export and import instructions. But this is not simply a matter of resolution, as theory and practice have proved. Between the individual elements of the mechanism as well as between the internal and external mechanism there is a strict relationship and there are strong interactions. It is unnecessary to repeat here the arguments relating to this. Accordingly, we have now arrived at a point where the subject could be closed with this summary. In order to bring about a genuine market in the external relations, with the corresponding price, value and money categories, it will be necessary to switch over to a controlled and planned domestic market economy which differs *qualitatively* from that based on a system of directive plan orders. This is the most important precondition for effecting multilateralism and transferability. All other problems, such as e.g. liquidity, important as they may be, will arise only afterwards. On the other hand, it is the higher efficiency of the economy brought about by the operation of a controlled and planned market economy that could, in addition to the external resources, create the reserves necessary to ensure liquidity in the international relations.

To introduce a money, multilaterally and regionally transferable in the CMEA region (or at least among three CMEA countries) it would be necessary to liquidate two important characteristics of the directive planning system, namely the lack of exchange rates working in their real function, connecting the domestic and foreign trade prices and influencing imports and exports, and also the directives relating to export and import quotas. These are, however, not matters of simple decisions. The individual elements of the domestic economic mechanism, and the domestic and

Committee for Foreign Trade on the subject of the mechanism of external trading it becomes clear that there is hardly any measure aimed at change and carried out in any of the countries where the system of directive plan instructions is in operation, which were not deliberately tried in Hungary in the period from 1957 to 1967. Now, it is well known that these measures, although they brought some improvement in the above sense as contrasted with the preceding period, did not and could not result in any qualitative change.

external systems are closely interdependent. We don't have to repeat our thoughts and arguments in this matter, and we could even conclude the chapter with the following remarks:

First, we have to change from the system of directive planning to a qualitatively different, controlled and planned market economy to allow the introduction of categories like money, value, commodities, corresponding to the real market also in international relations. This is a real *sine qua non* of multilateralism and transferability. Every other issue, like liquidity, no matter how important it is, could be raised logically and historically only afterwards. Moreover, only a greater efficiency due to the establishment of controlled and regulated market economies could create – beyond external sources – the necessary reserves required for greater liquidity.

The problem requires, nevertheless, further investigation:

(1) because of the great importance of the steps that can be undertaken within the framework of the present system and form a preliminary to the future qualitative changes; and

(2) because references to the possible limitations of such steps may contribute to the realistic assessment of the present possibility of the healthy, just and urgent claims for the introduction of multilateralism and the creation of a transferable and convertible currency.

Up to the present, of all CMEA countries it is only in Hungary that an economic mechanism which could serve as a basis for multilateral settlements has been established.

To the degree, however, to which the role of the commodity, value and money categories as incentives can be increased even in the conditions of the system based on directive plan orders, progress can and must be made in three fields, namely in those of:

(1) the system of 'quotas' (directive export and import instructions);

(2) the price agreements;

(3) the terms of credit and interest.

## (1) The quota system

It will be remembered that the system of quotas never covered the whole volume of trade, not even in the early 1950s. In the trade between Hungary and the CMEA countries, the goods for which individual quotas are fixed in volume terms amount to some 50 to 60 per cent of the total volume of trade.[1] Under the quota system, the enterprises can contract only

---

[1] This statement refers to the long-term five-year agreements. The annual agreements – which differ from the former ones to the same degree as the domestic five-year plans differ from the annual plans – show a higher grade of specification, and it is these that are really important.

for deliveries of the goods specified in the list of quotas. There exists also another, less strict form of quotas under which the enterprises are free to agree upon the quality, type and choice of the commodity in question when contracting. *Value quotas* fix only the volume of compulsory deliveries, leaving the enterprises a free hand to enter into contracts for any commodity belonging to the commodity group concerned. *Global quotas* allow a wider choice, even between commodity groups. However, the main thing is that strict quotas are established for the hardest commodities (raw materials), as well as for machinery and for all final products whose domestic production and distribution is based upon balances.

In a country like Hungary, where the economic system is in essential contradiction with the system of 'compulsory quotas', it is quite natural that numerous proposals should be put forward with the aim of rendering the latter more flexible. Thus, it has been suggested that 'in the case of products and commodity groups where productive capacity can be converted, the ratio of unspecified quotas fixed only in terms of value should be increased'; 'the exact quantitative and value limits of certain quotas should be replaced by upper and lower limits'; 'instead of fixing deliveries by calendar years, the delivery terms of the contracts entered into by enterprises should be taken as a basis'; 'the system of annual inter-government protocols should be reduced in scope and finally discontinued, and the functions of these protocols should be taken over by long-term agreements and by the contracting and management activities of the foreign trading enterprises systematically controlled by their own government organs'.[1]

However, from the point of view of our subject, these proposals have two shortcomings, namely that: (*a*) in the relations with a number of countries they represent wishful thinking rather than real possibilities; and (*b*) even if they were put into practice they would be insufficient to bring about multilateral trade and transferability.

(*a*) In the countries where the system of directive plan orders persists but an indirect interest in prices abroad is created by means of foreign currency bonuses, the granting of export and import rights to producing enterprises, the sharing of profits between foreign-trading and industrial companies, incentives to increase the 'efficiency' of foreign currency earnings, novel-type specialization agreements, etc., the role of the

The product list of the long-term agreements and annual contingencies is getting more detailed in the CMEA trade in most of the cases. The increase in the number of products entering the list is greater than that of the increases of the trade volume.

[1] Dr György Tallós, 'The Development of Trade among CMEA countries', *Közgazdasági Szemle*, 1966, no. 1.

enterprises in establishing the quotas will to a certain degree increase and so will their influence in widening the range of compulsory quotas fixed in value terms.

However, at present and for a long time to come, this will be limited by structural tensions and the striving for barter relations ('hard' and 'soft' commodities, the principle of 'machinery for machinery'), a well-known consequence of the whole system. What is, however, more important in the long run is the fact that as long as the system of directive plan instructions exists, the enterprises cannot be allowed to effect their purchases in the markets, in quantities and at prices of their own choosing; nor is it possible to establish a mechanism within the directive system that would enable or encourage the enterprises to do so. In such a system, they will ask for 'security', for specifications, and rightly so. (It is unnecessary to deal with this aspect of the question in detail; suffice it to refer for particulars to the preliminary material of the Hungarian reform of the economic mechanism.)

(*b*) For progress towards multilateralism, the initial condition must be the introduction of the quota system employed in bilateral trade of type I (see p. 68 above) and characterized by upper limits set to imports by the central authority, a system of licences etc. Such a system, although protectionist in character, leaves a higher degree of freedom than all the possibilities described above. Gradual liberalization should take place as related to this system. (Let it be pointed out that within EPU the share of liberalized imports in total imports rose from 47–57 per cent in 1950 to 91–98 per cent by 1958.)[1]

## (2) Price agreements

Even under the present system it will be possible to aim at more realistic and more flexible price agreements concerning the price proportions of the major commodity groups. These will, even against the wishes of some countries, assert themselves in the well-known manner through central decision-making, which will be realized in price agreements on the enterprise level (e.g. in the case of specialized products).

As the present prices are in contradiction with the interests and the legitimate requirements of several countries – primarily of the USSR – it is most desirable that considerable price changes should take place over the years to come.[2]

---

[1] OEEC, *Annual Economic Review*.
[2] Some practical experts are inclined to misinterpret this fact, believing it to be a sign of the tendency towards some form of free price formation.

In earlier published papers it was shown in detail that the system of directive plan targets is incompatible with frequently changing foreign-trade prices and does not make it possible for the foreign-market price to affect production (except within a narrow range, by means of special 'arrangements', and resulting in every case in imperfect solutions and conflicts of interest).[1] Consequently, as long as this system remains in operation in the domestic economy, no major unforeseeable price fluctuations can take place in bilateral trade either. Intentionally or unintentionally, the price agreements, and price proportions too, will be determined by the central links which are the necessary concomitants of the system of directive plan instructions and have been dealt with in detail in the article quoted above.

The price system required for the introduction of a transferable currency can be briefly characterized as follows: the prices must, in general, be market prices. Stable prices could be those which the enterprises, combines or governments deem expedient to fix (or allow to move in accordance with certain predetermined conditions, such as exchange quotation, magnitude of series, technical characteristics, etc.) within the framework of long-term agreements, on the basis of profit sharing. With the progress of integration,' it may be expected that multilateral price agreements will also be concluded for certain commodity groups, linked with one another by a suitable compensatory system.

## (3) Terms of credit and interest

Any progress either in the quota system or in the field of prices along the lines described above may disturb the balance of multilateral trade planned at the beginning of the year. In order for more flexible methods to prevail it will be necessary to agree upon credits for several years wherever there is a hope for later bilateral repayment. However, it should be clear that credits of this type will be granted only against structural guarantees. For example, it may be stipulated beforehand that credits will be extended on deliveries exceeding certain compulsory quotas to a defined limit. Such credits will in themselves not solve the problem; they will, nonetheless, enable progress to be made in other fields, such as quotas and prices, by

[1] E.g. Ausch and Barta, 'The theoretical problems of prices in the trade between CMEA countries', *Közgazdasági Szemle*, 1967, no. 1; Ausch, 'The possibilities of utilization of market relations in the co-operation of CMEA Countries', Institute of Economics, Hungarian Academy of Sciences, Budapest, 1965. [Both articles reprinted in English in *Socialist world market prices*, Publishing House of the Hungarian Academy of Sciences, 1969.] See, above all, 'Reform of the Mechanism of Economy in Hungary' (in English), ed. I. Friss, Publishing House of the Hungarian Academy of Sciences, 1968, pp. 223–45.

postponing the requirement of yearly equilibrium by several years. In the credits of this type, interest may play a greater role than it has till now.

In order to widen the field of balance compensation to some extent, it should be possible for the balances resulting from bilateral payments to be sold by the participating countries to each other at discounts which compensate for the structural and price-level differences between the individual countries.

What is called the 'liberalization' of trade in consumer goods may be considered as part of this process, as a variant applied to concrete commodity groups. Within the framework of the directive system, 'liberalization' cannot obviously go beyond the limits set individually and collectively by the factors described in paragraphs (1), (2) and (3).

The process will become more meaningful if carried out by two countries (such as e.g. Hungary and Czechoslovakia) which have switched over to a market mechanism in the domestic economy. In such a case, bilateral 'liberalization' of trade will, as regards the external conditions, be limited only by the fact that foreign-trade price agreements will have to be liberalized over a wide range and the old quota system discarded. As long as two countries are involved, this can in principle take place within the limits normally set by the clearing system type 1. This is because the bilateral equilibrium of the balances of trade and payments must be taken care of (not excluding, in case of long-term indebtedness, the requirement of payments in gold or convertible currency). The term 'liberalization' must, therefore, be interpreted in a relative sense, because it can bring about at best a state which would otherwise be characterized as 'extensive trade and payment restrictions'.

It is well-known that actual progress is rather slow and gradual, and this for the following reasons:

For well-known reasons, the domestic market is still highly imperfect. A large number of restrictions are still in force, temporarily, with temporary 'financial bridges' and even directive instructions among them, in some countries and in some fields of the economy, including foreign trade. For example, it will frequently be impossible to allow the import prices based on prices abroad converted at the foreign-exchange rate to assert themselves in the domestic market, because in several cases this would mean competition for the domestic producers which they cannot withstand. As a matter of fact, the amount of enterprise and central credits or budgetary means available is insufficient to enable the necessary changes in the pattern of production, not to speak of the measures to stop production in some plants and the creation of new productive capacities. In addition, the role of capitalist imports is particularly conspicuous in some product groups under present conditions.

The minimum of progress made up to now towards 'liberalization' in the trade of consumer goods, and its expected gradual extension to other products will, nevertheless, be of great importance from the point of view of the production structure of the two countries and of the greater choice of goods. Moreover, with the 'propaganda' being made for the international introduction of a market mechanism, it may constitute a preparatory school for a novel currency co-operation.

STRUCTURAL TENSIONS AND THE PROBLEM OF LIQUIDITY IN
THE TRANSITION TO A CONVERTIBLE CURRENCY

It is a generally known fact that over the past fifteen years the efficiency of the national economies of the CMEA countries (the ratio of social inputs to domestically produced goods available for final use) has not shown a favourable trend. Partly as causes and partly as effects of this inefficiency, considerable structural tensions have appeared both within the individual countries and with CMEA as a whole. Only an outline of the facts can be given here. The low degree of efficiency of the national economy has been proved in respect of every CMEA country by a number of socialist and western authors.

As regards Hungary, let us refer to our calculations based on the official data published by the Central Statistical Office. In the years between 1950 and 1965, a *unit increase* in final, non-productive utilization (private and public consumption, defence expenditure, non-productive fixed assets) required, taking into account foreign indebtedness, a 3.88-fold increase in the cost of productive fixed and current assets and the manpower employed in the productive sphere. Over the same period, this index was 2.2 in Austria, 1.9 in Italy, and 1.2 in the German Federal Republic.[1] Not exactly identical but similar indices for the CSSR show an equally unfavourable trend.[2]

In the domestic economy, the low level of efficiency finds its expression in the well-known phenomena of the 'scarcity economy', i.e. in the fact that there is a relative scarcity of every factor of production at the given

[1] See Ausch, 'CMEA Co-operation: situation, mechanism and perspectives', Publishing House of Economics and Law, Budapest, 1969, pp. 64–5 and pp. 249–77. (English edition in preparation.)
[2] O. Sik: 'Some problems of the analysis of economic development in Czechoslovakia', *Politicka Ekonomie*, 1966, no. 1, and articles by I. Nachtigal, *ibid.* In respect of other countries, too, a wide range of articles and books of a similar content could be quoted. (E.g. Miklós and Zsukova, 'Experiences of Economic Growth in some CMEA Countries', *Gazdaság*, 1968, no. 3.)

rate of development of the national economy. Another form in which the low efficiency finds its expression is the low technical level of the final products. In the final analysis, this is also the cause of the scarcity of raw materials, because the finished goods cannot as a rule be sold at a profit in the world market.

A further effect is the permanent scarcity of resources available for investment. In order to maintain the rate of development, a high investment level is required. Therefore, all countries are reluctant to invest for export purposes in the productive sectors where large amounts of investment are required at a time with a low rate of return; at the same time, in a number of processing industries, parallel development is taking place, and many products can be sold only with great difficulty, or not at all, either in the domestic market or in reciprocal trade, and even less in the capitalist markets. There is also a scarcity of a great number of high-quality products requiring a high level of technical competence; as a result, it becomes difficult to raise the standard of living at an adequate rate; indebtedness to capitalist countries shows an increasing trend.

Let us now imagine for a moment what would happen if the necessary precondition for a switch-over to multilateralism in trade and payments, the transition to a controlled market mechanism in every CMEA country, commenced with the required efficiency and the given production patterns. (It should be emphasized that this is merely an abstraction serving the purpose of outlining more markedly the problems under analysis. In actual practice, the transition could take place only gradually, by transforming the tools of the present 'super-protectionism', such as export grants and import levies, into the corresponding market categories of subsidies and customs duties. Starting from this basis, liberalization would be a slow process, with its degree determined by the rate at which the amount of reserves needed for transformation and rationalization become available as a result of increased efficiency.)

In order to further emphasise the problems involved, the terms 'controlled' and 'planned' will, as mere abstractions, also be discarded. As a matter of fact, 'control' should, among other things, serve to mitigate in the short run, and 'planning' to eliminate in the longer run, the tensions to be described here. The price of raw materials would immediately rise significantly. The enterprises producing raw materials, and the countries which are net exporters of raw materials, would thus make additional profits. The accumulation of these profits would after a certain time lead to an increase in the production of raw materials for export, provided that extraction costs at the new places of occurrence did not rise at a quicker rate than the raw material prices. The increase in raw material prices will, however, be limited by the purchasing power of the enterprises in the countries which are net importers of raw materials.

The following results, or some combination of them, are likely:

(1) The enterprises with a low rate of profitability reduce their imports of raw materials, and subsequently also production, which will lead to unemployment.

(2) The enterprises are allowed to compensate for the effects of rising raw material prices as a cost factor:

(*a*) by lowering their taxes or,

(*b*) by admitting price increases by the enterprises.

Variant (*a*), if not concomitant with a decrease in expenditures, will equal variant (*b*) in its inflationary effect. The effect of the decrease in government expenditure will vary from sector to sector but will be deflationary in every case (decrease in productive and non-productive investment, in the volume of credits, etc.) and thus also lead to unemployment.

(3) The CMEA countries could decrease their imports of raw materials from each other and increase those from third markets. This would be limited by the additional cost of one unit of foreign currency needed for the additional exports to those markets, as contrasted with the price increases within CMEA. As regards the effect on the economy as a whole, it amounts to the same as cases (1) and (2).

The shortages and surpluses in the trade of finished goods would lead to a decrease in the prices of one group and to a rise in those of the other; in the longrun this would result in an increase in the volume of production of the scarce or better products and conversely. However, this would greatly raise the demand for rationalization and switch-over capital, and would thus have the same effect on the economy as a rise in raw material prices.

These problems will pose themselves particularly in the countries where raw material shortage and the quality and choice problems of final products appear together.

Up to now, 'pure' free market effects have been assumed. Should these be replaced by controls and planning on the national level, and also on the international level, which should become *possible* with a mechanism of this type, then the problems of disequilibrium would not appear all at the same time and could be remedied with less total sacrifice.

What is most essential, however, is that the elimination of 'structural tensions' will in any case require additional capital. What amount would be needed to eliminate these structural tensions? It is naturally impossible to give any well-founded estimates, but this is also unnecessary because in the given conditions the elimination of structural tensions will be possible only gradually. Moreover, there is a strong interrelation between this process and the changes in the mechanism; quicker or slower progress in one field will enable or hinder the other and *vice versa*.

In the final analysis, it is only the changes in the internal and external mechanisms and the strongly related changes in economic policy, resulting in increased efficiency of the national economy, which will be able to produce the amounts needed for the transition to multilateralism and transferability and, from the financial side, to increased international liquidity, even if a recourse to external help should be both possible and necessary.

Will the structural changes described above be sufficient for a switchover to multilateralism and transferability? In themselves, certainly not. Suitable international agreements and institutions will also be needed, and fixed and working capital, which must be at the command of these institutions, even if all the requirements raised up to now were fulfilled. This capital will have to serve the maintenance of international liquidity in the case of more or less lasting difficulties in obtaining balance, which may – even in case of the structural changes described here – occur for most varied reasons. The amount of capital and the question in which foreign currency it should be kept, will depend on the degree of convertibility and transferability achieved in the trade between CMEA countries and on whether this can be extended to the world economy as a whole. These questions will be dealt with below.

To sum up: in order to bring about multilateral trade and payments and a transferable currency, controlled and planned socialist market economies and a corresponding foreign-trade system must be brought into being in the CMEA countries. Then the functions of money will be able to assert themselves on the international level. Furthermore, certain national and international economic disproportions will have to be eliminated. If, then, the control of foreign trade were not to exceed certain limits, and the necessary international institutions were to be brought into being, then the currency would become, at least regionally, transferable.

But can the necessary degree of government liberalization be brought into harmony with the requirements of a controlled and planned socialist market economy? In the knowledge of the achievements up to now of the Hungarian reform of the mechanism and of the further gradual progress, the posing of the question in this country may seem unnecessary. It is, however, not unnecessary to give a concrete answer to the related questions because the statement may be frequently met with in the literature, and particularly in practice, that multilateralism is a concept compatible with socialist production conditions but that convertibility is not.

First of all, the freedom of the flow of capital is not a necessary condition for multilateralism and transferability. It will be sufficient to abolish the restrictions on current payments. (It is, of course, another question whether the planning and influencing of structural proportions on an international scale, as well as the efforts to make the advanced countries interested in helping the less advanced ones, would also require the launching of international ventures and the flow of capital.)

Here, too, there are different possible degrees of transferability and later convertibility. For example, it is possible in principle that regional transferability should in the initial stage apply only to aliens under the Foreign Exchange Act (in this case only to CMEA countries and their enterprises). This entails the obligation that such aliens can effect purchases from Hungarian enterprises to the extent of their balances held in forints, or, if they cannot spend their money here, they should effect purchases to the debit of this country. (Should Hungary become in this manner a debtor country, then the necessity of payment in gold or some reserve currency would arise. The possible variants of this will be considered below.) The total imports of Hungarian enterprises could in this case be under the strictest control and burdened with quotas and deposit regulations etc. (as e.g. in Greece where only external convertibility exists). Should internal convertibility be also introduced, this means that domestic enterprises may also freely effect purchases from and sales to any socialist country (clearly this will be influenced by customs duties in the case of imports, by subsidies in that of exports, and in some cases even made dependent on licences). This should be entirely possible if the initial conditions are fulfilled in every country.

The objection which would be made in the literature on the subject is this: would it then be possible for anyone to import capital goods?[1] The question is, obviously, hardly justified. Anyone can import and export who has the right to do so; under socialism this will be no private person but an economic unit invested with the right by the government.

As regards private persons, in the case of internal convertibility they will be entitled to convert the domestic currency into foreign currency and use it for any purpose of consumption, and in a restricted sense, by artisans, even for the acquisition of means of production. As regards the

[1] See the proceedings of the 1967 CMEA Conference on Prices, Budapest (in English: *Socialist World Market Prices*, eds. T. Földi and T. Kiss, Akadèmiai Kiadó, Budapest, 1969.

extent of this freedom, it is a well-known fact that even the most advanced capitalist countries may from time to time restrict the amount of foreign currency available to private persons (e.g. for travel abroad). The capital exports and imports which should later on become possible for the state-owned enterprises with other socialist countries will obviously be governed by regulations of the state (and the CMEA's Bank for International Economic Co-operation as well as the other international organs that will be established by mutual agreement). In the relations with capitalist countries the regulations will certainly be more strict and centralized, and the individual cases will be judged from the point of view of expediency in such a way that the basic principle of social ownership of the means of production, which is embodied in the constitution, is not damaged. But even in the capitalist world there are very few countries where the export and import of capital is entirely free. These questions are, accordingly, hardly relevant from the point of view of currency convertibility.

Therefore, if we consider the controlled and planned market economy within a socialist country to be a possible concrete form of the socialist production relations, then we have already taken a stand also for the mutual transferability of the currency.

How could this convertibility and transferability operate in principle, temporarily only within the CMEA region?

If the two basic conditions of the external mechanism ('price and quota', as described above) changed and the means necessary for liquidity came gradually into being, then all that would be needed for the purpose would be:

(1) an alteration and extension of the credit terms of the already operating BIEC;

(2) the charging of real (higher) interest rates on credits.

This means, of course, that real rates of foreign exchange must function in all (or, at least, in three) CMEA countries, whereby the present 'clearing rouble' must come into connection as real money with the domestic currency of all (or, at least, three) CMEA countries, primarily with the Soviet domestic rouble. In this case and in this region, provided, and this should be again emphasized, that structural tensions such as the shortage in raw materials are also eliminated, the rouble, as the currency of the strongest and dominating economy within CMEA, could become the reserve currency of that region.

This would not as yet presuppose by any means the obligation of payments in gold or in capitalist convertible currency, because the creditors could buy with their credit balances any commodity physically available within the region, with a minimum of trade restrictions.

Practically – and especially in the initial stage of the existence of the system of transferability – it would be necessary for the reserve currency to be convertible within certain limits and under certain conditions into gold or some capitalist convertible currency. This is because within the region a large number of structural tensions may be expected to persist, especially in the first stage, the rapid elimination of which will only be possible by ensuring the connection with the convertible-currency markets.

There is only one further condition for the realization of a multilateral trading system, namely that the exchange rates remain fixed and the stable relative value of the rouble ensured. The Soviet domestic price level should not rise at a quicker rate than the price level of the rest of the CMEA countries.

As contrasted with a system of financial co-operation on a world-wide scale, which is only likely to become a reality in the very distant future, this type of regional multilateralism and transferability is, of course, less desirable in effect, because it would serve to perpetuate regional autarky and protectionism. In order to make the rouble, and through it the currency of all member countries, convertible outside the region, its convertibility into gold or another reserve currency would have to be ensured. Would this bring any advantage, in financial terms, to the USSR? Obviously so, because every capitalist country or enterprise would, to the extent of its rouble holdings, automatically grant a credit to the USSR as the issuer of that currency.[1]

In order to examine the *realistic* possibilities of multilateralism and convertibility in the given economic and political situation of the CMEA countries, we must start from the expected possibilities and attitude of the USSR, the dominating economy within CMEA and the main supplier and purchaser for the rest of the CMEA countries.

Nobody who knows the situation is likely to dispute the fact that, for economic, ideological, traditional and, last but not least, military reasons, the USSR is not likely to abandon in the foreseeable future her system of a planned economy based on directive plan instructions, although even there the mechanism tends towards flexibility. This fact itself sets certain objective limits to the progress towards a system of multilateralism. For political as well as economic reasons the USSR will also for a long time to

---

[1] It is another question, what obligations this would involve on the part of the USSR, and whether it would be acceptable in the foreseeable future from other – political – points of view to the USSR *and* the capitalist countries. We shall revert to the subject below, when discussing the short-run possibilities, which differ considerably from those mentioned above.

come strive for bilateralism in her trade with capitalist countries. Profound changes would have to occur in the world's entire political pattern to induce the USSR to enter into multilateral trade with the latter and to introduce convertibility either on the basis of the capitalist reserve currencies, which are undergoing a crisis, or on that of the system described above (the rouble as the world's third reserve currency), or based on a uniform world reserve currency to be established sometime in the future.

Until then the USSR will, relying on her immense economic resources and gold reserves, most probably prefer centrally directed bilateralism. For this form ensures her the greatest freedom of manœuvre in the political and economic field, exposes her least to the effects of changes in the monetary position of other countries, and does not require a coordination of her monetary policies with the latter. There is, of course, steady pressure on the USSR from the developing countries to bring about the *external* convertibility of the rouble. It is possible that the USSR, after taking into account the position of the dollar, will meet these demands in some form, with suitable restrictions. However, we shall not engage here in the discussion of this question, because it is hardly relevant from the point of view of transferability and multilateralism within CMEA.[1]

All that can be expected in the trade between the USSR and the other European CMEA countries is that in the not too near future some progress will be made towards the application of non-specified quotas in value terms. This expectation is motivated by the prospects of changes in the economic mechanism of the other socialist countries and of the USSR herself. In the field of price agreements, it may be expected that on the basis of the well-known attempts to increase the price of raw materials relative to that of finished products more realistic prices will be worked out which are more in harmony with world market prices. However, as has been said above, it can hardly be expected that a transition to a system of variable market prices can take place in the foreseeable future.

Therefore, for various reasons which all act in the same direction, trade between the USSR and the other European CMEA countries will for some time to come be transacted under conditions similar to those of the former mechanism; the same applies also to settlements.

[1] Discussions were going on, and statements were made in different socialist countries in recent years about the conditions of introducing convertibility – basically external convertibility – of their currencies. There are several conditions of such steps even on a limited scale, and with a limited group of currencies. The possibility of introducing such a type of convertibility depends really only on a general increase in the efficiency of the national economy, on the accumulation of adequate foreign-exchange reserves, and on the establishment of co-operation with the international financial institutions and the central banks abroad.

If the above can be accepted as likely, and if the assumption is justified that the probability of doing away with the system based on directive plan instructions in the long run is greater in the other CMEA countries than in the USSR, the question may arise whether it should not be possible to create regional multilateralism and transferability in the trade between the other socialist countries.

It must be emphasized that the question is a purely academic one because at the moment, of all CMEA countries, only Hungary has introduced a system of controlled and planned market economy. Moreover, a smaller group of countries, since it could not rely directly upon economic and financial potential of the USSR, would be weak on purely economic terms.

From the economic point of view, in the case of the realization of sub-regional transferability of this type, the following difficulties can be expected to appear:

(1) Within the sub-region there will be structurally debtor countries whose deficits will have to be covered. However, the whole concept is conceivable only in the rather distant future; in the meantime

(*a*) the development level will rise in the countries concerned;

(*b*) the efficiency of their economies will increase and so will their credit-granting capacity;

(*c*) continued assistance on the part of the USSR and the international financial organs may be counted upon.

(2) Should the system of trade and settlements with the USSR remain similar to that at present in force, then in the stage of the emergence of a sub-regional multilateral group, with the formation of three price levels (capitalist, sub-regional and Soviet), the participating countries would have to work with at least three exchange rates,[1] which would lead to well-known difficulties. In the course of time the number could be reduced to two, to the extent to which the domestic price system and the prices in reciprocal trade approach the world-market prices.

The switch-over to multilateral trade and payments, to transferability and varying degrees of convertibility within CMEA cannot thus be achieved by simple measures of monetary reform. All this can emerge only, on the one hand, as the concentrated expression of gradual changes within the individual countries and in the mechanism of co-operation, changes which must lead to *qualitative transformation* and to the abolition of the system of

---

[1] For the present we can ignore the situation in which – for well-known reasons – two basic exchange rates are in operation *in every relation*: a foreign-trade 'price multiplier', and another rate which is more in harmony with the purchasing power of personal consumption.

directive plan instructions; and, on the other hand, as a result of a general rise in the efficiency of the individual economies and of fundamental changes in the political pattern of the world.

On the other hand, it is also obvious that a convertible currency will be needed in order to solve several present-day difficulties of co-operation, and to raise thereby the efficiency of the national economies. And there are also external causes such as the existence and the prospects of the Common Market, which make progress in this direction imperative, and which compel us to seek a solution, distant as it may seem at present, of the problem and to accelerate the process as far as possible. For this reason, it is imperative to press now the undertaking of such steps as can be realized even in the present situation. It is also important clearly to see the goals and, as far as possible, the ways that lead to them. This means at the same time that a serious attempt should be made to evaluate the numerous ideas which have been put forward, in discussion or in writing, in connection with the problem.

Therefore, having outlined above our own views on the subject, we shall now proceed to survey briefly some characteristic opinions and to evaluate them critically.[1]

According to some views expressed during the debate on the problems the convertibility of the domestic rouble should first be attained – this would then solve the problem of the mutual convertibility of the other CMEA currencies as well.

What does this mean in actual practice? It means that if some exporter were not interested in the Soviet commodities offered in barter trade – for reasons of choice, quality, or for unspecified reasons – and asked for payment in dollars of gold, the Soviet bank would pay.

Accordingly, this concept also means that the same principle would be applied to imports of any socialist country from the USSR.

Although this would not render formally convertible the accounting unit in the trade between the other socialist countries (nor their domestic

---

[1] In view of the fact that most of these opinions have not been presented in the press, but were put forward in the course of debates and in contributions to conferences dealing with the question, no names will be mentioned here. Nor is the list a complete one. As in innumerable similar cases when some harmful phenomenon is the result of the operation of the whole system (e.g. fluctuations in production, growing inventories, concealed price increases, etc.), numerous 'radical' proposals have been put forward and decisions taken to overcome the difficulties. However, it is not possible to cure the symptoms without eliminating their causes. There is probably no other field where proposals relating to some 'panacea' appear in such great variety as in that of creating transferability within CMEA. Many of these proposals are like advertisements for hair-restorers; the 'certain remedy' was advertised as long ago as 1868, in Jókai's newspaper called *Hon* and in the 1914 volume of *Érdekes Ujság* but will be hailed also by the current issues of the Swiss periodical *Sie und Er*.

currencies), in practice – as the share of the USSR is considerable in the trade of each country – nothing would be easier than to ask the USSR for dollars or gold in payment for the exported goods. This would probably be sufficient to pay off the payments deficits arising from the trade with the capitalist countries, to increase imports from these countries, and also to effect payments partly in dollars or gold in inter-CMEA trade, thus doing away with all the structural tensions. However, in our opinion, this is an unrealistic concept, if for no other reason, because it would – owing to the actual production patterns and commodity qualities, the price levels formed in the course of bilateral barter trade, the debts to capitalist countries accumulated over a long period, and the established 'production' (acquisition) cost of convertible currencies – put the USSR under the obligation to pay out continuously amounts of dollars or gold which would far exceed even her possibilities.

According to another view 'debtors should be obliged, under the existing economic mechanism and structural conditions, to pay off interest charges and part of the end-year balances (a part that would gradually rise to 100 per cent) in gold or freely convertible capitalist currencies'. This proposal was published years ago in the Polish official press, where it has recently reappeared.[1]

With some changes – concerning the so-called swap construction, to which we shall revert below – this idea was also adopted by the German Democratic Republic and Czechoslovakia. It will be expedient to examine the possible effects of this proposal – in case it were realized within the framework of the existing planned economy, or with only gradual changes in that framework – separately for the 'hard' and the 'soft' commodities.

(*a*) Should the obligation of payment in gold, the 'gold sanction', be extended also to the field of 'soft' commodities (or to a physically delimited part of them), this would only lead to an even stricter bilateral balancing of trade than hitherto, since no country would risk becoming obliged to effect payment in gold. According to Gresham's law and by all practical experience (such as that of the 1957 'multilateral clearing') bad money will drive out good money from circulation.

(*b*) Should the 'gold sanction' be confined to the trade in 'hard' commodities, this would hardly lead to a multilateralization of trade. According to the proposal, this goal should be approached by introducing certain discounts on the exchange rates. However, due to the existing price differences and physical interconnections, it is impossible to work out discount rates which would be acceptable to all countries participating

[1] *Trybuna Ludu*, 1967, and *Zycie Gospodarce*, 1968.

in a multilateral clearing agreement and which could at the same time be brought into line with the cost for each country of acquiring convertible foreign currency. But even if we disregarded this aspect, the problem would remain that the countries with a 'soft' price structure would be unable to pay in gold or capitalist currency. Nor can this difficulty be overcome by means of the so-called swap construction, under which the debtor would be given the right to reacquire in a year or two the convertible currency used in payment. As a matter of fact, it is wholly unrealistic to expect that a country with a 'soft' price structure and running into debt with her CMEA partners under the existing conditions, should in the same period be able to acquire in her trade with capitalist countries the convertible currencies lent to her under the swap terms.

(*c*) Were the 'gold sanction' to apply only to transactions over and above the bilaterally fixed quotas, then the system proposed would hardly differ in substance from the actual practice; certain 'hard' commodities, delivered over and above the quotas, are already paid for in convertible currency. This, however, has nothing to do with settlement in roubles.

There is also a view expressed in the debate according to which multilateral and transferable settlement should be introduced in the trade in certain bilaterally or multilaterally specialized products, and a central fund be created to cover the reconstruction and rationalization costs arising in connection with this specialization.

Assuming that the effect of the price and other conditions of the specialization agreements will be to make the products concerned as 'hard' as, for instance, the most important raw materials are at present, then what has been said in the second paragraph of section (*b*) above will apply also to these products. The 'central fund' mentioned above would also have to consist of capitalist convertible currency because, for the time being, no other 'money' actually exists.

The less important proposal, according to which 'the capital of the Bank for International Economic Co-operation (BIEC) should be composed partly of gold and convertible currency' is related to the above and has already been partly realized.

This capital is, for the time being, of minor importance only, because the member countries may also draw on their shares. Additional funds would have an advantage over the short-term capitalist credits which could be obtained bilaterally; it would, however, require a considerably larger capital to make the amount of such funds really significant. A major capital increase has been proposed again recently and is more likely to materialize now than it was earlier.

If the CMEA countries had at their disposal adequate stocks of gold and convertible currency for the purpose, it would be possible for BIEC to create a corresponding gold and convertible currency fund, and this would enable it:

(*a*) to grant short-term credit for trade in specialized products which have become 'hard' and in the commodities which have previously been paid for in convertible capitalist currency;

(*b*) to grant long-term credit in capitalist currency for the reconstruction and rationalization purposes connected with specialization and for investment aimed at increasing the production of commodities in short supply. Moreover, these long-term credits could be combined with the long-term investment credits raised bilaterally by the individual member countries in capitalist countries and probably also with deliveries in a framework of co-operation projects. Recently, this proposal has been again put forward in the form that a common Investment Bank should be set up for CMEA. If enough capital is paid up in convertible currencies and other means are also drawn in, this is, of course, possible.

These proposals were not implemented for the simple reason that the individual countries were either unable or reluctant to set up a fund of this type and of adequate size.

It is, however, more important that the whole construction has but a minor and, as will be clear from the above, only a highly indirect bearing on rendering actually multilateral the trade which is at present being settled in so-called 'transferable' roubles; it could only contribute by facilitating structural improvements.

Another proposal would make the present-day clearing rouble transferable. The basic characteristic of this concept is that, according to its advocates, it is not an essential condition of transferability that the international currency (transferable rouble) should be related to the domestic currencies through actually operating exchange rates, and influence both trade and production in this way.

In their opinion, even if this were necessary in principle, it cannot be expected in the next twenty years that a system of this type could come into being in the CMEA countries. All that should be done is, accordingly, to liberalize foreign-trade prices and to abolish the quota system. This is only a question of decision taking. Should it cause difficulties for any country, that would be her worry. Thus, according to this proposal, the whole transition should be started from the monetary side, on the basis of agreement.

It is not our intention to challenge this opinion here again. We believe that our earlier arguments have already proved its illusory character. We should only like to draw attention to the fact that a 'transferable rouble' of this type (the term is applied in an entirely arbitrary manner) – even if it could be brought into being – could not perform any of the functions of a genuinely transferable currency. The only respect in which it would make things easier would be in the 'compensation' of balances emerging in bilateral relations.

There exists also in Hungary a view according to which the transition to transferability and convertibility should be approached from the point of view of liquidity. Substantial stocks of gold and convertible currency would first be needed. It is, however, not easy to build up such stocks, nor is it reasonable. It is well known that the 'price' of gold depends on the power position of the capitalist countries and on speculative factors, and that the convertible currencies may be devalued. Accordingly, it would be necessary to build up huge stocks of raw materials of high value and comparatively small volume, which could at any time be sold on the commodity exchanges or in re-export, or to earmark part of such stocks in the individual countries for the BIEC. Besides, the prices of such commodities are also liable to fluctuate extensively and to fall in the long run. But apart from this, in our view, the concept may also be challenged on more general grounds. The answer may be similar to what has been expounded in connection with the first view outlined above. Commodities are not money, nor does any of them represent a universal equivalent (not even those with the smallest volume, with the single exception of gold). But aside from this, somebody or some country would have to make these commodities available continuously and in unlimited quantities, as would be the case with gold according to the concept first mentioned. And the one is just as impossible as the other.

Yet another view would agree with all that has been said above on the subject, with a slight difference in one aspect only, namely in judging the possibilities of future development. The argument runs as follows. True, the primary condition for multilateral trade and payments and for convertibility in reciprocal trade is the existence of the market. This necessitates certain changes, at least in the areas in which the external relations occur (prices, quotas, credit, etc.). However, as up to now only one CMEA country has introduced a regulated and planned market economy, let us not wait idly any longer nor content ourselves with the minor steps discussed up to now. Let us act, starting from the financial side. Let us agree on changing its elements, irrespective of the type of economic system prevailing in the individual countries. As a matter of fact, the systems based on directive plan instructions are also in a state of flux. In the course of gradual development, they will be 'adjusted' to the requirements of transferability with the aid of 'financial bridges'. This should be possible. (In the course of the debate, it was not possible to clarify the arguments on which the latter contention was actually based.)

Nor do we wish here to draw the argument out to greater length. Let us remind ourselves only of the facts that: (1) theory has long ago clarified the difference between the use of the categories of commodity, value and money as incentives within the framework of directive plan instructions, and a system which permits an active assertion of these categories and the laws governing them; and (2) if the categories of commodity, value and money really exert an influence through the market mechanism on enterprise management and on the decisions of the enterprises in matters of detail, then this economic mechanism will no longer admit any detailed directives from above. If, on the other hand, the basic characteristics of the system of directive plan instructions are retained, it will not be possible to change the economic mechanism into a system operating on the basis of a planned and regulated market mechanism. These facts are borne out by the experience of the gradual transformations between 1957 and 1967 as well as by the numerous volumes of critical analysis which preceded the reform of the economic mechanism in Hungary.

These problems have already been often discussed in analysis of the assertion, under socialism, of the categories of commodity, value and money as well as of the laws relating to them, the interrelations between plan and the market, and the operation of the economic model regulated by direct and indirect means. This discussion occurred in another context, but the results are valid in this connection as well. We consider the possible views on these questions both theoretically tested and proved by Hungarian experience. However, as has been pointed out in this paper, when the question to be decided affects more than one country, the possible standpoints and their practical implementation are largely dependent on the situation in fluctuating struggle between the forces of progress and those tending to conserve the old system.

As a result there emerge the views, explicable only on tactical grounds, which we have discussed in this section. The trouble begins, however, when we begin to believe in such reasoning ourselves. Only yesterday, we had proved to ourselves that:

Commodity relations between sellers and buyers, the use of the market mechanism, will rid central planning of the insoluble problem of taking into account the millions of ever changing partial processes and relationships.

It is impossible, even with the application of the most up-to-date computer techniques, to control the national economy as if it were a single enterprise which could be controlled from a centre, taking into consideration every economic detail. The creation of active market relations, accordingly, does not constitute any 'backward step' in the direction of less developed methods. On the contrary, it constitutes an acknowledgement of the fact that socialist society is a commodity-producing society, and that only the forms and methods of control which conform to this fact can ensure an adequate utilization of the possibilities existing under socialism.

The regulated market mechanism will take care that production [supply] structurally adapts itself to demand, that the requirements of the buyers are met, and that the enterprises manage their affairs economically and effectively under the effect of economic compulsion and incentives.[1]

In other words, even in the domestic economy, without the existence of a genuine market, no money fulfilling all the functions of money can emerge. This applies to an even greater extent to the world money.

However, there are many people who will not be convinced by theoretical arguments. Let us, therefore, take a practical example. The motor-car is now a scarce commodity in Hungary. For example, a Trabant car costs 45,000 forints, and as demand remains unsatisfied, those granted an allocation may easily be able to resell at a profit of as much as 10,000 forints. Thus, at the present moment – disregarding for the time being the elasticity of demand with respect to price – several thousand cars could be sold at a price about twenty per cent higher than the actual one. Mogüt, the Hungarian distributors, and Sachsenring-Werke, the producers, could share the additional profits at a predetermined rate, let us say, on a fifty-fifty basis. Any enterprise in any market economy of the world, given the opportunity of making an additional profit of this size, would quickly expand its production until increased output and demand brought about an equilibrium price. However, under a system of directive plan instructions, where the material, labour and import inputs, as well as the production and investment possibilities of a great number of co-operating enterprises are decided centrally, even the additional profits will not induce an enterprise to expand its production to conform to effective domestic and foreign demand. The Trabant car was taken as an example only because it is widely known. The situation is similar in the case of a great number of means of production which are highly important from the point of view of the smooth running of the production process. The example applies not only to the expansion of production, but also to the

[1] Dr L. Csapó: *Tervgazdálkodás és központi irányítás az uj gazdasági mechanizmusban* [Planning and central control under the new economic mechanism], Kossuth Kiadó, Budapest, 1957, pp. 6, 7, 9, 13.

curtailment or closing-down of production, should this become necessary for lack of demand.

Thus, a transferable and convertible world money will in its main content, and primarily, call for the availability of goods which answer world market conditions.

Finally – and in order to admit our own earlier mistakes – we will have to deal with a concept which essentially differs from those discussed above, i.e. the concept of what is called 'planned multilateralism'. This would consist in working out for each country centrally, on the basis of central coordination of some important elements of production and the volume of external trade, the annual foreign-trade (active and passive) balances; and decisions on their compensation would also be taken centrally.

This idea was born at a time when we thought we could solve the increasing difficulties of CMEA co-operation in the long run by international planning of a central directive character.

As originators of this proposal, we pointed out at the time the structural features of the mechanism of foreign trade and of the price system which would have rendered its actual implementation impossible (admitting, however, *ex post* that we did not see clearly the substance of the question). This proposal survived until after the experiment of 'international planning', carried out under CMEA rather hastily and with unsuitable methods, had failed in practice and had to be removed from the agenda. Moreover, even now, this proposal is frequently voiced as a practical alternative by those who (tacitly) disapprove of the adoption of a controlled and planned market mechanism within a socialist country, and openly disagree with the introduction of this reform in the mutual relations of the CMEA countries.

It should be clear that, as far as foreign trade is concerned, no country with a system of directive plan instructions can avoid specifying her bilaterally balanced export and import trade over a rather extensive field in physical terms. Neither the central organs nor the collectively taken decisions of the countries concerned will be able to 'plan' for the bilateral active and passive balances of various degrees of 'softness' and 'hardness', and their compensation with the balances of third countries, to be smaller or different in direction than would be the case within the framework of the rather insignificant balance compensations actually taking place. (The possibility of trade combined with possible discounts on exchange rates has already been mentioned above.)

*The most recent (1969–1970) discussions on the problems of CMEA integration only confirmed the theoretical and practical conclusions of this paper.*

# 5. Some theoretical problems of the price system in the trade between CMEA countries

## BÉLA CSIKÓS-NAGY

With the growth of trade between the socialist countries and the development of multilateral economic relations, the need increases to establish a system of foreign trade prices that best promotes co-operation based on planning and mutual advantage. This unsolved problem is closely connected with the general principles and theoretical questions of the system of a socialist world economy. A decade ago the problem of the price system in trade between CMEA countries was raised in the form of the problem of 'own price basis'. Up to now, no practical solution has been found.

Economists approach the problem of 'own price basis' in various ways. Behind the differing opinions there are differing ideas about the criteria of a rational international division of labour. Two main schools of thought exist. Some economists are of the opinion that the present economic mechanism of international co-operation is generally adequate, the only problem to be solved being to make foreign trade prices reflect the value relations in the socialist world market. Others think that the whole mechanism of economic co-operation should be reformed and that the price problem can be solved only within the framework of such a reform.

The existence of these two opinions presents no unsurmountable dilemma for socialist economics. The problem to be solved is well known from the discussions concerning domestic prices in the various CMEA countries. In several countries the price debate first started as one dealing exclusively with the price problem, only to continue later as a discussion about the general problems of the economic mechanism.

The so-called 'pure' price debate started from the hypothesis that the problems faced in the socialist economy are due mainly to deficiencies in the price system. The conclusion then follows that the operation of the socialist economic mechanism can and must be improved by improving the price system. This critique of the price system started from the postulate of economic clear-sightedness. The requirement is that prices should reflect the socially necessary labour inputs. In this case – according to the assumption – every economic decision will ensure a rational solution and reiteration can be regulated by the state with due consideration for economic efficiency. Later, the opinion gained ground that the price problem can only be raised and successfully solved as a part of the problem of state economic control and management. Thus, attention has been directed to the regulatory function of prices.

If any parallel may be drawn between the national and international discussions about prices, it seems justifiable to say that in the debate about the 'own price basis' some economists took a standpoint similar to that which characterized the first stage of the national price debates, while others are nearer to the concepts which emerged in the second stage of these discussions. The CMEA countries are united in their efforts to solve the problem of foreign trade price in order to improve international co-operation, secure greater economic efficiency and thus achieve quicker development. The differences in viewpoints could be eliminated or at least approximated, if a common denominator were reached concerning the rational organization of the economy and if the hypothesis which now serves as a foundation for the study of the price basis were revised.

The foreign trade price prevailing in the socialist world market has a role in the distribution of national income among countries but only a very limited scope in determining the volume and commodity pattern of foreign trade.

The role of foreign trade prices in the distribution of national income among countries necessarily follows from the fact that the international division of labour assumes the form of an exchange of commodities. Individual countries participate in foreign trade as independent partners and settle the commodity deliveries at fixed prices. In this manner, there necessarily emerges an organic connection between the distribution of the combined national income produced by the different countries and the foreign-trade price relations. Should the category of foreign trade prices be judged only from the point of view of this single function, there would be no other requirement in connection with the foreign-trade price relations than that no re-distribution of national incomes should take place through their effect. Such price relations would approximately reflect the socially necessary inputs as measured on an international level. In the absence of other factors, this would secure equal advantages for all countries participating in international co-operation. A deviation from the socially necessary inputs would mean a disparity between the export and import price levels.

The role of foreign trade prices in determining the volume and pattern of foreign trade may assert itself on a broader basis or within strict limitations; in principle, it may even be eliminated. This essentially depends on the system of the international division of labour. With the existence of commodity and money relations all countries will endeavour to secure the best results for their own economies and to promote the most efficient utilization of their own productive forces through the exchange of commodities. Now price relations will determine the optimum volume of the international exchange of commodities, from the point of view of the individual countries, and the most efficient commodity pattern of trade. Concrete price relations are needed in order to determine the volume at which the relation of the foreign trade price level to the domestic input level is still more favourable in exports than in imports. Only with given foreign-trade price relations can the ranking of products according to economic efficiency take place. Since foreign trade improves the efficiency of the economy, it may offer advantages for a given country even if it involves a re-distribution of national income, i.e. even if there exists a disparity between the price levels of exports and imports.

Under the present system of international economic co-operation within CMEA, the regulatory role of commodity and money relations asserts itself only in an extremely limited way. International agreements on the exchange of commodities between CMEA countries are based on the international co-ordination of national plans and are regarded as central state affairs. Accordingly, prices play hardly any role in shaping the volume and pattern of foreign trade.

The limitation of commodity and money relationships between CMEA countries is ensured by a peculiar currency mechanism. All CMEA countries have separately retained the gold parity of their currencies but apply a strict management of foreign exchange. In fact, unlike the commodity exchange occurring outside the CMEA, the socialist world is not based upon a highly developed monetary system. A so-called currency accounting system is substituted for the regulated paper money mechanism.

According to some views, even under such conditions price will have an effect on the commodity pattern, since the CMEA countries take into consideration the price relations in their international trade agreements. But it is one thing to take into account the law of value in an administrative way and another to operate it. Though prices in fact influence the international exchange of commodities, their influence is very indirect and works only through the administrative rules (or precisely against them), but it cannot be claimed that prices have a regulatory role in respect of the commodity pattern of foreign trade. The law of value asserts itself through the market mechanism; it cannot be operated in an administrative manner, nor can it be assumed that it may be effectively limited in that manner. The operation of the law of value requires a mechanism in which the market is regulated by economic measures instead of administrative ones and in which the price is, accordingly, a market price.

If prices had a regulatory role in the international division of labour, the situation could not have arisen in which various principles are laid down in respect of prices and, particularly, where decisions are taken in an arbitrary way. A price system would have existed from the beginning, one which could be changed only in conformity with commodity and money relationships prevailing on the market. When prices have a regulatory role in trade, price problems can be solved only by starting from prevailing prices and by accounting for the effects of price changes on the commodity pattern. To abolish the entire price system and to replace it by a new one – merely in order to express inputs in a better way – is possible only where there is no market and the role of prices is restricted to clearing accounts.

The question may now be reformulated: What is the realistic economic way to solve the problem of foreign trade prices within CMEA? Should the system of accounting currency be retained and the function of prices be essentially restricted to the distribution and re-distribution of national income between countries; or should the mechanism of co-operation under CMEA be reformed by giving greater weight to commodity and money relationships and enabling prices to play a role in the formation of the pattern of production and the international exchange of commodities?

The possibility of transforming the mechanism of co-operation under CMEA cannot be excluded. As a matter of fact, the resolution which gave rise to the study of the own price basis already advocated an examination of the conditions and criteria of transition to the own price basis. Still, up to recent times the opinion has generally prevailed that placing the international division of labour on a planned basis will entail abolition of the monetary system, this being the only way to regulate commodity trade in conformity with co-ordinated plans. For a long time the CMEA countries did not consider the abolition of the monetary system as likely to be inconvenient. On the contrary, this was thought to be the way to ensure economic efficiency based on macroeconomic considerations. However, as a result of experience, criticisms of the regulating methods applied up to now in the co-operation of CMEA countries have become more and more frequent.

Particular attention should be paid to two restricting factors:

(1) The co-ordination of plans based on physical indicators gave rise to a tendency to replace the exchange of equal values by an exchange of identical commodity patterns. Actually, it is not price values but use values that are internationally equated, and efforts are made to keep the share of raw materials, intermediary and finished products, approximately identical. In other words, what is aimed at is an exchange of equally 'hard' commodities. Earlier, this regulatory role appeared in the form of the principle of specialization in engineering. It has grown, however, into a general convention of trade.

(2) Commodity trade between the CMEA countries is organized on a bilateral basis. This co-operative mechanism has brought about a divided world market where the advantages of a united socialist world market cannot assert themselves.

The system of bilateral relations puts a brake on the efficiency of foreign trade. And the principle of identical commodity patterns simply contradict the requirements of efficiency. Starting from these facts, some economists have reached the conclusion that the above principle should be replaced by that of an identical tying-up of assets in exports and imports. Those believing that this conception is correct base their reasoning on the fact that efforts aimed at identical commodity patterns hinder the emergence of a rational international division of labour but that for a country with a capital-intensity of exports above the average it would be right to try to mitigate the attendant disadvantages by measures outside the price system. But the replacement of the exchange of equal values by an equalization of investment is just another variant of the barter-economy approach.

It seems, therefore, that the unity of the socialist world market and a rational division of labour in this market can best be assured by establishing a highly developed monetary system. Under such a system clearing is multilateral, currency is convertible and inter-state agreements on the exchange of commodities offer the possibility of flexible management of commodity trade. If, however, one acknowledges this fact, one has to acknowledge also that a monetary system of this type requires an entirely different price system. In the case of a highly developed monetary system the price problem has to be approached quite differently than in the case of an accounting currency. Here price will play an active role in shaping the commodity pattern of foreign trade.

If price regulates the commodity pattern – however restricted this function may be by plan co-ordination agreements – it will have to conform to the conditions under which a division of labour among CMEA countries can exist and develop at all. A price functioning as an accounting medium may be constructed on any basis and may even be adopted from foreign markets. But a price which is to function as a market price cannot be simply specified; it can only be the product of the market in which it operates.

Approached in this way, the problem of own price basis will gain economic reality through the existence of the CMEA world market; it will not be a system of accounting prices but a type of market price system. Under such conditions, it will be possible to deduce the differences between the socialist and the capitalist world market price systems from the territorially limited characteristics of commodity and money relations, in the same manner as an economically meaningful answer can be given to the variations in price relations between the various major world markets.

In the knowledge of the relationships underlying the category of prices, what conclusions may now be drawn regarding the prices to be applied in trade between CMEA countries? This question should first be answered within the framework of the existing mechanism of economic co-operation.

The question poses itself in the following form. Considering the present economic mechanism, which of the two methods would yield better results: an adaption of capitalist world market prices, or a regulation of prices conforming to the value relations in the socialist world market?

In spite of all the differences arising in connection with the adaption of capitalist world market prices, it seems that – in view of the actual mechanism of co-operation – it would be unrealistic to expect to be able to change over to a price basis reflecting the particular production conditions and exchange relations of the CMEA countries. In the given situation the real problem is not whether the principle of applying capitalist world market prices should be given up for the pricing principle based on own inputs, but consists much more in doing away with the distortions which assert themselves – in contrast with the terms and the spirit of the Bucharest agreement – in the course of the practical application of the world market price principle.

But neither should we be blind to the problems emerging from the adoption of capitalist world market prices, since they may sooner or later become serious hindrances to the progress of a purposeful division of labour.

CMEA market co-operation takes place among relatively developed socialist countries. The more developed the productive forces and the more diversified international co-operation in production, the greater will be the difficulties arising from adopting prices from external markets.

Co-operation in production, specialization and the problems of exchange must not be judged exclusively on the basis of the technical advantages to be derived from a more rational organization of production. They should be based on economically determined prices in order also to safeguard mutual material interests.

It is only natural that countries co-operating in an industrial sector or exchanging a range of their products should examine the export and import prices (in terms of roubles) or products turned out both in identical and in different production stages. They will consider co-operation disadvantageous if in the case of related articles produced in the same production stage they have to pay relatively higher prices for the import assortment than for the export assortment or if the import prices of materials, intermediate products and accessories used in production are fixed too high, in comparison with the export prices of finished goods. In a horizontal exchange of commodities the price proportions have to conform to the technical parameters. In vertical production co-operation, however, relative prices have to be derived from the production conditions under which it is possible for such co-operation to come about at microeconomic level.

Still, the road to the solution of these problems leads not through the reform of price formation but through the solution of the market problem. The immediate objective should be the creation not of a common price basis but of a common market. This again assumes:

(*a*) the solution of the currency problem and of the problem of convertibility;

(*b*) the transition from bilateral to multilateral connections and to multilateral clearing;

(*c*) a change in the forms of production co-operation, a synthetic unification of plan and market, and a greater independence for enterprises.

These tendencies assert themselves mainly in the initial stages, but their connection with the own price basis is not sufficiently well known. Thus, it is of great importance to realize that:

(1) the mechanism of co-operation under CMEA needs revision;

(2) the latter involves not simply the introduction of the own price basis but a change in the mechanism of commodity exchange with, among other things, the creation of conditions for the convertibility of the currency;

(3) the own price basis will assure the positive results expected only if a general reform of the mechanism is undertaken and its requirements are met.

*Béla Csikós-Nagy*

In a monetary system the prices to be applied in trade between CMEA countries must be based on: the costs of production; the market-value judgements of the CMEA countries; the co-operation preferences determined for the CMEA world market.

It is these factors and their interactions that will determine prices. Owing to changes in production costs and in value judgements of the market, this determination becomes possible only if the number of goods for which contractual prices are fixed in long-term international agreements is small, while the rest are allowed to be agreed upon directly by the enterprises actually transacting the exchange. It follows that the price system thus emerging will essentially be of a market type, in contrast with the former, officially manipulated one.

(1) The principle of production costs

In the trade between CMEA countries the foreign trade prices must, as a rule, cover the production costs.

A well publicized debate was carried on for several years between the CMEA countries on the question whether national producers' prices can serve as a basis for the formation of foreign trade prices. The argument took place within the present concrete framework of CMEA economic co-operation. Under that mechanism the national producers' price could not provide a satisfactory basis for the formation of the foreign trade price. If the foreign trade price regulates only the balance of payments and the commodity pattern is regulated by collating the plans in physical units, the producers' price cannot provide a basis for foreign trade price formation. The national producers' prices deviate from national inputs to varying extents and it is inadmissible that one country should acquire a more advantageous position than another merely as a result of different principles of price fixing.

However, with an international market in operation and with prices actively fulfilling their function, nothing other than national producers' prices can provide a basis. This does not even require a consensus of CMEA countries in respect of a common principle to be applied in the formation of national producers' prices. It is not a pre-condition of the market-type own price basis that national price systems (principles of price formation, price structures, etc.) should be brought into alignment. This will automatically come about in a definite manner as soon as the market-type own price basis is introduced in practice. Of course, the national producers' prices of individual export–import goods will not automatically become international prices even with the market mechanism at work. From the actual labour inputs of the individual countries only as much will be returned in international trade as represents the international value (the inputs necessary under the production conditions of the CMEA market) embodied in them.

(2)  The market-value judgement of the CMEA countries

The foreign trade price may deviate from the CMEA international value. The level of the foreign trade price will also reflect the value judgement of the market with respect to the commodity in question. Under real market conditions the CMEA countries will also have to take into account the conditions of supply and demand, i.e. the fact that in the case of excess supply the price of a commodity will tend to decline below the international value while in the case of demand pressure it will tend to rise above that value.

It is precisely this criterion of price formation which renders the price a market phenomenon. Thus, the criterion involves not only the requirement that in certain cases price ratios may deviate from input ratios but also the requirement that the extent of this deviation from input ratios can be determined only in the market and cannot therefore be fixed for any longer period.

Why should this be so strongly emphasized? Because in the official, administrative price systems of the CMEA countries as well prices are sometimes made to deviate from input ratios. The following are well-known cases in point:

(*a*) When prices of mutually substitutable products are made proportional to use value;

(*b*) When price ratios of an incentive character are established in order to channel demand in a certain direction.

However, the fact that these measures are applied under conditions where the function of prices is highly restricted and commodities are centrally allocated should also be taken into account. Thus the users have no choice. In this way, the type of price manipulation in question is intended to solve – with more or less success – the task of co-ordinating product allocation with the price system for the purposes of independent enterprise accounting.

This does not imply that a system of foreign trade prices which conforms to market requirements would necessarily contradict an active price policy to be uniformly established by the CMEA countries. It should, however, only exceptionally aim at fixing prices. The most essential methods of this price policy would be the indirect ones to be applied with the aim of assuring certain co-operation preferences for the CMEA world market. Thus, a market-type price should not only ensure a freer movement of prices and the possibility of bargaining between co-operating enterprises, but also create a situation in the co-operation between the countries in which prices act towards the development of a planned division of labour.

### (3) CMEA preferences

The price problem of the international market within CMEA cannot be solved without taking into account the connections with the world market as a whole and the extent of separation between CMEA and the rest of the world market.

The connection between the international market within CMEA and the world market outside it means that the market value judgements of the CMEA countries about the prices of individual products and about the relative prices of different products can be formed only by taking into consideration the price relations in the capitalist world market. Quite independently of the fact whether and to what extent a CMEA country has the opportunity of choosing between the various main world markets, the concept of a 'realistic' price necessarily involves the consideration of the price of the product outside the CMEA market.

The price relations of the various major world markets obviously differ from product to product. No scheme can be set up in this respect since the consequences of this are determined in concrete form in a system where bargaining between enterprises has a role in price formation.

It is, however, equally important to remember that no organized main world market can leave international co-operation at the mercy of spontaneous market processes. It has always been characteristic of international integrations that the countries participating influence the market processes through deliberate price policies. Apart from such deliberate exceptions, prices function automatically in the market, but the latter is often used only as a technical medium to ensure that the price tendencies which are thought to be correct assert themselves. Thus, the price has also a norm abstracted from the market, and the market should be made suited to its absorption. This can be achieved by offering CMEA preferences, the main form of which may be a customs tariff system. Beyond that, if necessary, price preferences may also be offered in long-term inter-state agreements.

As a matter of fact, we are dealing here with a double system of customs duties: the national system of each CMEA country, and a uniform

CMEA tariff system to separate the CMEA market from the rest of the world market.

The national tariff systems of the CMEA countries are actually functioning, although instead of customs duties they operate through export subsidies and import levies. If, however, a connection is to be made between the domestic and foreign trade prices, this must give way to a system of customs duties. The latter will safeguard, though in a more limited manner, the general national interests existing within CMEA, which cannot be abolished overnight by legal measures.

The real task in connection with the transition to the own price basis is to bring about the CMEA customs union, taking into consideration the particular interests of the CMEA international market. These particular interests and thus the uniform customs system of the CMEA are determined by two factors: (1) the deviation of production conditions in CMEA countries from the price relations in the world market; and (2) the interests of co-operation, because of which it is expedient to develop co-operation even in cases where – considering only the market relations – economic ties should be strengthened with the markets outside CMEA.

The establishment of a uniform system of customs duties for CMEA presupposes a knowledge of production conditions prevailing in the member countries or, rather, a knowledge of the extent of deviations from general international conditions. It is precisely from this point of view that the systematic experiments with price models at present going on in the member countries are of the highest importance, providing a practical opportunity for a comparative international analysis of value relations.

The knowledge of the value relations of the CMEA international market and their differences from world market value relations is – as has been pointed out – one of the criteria of creating a CMEA customs system. As a matter of fact, if the system were established solely in order to bridge over these differences, conditions would actually be created for the CMEA market under which the prices in trade within CMEA would conform to input relations. Fundamentally this would be an autarkic price system which, though promoting further co-operation between the CMEA countries, would neglect the advantages to be derived from international co-operation on a wider basis. The real problem is to determine what range of products should actually be given preference in the trade between CMEA countries in order to increase trade between them and to benefit the economic progress both of the CMEA community as a whole and of the individual member countries. This criterion cannot be derived from the customs system itself but only from the co-ordination of the national economic policies of the individual member countries. Customs duties can thus take a concrete form only in the service of a given economic policy.

Surveying the various systems of economic integration, and the major principles and methods by which such groups separate themselves from the world market, two essential features may be observed:

(*a*) The supply of products within an integrated market is generally secured by a customs system in respect of industrial goods and by price systems in respect of agricultural produce. In the case of industry, it is deemed sufficient to charge the imported products to an extent that will put them at a disadvantage in competition. In the case of agriculture, however, price constructions are applied.

(*b*) Raw materials for industrial use can generally be imported duty-free from all over the world. The duty imposed on manufactures is usually higher in the case of the more labour-intensive products. The greatest degree of protection is generally enjoyed by agricultural products.

These characteristics of integration efforts have, of course, emerged in a given historical situation and under given conditions. They do, however, allow certain conclusions to be drawn which may be useful for setting up tariff and price structures under CMEA.

*Since the writing of this paper, the views of the author have been changed in one important respect. He does not think any more that the CMEA integration will be established on the basis of a unified tariff system. It seems to be possible however to declare the CMEA region as a tariff-free belt of the World Economy.*

# 6. Exports and export performance

MIHÁLY SIMAI

The foreign trade of a country in a given period is determined by factors arising in the process of her economic development and by international political and economic conditions. These latter are important sources of uncertainties since, in general, they are beyond her control. The external limitations of export expansion are the major 'unknowns' in planning or economic policy decisions.

Analysing the data on the fulfilment of medium-term plans in many countries we have found serious errors in export planning, especially for periods of four to five years or more. This was to a certain extent true even where economic relations between countries had been established on the basis of their long-term economic requirements and these requirements were incorporated in long-term trade agreements.

Export planning, connected as it is with domestic planning, proved to involve not only a forecast of external consumption, which is itself a highly complex task, but also a process of comparative projection of technological development and a marketing programme for new products. Export planning involves forecasting the policies of those countries which are considered the most important markets. Export planning and corresponding policies are supposed to contain the required tools for export incentives, subsidies, credits, marketing, market research, etc., the aim of which is to counter unfavourable conditions. It must be remembered that export planning cannot be separated from the planning of imports.

In this paper we intend to examine only one of the many complex problems of foreign trade planning. We propose to analyse the reaction of seven socialist countries, given the changes in their export markets, to the new conditions which they had to face and also to examine the effect of their reactions on their exports between 1961 and 1965. The countries are the members of CMEA: Bulgaria, Czechoslovakia, Eastern Germany, Hungary, Poland, Rumania and the USSR. The period in most of the countries covers the years of the medium-term plans, so the analysis may provide an answer to the question: how realistic had these plans been in forecasting exports? There were differences in domestic output patterns and market sizes and in international trade positions. Therefore, the ability of these countries to implement certain adjustments in their economies, according to the requirements of the export markets, varied substantially.

### I. TRENDS IN THE 1961–5 PERIOD

The development of the external economic relations of the CMEA countries between 1961 and 1965 differed in many respects from the patterns of the fifties.

One of the most important indicators is the comparison of export and import growth with the increase in national income, i.e., the export and import elasticities. From the data presented in Table 1, it is evident that only in the case of Rumania was the importance of export demand smaller, compared to the previous period. On the other hand, the import intensity of economic development has increased in four countries, especially in Czechoslovakia and Hungary. In Bulgaria, the German Democratic Republic and the Soviet Union, the import requirements of economic growth were somewhat smaller than before.

TABLE 1. *Changes in export and import elasticities*

| | Import elasticities | | | Export elasticities | | |
|---|---|---|---|---|---|---|
| Country | 1951–5 | 1956–60 | 1961–5 | 1951–5 | 1956–60 | 1961–5 |
| Bulgaria | 1.30 | 2.09 | 2.03 | 1.47 | 2.02 | 2.04 |
| Czechoslovakia | 1.28 | 1.66 | 4.20 | 1.05 | 1.49 | 3.57 |
| German Democratic Republic | 1.97 | 1.93 | 1.40 | 2.53 | 1.69 | 1.91 |
| Hungary | 1.90 | 1.82 | 2.02 | 2.05 | 1.20 | 2.52 |
| Poland | 1.23 | 1.57 | 1.59 | 0.91 | 1.21 | 1.84 |
| Rumania | 0.99 | 1.01 | 1.20 | 1.06 | 1.62 | 1.01 |
| USSR | 1.40 | 1.40 | 1.17 | 1.21 | 1.11 | 1.17 |

Sources: National Statistical Yearbooks. Note: The relation of imports and exports to net material product.

The differences in export elasticities were substantial not only between countries but also between sectors within the countries. According to the available statistics, the export elasticities in *Bulgaria* increased at the highest rate compared to the previous five years in the output of foodstuffs and also in the engineering industries. In *Czechoslovakia*, the ranking of sectors according to export elasticities was: chemicals, raw materials, semi-manufactured goods, engineering. In the CMEA region the increase of export elasticities in food production compared to the period 1956–60 was the highest in *Hungary*. In that country, higher export elasticities also characterized the group of raw materials and semi-manufactured goods. Food products, consumer goods and raw materials achieved the greatest increases in export elasticities in *Poland*. *Rumania* increased the export much faster than the output of chemicals, but in the engineering, raw materials and semi-manufactured goods sectors, the ratio of exports to output declined. The *Soviet Union* was the only country among the CMEA members where there was a decline in the export of foodstuffs in relation to output. However, the share of exports in the engineering and consumer goods sectors increased during the five years. There are no comparable figures for the Soviet Union in the group of raw materials and semi-manufactured goods. Calculations for individual products, however, show an increase in export elasticities in this group.

Table 1 also indicates that between 1961 and 1965 there were no such spectacular changes compared to the previous five years, as between 1956–60 in comparison to 1951–5. The slower changes are reflected also in the fact that while the share of the seven countries in world exports increased by nearly one third between 1956 and 1960 in comparison to 1951–6, there was a much slower increase between 1961 and 1965. The seven countries supplied 10 per cent of world exports between 1961 and 1965. Their share in the preceding five-year period was 9.5 per cent on average.

Trade policies in individual countries often changed between 1961 and 1965 but they were more constant concerning the interrelations of the principles and practices laid down in the annual plans with those of the medium-term plans. At the same time they reflected the short-term changes induced by the internal problems of the countries. For example, there was increasing pressure on the foreign trade sector due to the structural inconsistencies between supply and demand in almost every country, with the possible exceptions of Bulgaria and Poland. These disproportions occurred as a consequence of the slow reaction of the economy, and especially of industry, to the changes in demand patterns. Short-term factors were also responsible for some of the bottlenecks which could not be anticipated by the planners, such as the decline in agricultural output in 1962 in Czechoslovakia, the German Democratic Republic, Poland and Rumania, in 1963 in the Soviet Union, in 1965 in Czechoslovakia and Hungary, and in industrial output in Czechoslovakia in 1963. In addition, in some of the countries the higher than planned increases in consumption and investment restricted export expansion, contributing to the creation of new import needs.

The CMEA member countries made new credit commitments of some 3.6 billion dollars to developing countries between 1961 and 1965, 20–25 per cent more than in 1956–60. This was almost equal to the total value of their engineering exports to developing countries in the same period. There was also an increase in the importance of medium-term commercial credits.

Commercial policy was concerned mainly with increasing exports. Every country of CMEA except the Soviet Union increased her exports faster than her imports, compared with the previous five-year period. Despite trade surpluses with CMEA and developing countries between 1961 and 1965, the Soviet Union had to increase her gold sales temporarily to pay for her deficits in other markets.

The cumulative deficit of some CMEA countries in their trade relations was so high that it endangered possibilities of further increases in foreign trade; for example, Poland in her trade with other CMEA countries.

The analysis of exports and imports by commodity groups shows a further increase in the disproportions between the manufacturing capacities and the raw materials production in the area. This was expressed in the fact that, with the exception of Bulgaria and Hungary, the countries characterized as new raw material importers further increased their deficits. Rumania, which had an export surplus in this category in 1960, had a deficit in her raw materials balance by 1965. The Soviet Union, on the other hand, increased her trade surplus further. So, with one exception, all the other members of CMEA became net importers of raw materials. As a result, the raw materials integration between the members of the CMEA was further strengthened.

There was an increasing trend in imports of machinery over exports, with the exception of two countries. Bulgaria reduced her deficit and Poland had balanced trade in this group. Hungary and Czechoslovakia reduced their surpluses, while Rumania and the Soviet Union increased their deficits.

All the members of the CMEA, except the Soviet Union, improved their balance in the foreign trade of foodstuffs. The Soviet Union had a deficit. In 1965, Bulgaria, Hungary, Poland and Rumania increased their trade surplus and Czechoslovakia reduced her deficit between 1961 and 1965. In the trade in consumer goods, the passive balance of the Soviet Union was reduced, and the other countries increased their exports surplus, with the exception of Czechoslovakia.

Despite temporary difficulties, the foreign trade sector played a more active role in economic development than in the preceding period. This was the result of changes in the system of planning and management, and also of the favourable changes in economic structure which increased the possibilities for certain countries to use their external economic relations more actively to further their development strategy.

The role of the specialization and co-operation agreements increased somewhat between 1961 and 1965, and their impact on exports was greater. However, the importance of these agreements was very different from the point of view of individual countries and commodity groups. The exports of machinery and equipment can be considered as the most important commodity group among those covered by the specialization agreements. The role of the agreements in this group is reflected in the share of 'specialized' products in the total exports of machinery and equipment within the CMEA. In the case of individual countries, this share was as follows in 1964:

|  | % |
|---|---|
| German Democratic Republic | 20.7 |
| Poland | 16.7 |
| USSR | 10.0 |
| Rumania | 9.8 |
| Hungary | 8.3 |
| Bulgaria | 6.0 |
| Czechoslovakia | 4.5 |

These agreements did not induce substantial changes in export patterns since they were based on the existing division of labour. Their aim was not so much the narrowing of the list of commodities produced and exported, but the limitation of further diversifications.

The socialist countries had to face much sharper competition in their export markets between 1961 and 1965 than in previous periods. Considerations of choice, quality, terms of delivery and sometimes even of financing, increased in importance in inter-CMEA trade. There was an especially marked increase in the quality requirements of the Soviet market in almost every product group.

The most important change in the conditions of trade with the developed industrial countries was the declining role of political embargo and discrimination in trade relations, with the exception of the United States. There were changes in the United States market, but the conditions of trade for most of the CMEA countries remained unfavourable. The new political atmosphere also played a role in the shift among different relations between 1961 and 1965. With the changes in the political atmosphere, the share of Western Europe in the trade of all CMEA countries except the Soviet Union, Poland and Hungary, increased; also, the developing countries became increasingly important.

The non-European developed countries are not included in Table 2 because their share of exports was in general very small. But there was a remarkable increase in the importance of Japan as an export market.

## 2. THE CHANGES IN EXPORT PERFORMANCE

Export performance means the ability of a country to utilize the expansion of her external markets in her exports. My assumption in the calculation of the indicator for export performance is that the opportunities for increasing the exports of a given country are not determined by the expansion of the world economy in general but by the growth of her export markets, especially within five years or shorter periods. According to the experience of several countries, the main export markets are changing very slowly because of the concluded trade agreements and other factors.

TABLE 2. *The increase in exports according to destination, 1961–5* (annual percentage average)

| | | | Destination | | | |
|---|---|---|---|---|---|---|
| | | | Socialist countries | | | |
| Exports from: | Total exports | USSR | Eastern Europe | Asia | Western Europe | Developing countries |
| Bulgaria | 15.9 | 14.9 | 11.5 | − 5.6 | 22.4 | 36.8 |
| Czechoslovakia | 6.8 | 9.2 | 8.1 | − 20.8 | 8.5 | 3.1 |
| German Democratic Republic | 6.7 | 7.3 | 7.7 | − 18.0 | 7.0 | 11.5 |
| Hungary | 11.6 | 15.4 | 10.9 | − 13.0 | 9.7 | 16.6 |
| Poland | 10.9 | 14.9 | 9.3 | − 11.4 | 9.6 | 10.1 |
| Rumania | 9.0 | 9.3 | 6.7 | − 3.7 | 11.5 | 12.2 |
| USSR | 8.0 | . | 8.7 | − 18.1 | 7.6 | 27.3 |

Sources: National Statistical Yearbooks and *Yearbook of International Trade Statistics*, 1965.

According to my definition, export performance is the difference between the rate of growth in import volume of the markets and the rate of growth of exports of a given country to the same foreign markets. The starting point in evaluating the increases in export markets was of course the export structure of the given countries according to destination.

I used the weighted average of import increases in the thirty most important markets to characterize the changes in the size of the markets. The share of a given market in the total exports of the country for which the performance index was calculated was used as weight in the corresponding years. The rate of growth obtained from these calculations was the increase of the export market. I compared these figures with the actual increases of exports. A calculation for the most important commodity groups was made by using similar methods.

The export markets of the seven socialist countries are highly concentrated. About 75 per cent of their exports are purchased by fifteen countries. Outside the CMEA group, Yugoslavia, China, the United Arab Republic, India, Western Germany, France and Italy are the most important markets. The share of these countries in world imports in 1965 was 31.2 per cent; in 1961 it was 30.4 per cent. Apart from these main markets, there are twenty to fifty other countries important enough to be mentioned in the export statistics of the CMEA members. Many of these countries have only a marginal share, but their importance can be substantial in the cases of some commodities.

Such a concentration of markets proved to be a favourable situation from the point of view of the individual socialist countries and, with some recent exceptions, it is so evaluated. But it can be argued that extension of the markets would be more advantageous for economic and for political reasons.

Can export performance be valid as an indicator for inter-CMEA trade? It is well known that, in the group, foreign trade is regulated by long-term trade agreements based on plans. According to our views, the use of the indicator is completely justified in this connection as well.

It has been already stated that trade among the socialist countries is no longer simply the distribution of goods according to previously determined quotas. Efficiency, quality, etc., are playing an increasing role in trade negotiations and in the actual deals. Despite the fact that trade is regulated by long-term agreements, it is not an easy task to fulfil requirements. In addition, the plans reflected in the agreements are usually modified. Sometimes they have to face a quite new situation compared to the plans.

The differences between the growth of the markets and the growth of the exports could be the result of statistical errors. This factor is, however, statistically insignificant.

I was not able to eliminate the effect of structural changes, and data which would have facilitated the calculation of unit value indices were not available for every socialist country. For the Soviet Union, Czechoslovakia, Hungary, the German Democratic Republic and Poland, the available data indicate that there was very little change in the unit value of exports during the period. In the case of the Soviet Union, Czechoslovakia and the German Democratic Republic, there were declines in unit value of 1.5,

1.6 and 2.9 per cent respectively between 1961 and 1965. The export unit value increased by 2 per cent in the case of Hungary, and for Poland it remained unchanged. The rise in the Hungarian index corresponded to the rise in the world index (4 per cent) and also to the rise in the index for the developed countries (2.9 per cent). In the other countries for which data were available, the movement of the export unit values was in the opposite direction.

TABLE 3. *The export performance of the CMEA member states, 1961–5*

| Country | 1961 | 1962 | 1963 | 1964 | 1965 |
|---|---|---|---|---|---|
| Bulgaria | 14.4 | 7.3 | − 0.8 | 7.1 | 14.0 |
| Czechoslovakia | 2.4 | − 1.8 | 1.5 | − 6.0 | − 1.9 |
| German Democratic Republic | − 0.4 | − 5.1 | 6.0 | − 1.6 | − 1.4 |
| Hungary | 13.0 | − 2.1 | 1.1 | 0.9 | 5.0 |
| Poland | 9.4 | 0.6 | − 1.2 | 7.7 | 0.1 |
| Rumania | 6.0 | − 6.0 | 3.1 | − 1.2 | 4.0 |
| USSR | 4.4 | 10.0 | − 4.0 | − 5.3 | − 1.2 |

Source: National Statistical Yearbooks and *Yearbook of International Trade Statistics*, 1963 1965.

Table 3 compares the export performance of the seven CMEA countries and reflects annual changes. According to the data, the export performance of Bulgaria, Hungary and Poland was the steadiest during the five-year period. In four years out of five, these three countries increased their exports faster than their markets expanded. The export performance of Rumania was positive in three years, Czechoslovakia and the Soviet Union in two years, and the German Democratic Republic in one year. As indicated, great variation exists among the countries even though they faced broadly similar external problems. It is suggested by the analysis that supply factors, choice, quality, price, competitiveness, etc., played an important role in the differences.

As an illustration, we compared the export performance of the seven CMEA countries with a few developed industrial countries between 1962 and 1965 (Table 4). These latter countries have a different production and export structure, their markets being much less concentrated than those of the CMEA countries. The export patterns of Czechoslovakia and the German Democratic Republic are the nearest to them.

Comparing these data with the export performance of the seven CMEA countries, it is interesting to note that the German Federal Republic, France and the United States of America increased their exports more or

TABLE 4. *The export performance of some developed industrial countries, 1962–5*

| Country | 1962 | 1963 | 1964 | 1965 |
|---|---|---|---|---|
| Japan | 8.4 | 2.6 | 9.0 | 17.2 |
| Austria | – 4.0 | – 5.7 | – 1.1 | – 1.5 |
| Italy | 4.4 | – 0.4 | 3.2 | 7.4 |
| German Federal Republic | – 2.2 | 0.0 | – 1.6 | 0.0 |
| France | – 2.0 | 0.8 | 0.3 | – 1.1 |
| Denmark | 0.3 | 6.3 | – 2.3 | – 1.5 |
| USA | 0.0 | 0.4 | 1.8 | – 3.0 |

Source: *Yearbook of International Trade Statistics,* 1966.

less in line with their market increases and the deviations between export increases and the market increases are relatively small. The fluctuations are smaller than in the export performance of the CMEA countries in the period between 1961 and 1965.

Changes in the export performance of the other countries are quite substantial both in size and direction. We have to take into account the fact that the developed capitalist countries are much more interdependent than the CMEA countries. Though the requirements of the two types of markets are similar, the sales conditions are obviously different.

In the CMEA group, the differences between the planned export increases and actual market increases were smaller than the actual differences between the increase of exports and the growth of the markets. This is due to the great differences between the planned and actual export increases in individual years. These deviations from the plan were the result of the importance of agricultural produce in exports; for instance, Bulgarian exports were well above the planned level. For several other countries this created important strains in their exports in some years. Sometimes the deviations from the targets in the export plans were of similar magnitude to the changes in imports compared with the planned import level. They reflected the fact that the unplanned import requirements had to be met from export resources. However, it is interesting to note that, in many CMEA countries, the annual deviations tended to balance within the five-year period as an average.

The deviations from the export targets represented in many cases changes in the destination of the outflow of goods compared with the plan. We have data only for CMEA trade, which compare the long-term agreements concluded at the end of the 1950s and valid until 1965 with the actual trade flows. According to this, the actual increase of exports within the

CMEA was much higher than what was anticipated in the long-term trade agreements. The range of the changes is between 4 per cent in the case of the German Democratic Republic and 100 per cent in the case of Bulgaria.

### 3. COMMODITY STRUCTURE AND EXPORT PERFORMANCE

The consistency between the changes in the commodity pattern of exports and the changes in the pattern of demand in the main markets is a basic issue from the point of view of export performance.

The commodity pattern of both exports and demand should be analysed in the greatest possible detail. In the framework of this paper, however, we can compare only the changes which occurred in the main commodity groups. Such an aggregation distorts the export performance of given countries in individual commodity groups. It often happened that in one market or another, in one article the export performance of the countries was very good, while in the commodity group as a whole it was weak. In spite of this, the analysis according to commodity groups reveals the most general trends.

The annual average change in export performance of the seven CMEA countries between 1961 and 1965 was as shown in Table 5. The figures in the table provide an answer first of all to the question: to what extent do the changes in export patterns for the seven countries correspond to the changes in the structure of demand? The changes were the smallest in the case of Poland, Hungary and the German Democratic Republic. This reflects the fact that with some exceptions their share did not change substantially in the major commodity groups. There are very important positive changes in some commodity groups in the share of Bulgaria and Rumania in their export markets.

It is of course true that countries with very small shares in the market of a product can show a very good initial export performance.

The data also shows which countries changed their export patterns in the direction of a higher degree of processing, more than the increase of the demand for such types of goods in their export market. In the case of chemicals, Rumania; in the field of machinery and equipment, Bulgaria, Poland, the Soviet Union and Rumania; in the case of other industrial goods like industrial consumer goods, Rumania, Poland and Hungary, the German Democratic Republic and Bulgaria improved their export performance.

It is clear from the table what percentage of exports showed an improvement in export performance and what percentage declined.

According to the table, the commodity groups which showed an improvement in export performance provided 97.8 per cent of the exports of

TABLE 5. *The changes in export performance of the CMEA member states by main commodity groups (1961–5, annual averages)*

| Country | Commodity groups | | | | | |
|---|---|---|---|---|---|---|
| | Foodstuffs | Raw materials and semi-manufactured goods | Fuels | Chemicals | Machinery and equipment | Other industrial goods |
| BULGARIA | 3.4 | 6.5* | . | -4.1 | 27.6 | 2.4 |
| Share of the product group in total exports of 1965 (%) | 36.6 | 23.1* | . | 2.2 | 24.6 | 13.5 |
| CZECHOSLOVAKIA | -9.4 | 2.3* | . | 0.9 | -2.4 | -4.2 |
| Share of the product group in total exports of 1965 (%) | 4.6 | 26.6* | . | 3.8 | 48.5 | 16.5 |
| GERMAN DEMOCRATIC REPUBLIC† | -0.4 | -2.6‡ | . | . | -7.0 | 3.8 |
| Share of the product group in total exports of 1965 (%) | 4.0 | 30.0† | . | . | 49.0 | 17.0 |
| HUNGARY | 1.4 | 7.3* | . | -1.4 | -3.5 | 4.0 |
| Share of the product group in total exports of 1965 (%) | 22.1 | 20.4* | . | 3.5 | 32.7 | 21.3 |
| POLAND | -2.6 | 3.4* | . | -0.7 | 4.3 | 6.5 |
| Share of the product group in total exports of 1965 (%) | 18.1 | 31.4* | . | 3.8 | 34.4 | 12.3 |
| RUMANIA | 0.2 | -1.6 | -2.6 | 20.1 | 1.5 | 17.7 |
| Share of the product group in total exports of 1965 (%) | 21.3 | 30.2 | 12.6 | 6.4 | 18.5 | 11.0 |
| USSR | -9.6 | 3.0 | 2.1 | -6.1 | 2.9 | -3.0 |
| Share of the product group in total exports of 1965 (%) | 8.4 | 48.4 | 17.2 | 3.6 | 20.0 | 2.4 |

Sources: *Yearbook of International Trade Statistics*, 1963, 1965. National Statistical Yearbooks, Nauchno Issledovatelni Koniuncturni Institute: Razvitie Vnieshnieh Torgovli Sichialisticheskih Stran, 1965.

Notes: * including fuels;    † 1960–3;    ‡ including fuels and chemicals;

Bulgaria, 26.6 per cent of the exports of Czechoslovakia, 63.8 per cent of the exports of Hungary, 17 per cent of the exports of the German Democratic Republic, 78.1 per cent of the exports of Poland, 57.2 per cent of the exports of Rumania and 85.6 per cent of the exports of the Soviet Union.

Further research would be needed to decide whether or not the improvement in export performance in the given areas was advantageous for the national economies.

The changes of export performance by destination and by commodity groups with a few exceptions followed the traditional trends. As a new trend, the better performance of the Bulgarian, Rumanian and Soviet exports of machinery and equipment in western Europe was probably the only change. Generally, in the category of machinery and equipment, the improvements occurred in the CMEA market or in the market of the developing countries. The CMEA countries strengthened their export positions in the developed western European countries in the category of raw materials and semi-manufactured goods and to a smaller extent in that of consumer goods.

It is remarkable that countries on a lower level of economic development, which a few years ago did not export machinery and equipment at all, achieved a very good export performance in this category. Particular products of these countries proved to be very good and competitive, capturing the demand even in the most sophisticated markets.

Among the exported goods, the group of machinery and equipment has special importance. The products in this group reflect clearly the technical progress of the exporting country. I therefore compared the export performance of the CMEA countries in this commodity group in one important socialist market (Soviet Union) and in one western market (West Germany). The conditions were favourable during the period analysed for the exports of the CMEA countries in both markets. The Soviet Union increased her imports of machinery and equipment from the CMEA area above the planned level. In the West German market, there was a boom in these years, and the conditions of sales for the CMEA countries were in general not bad. One has to take into account of course that, with the exception of Czechoslovakia, the share of machinery and equipment in the exports of socialist countries to the West German market is not more than 5 per cent of their total sales, but in the case of exports to the Soviet market it is much higher. Still it is interesting to note that the trends in export performance of the countries are very similar in both markets, even though there are great differences in proportions. Taking the average export performance of the CMEA countries together as 100, in the Soviet and West German markets, the position of individual countries in the commodity group of machinery and equipment between 1962 and 1965 was as shown in Table 6.

TABLE 6. *The relative export performance in machinery and equipment* (*1962–5*)

(CMEA average: 100)

|  | Soviet market | German Federal Republic market |
|---|---|---|
| Bulgaria | 435 | 132 |
| Czechoslovakia | 87 | 42 |
| German Democratic Republic | 29 | n.a. |
| Hungary | 26 | 33 |
| Poland | 206 | 191 |
| Rumania | 161 | 179 |
| USSR | . | 452 |

Sources: *United Nations Commodity Trade Statistics*, 1965. *Vnesnaia Torgovlia S.S.S.R.*, 1959–1963, 1965. National Statistical Yearbooks.

The export performance of five socialist countries can be compared in both markets. It is evident from the data that in relation to the CMEA average, the export performance was best in Bulgaria, Poland and Rumania. Czechoslovakia and Hungary showed a poor export performance in both markets.

In addition to the previously discussed 'individual cases', we tried to reveal the export performance of the CMEA countries taken together in the most important commodity groups. In calculating this indicator, we took the world market as the basis. Between 1961 and 1965 the CMEA countries, as a group, improved their export performance in the group of machinery and equipment, which was the second fastest-growing commodity group in world trade, and in the export of raw materials, which was the slowest expanding group in world trade. As a consequence of this improvement, the change in their share in world exports was as shown in Table 7.

The commodity structure of the exports of the CMEA countries in both 1961 and 1965 was nearer to the structure of world exports than the export pattern of the Common Market. It is a remarkable feature that by 1965 the CMEA countries were nearer to the Common Market countries in the share of machinery and equipment in their exports than to the world export patterns. In 1961, the share of machinery and equipment in world exports was 22.6 per cent; in CMEA exports, it was 26.5 per cent; in the

*Mihály Simai*

TABLE 7. *Changes in the share of CMEA countries in world exports* (by commodity groups, in percentages)

| Years | Foodstuffs | Raw materials and semi-finished goods | Mineral fuels and products | Chemicals | Machinery and equipment | Other industrial products |
|---|---|---|---|---|---|---|
| 1961 | 9.2 | 9.0 | 13.5 | 8.8 | 12.4 | 15.3 |
| 1965 | 7.3 | 9.4 | 12.6 | 8.3 | 13.1 | 10.5 |

Source: *United Nations Monthly Bulletin of Statistics*, March 1967.

exports of the Common Market it was 31.7 per cent. By 1965, the corresponding shares were 24.6 per cent, 30 per cent and 32.8 per cent.

It is very interesting to compare the export performance of the CMEA countries and the Common Market countries in different markets in the category of machinery and equipment.

The export performance of the CMEA member countries in Western Europe in this commodity group was 1.2; the export performance of the Common Market countries was 1.5. In the developing countries the export performance of the CMEA member countries was 7.6, whereas the export performance of the Common Market countries was −2.2.

The export performance of the Common Market countries in the markets of the CMDE countries in the commodity group of machinery and equipment was −3.0, while the export performance of the CMEA member countries in the Common Market was −6.0.

The export performance of the CMEA members and members of the Common Market in trade within the groups in machinery and equipment was as follows: the export performance of the CMEA countries in their mutual trade: 4.5; the export performance of the Common Market countries in their mutual trade: 2.1. This means that the CMEA countries increased their mutual trade at a faster rate in this commodity group than the members of the Common Market.

In comparing the planned and actual export performances of the CMEA countries in the main commodity groups, we have, due to lack of data, to limit the research to the CMEA area based on the trade agreements. If the trade had grown according to these long-term trade agreements, the trade pattern of the intra-CMEA exports by 1965 would have been as follows:

|  | % |
|---|---|
| Machinery and equipment | 38.0 |
| Raw materials and semi-finished products (including fuels and chemicals) | 27.5 |
| Foodstuffs | 7.8 |
| Consumer goods | 26.7 |

Actually, the share of machinery and equipment was 35.1 per cent, the proportion of raw materials and semi-finished products was 25.5 per cent, the share of foodstuffs 9.9 per cent, and of industrial consumer goods 29.5 per cent.

Intra-CMEA trade increased more than planned in every commodity group. Taking the planned 1965 level as 100, the actual exports in individual commodity groups were as follows:

| | |
|---|---|
| Machinery and equipment | 113 |
| Raw materials and semi-finished goods | |
| (including fuels and chemicals) | 114 |
| Foodstuffs | 155 |
| Manufactured consumer goods | 134 |

Since the exports of the seven countries between 1961 and 1965 were only about 8 per cent below the planned level (the annual average increase was 9 per cent compared to the 9.8 per cent planned), it is evident that the intra-CMEA trade was planned, in general as well as by commodity groups, below the actual rates of increase. Comparing these data with the expansion of the market, one can draw the conclusion valid in every commodity group, that in the case of CMEA exports, the export performance was somewhat better, and in other relations somewhat worse, than planned. The deviations from the plans and especially the better export performance in CMEA trade can be explained partly by the greater sales difficulties in other markets, partly by the fact that the CMEA relations served again as a safety valve for the CMEA members which, particularly when deliveries exceeded the planned level, helped in the bridging of temporary difficulties, the elimination of bottlenecks in supplies for consumption or for industry.

One has to take into account the fact that the data are aggregates and that there are deviations from the general trends in the cases of individual products in different countries. In some bilateral relations the contracted quotas were not completely utilized; in other cases, however, they were surpassed.

The inter-relations between the changes in the patterns of output and exports are beyond the scope of this paper. It is interesting to note, however, that the changes in the output patterns of individual CMEA member countries were more similar to the changes in demand patterns in their markets than to their actual export patterns.

This reflected the fact that the CMEA countries could not fully utilize in their exports the technologically progressive structural changes in their output. In this respect, one can generalize the statements of Imre Vajda, referring to the position of Hungary.[1]

[1] *Közgazdasagi Szemle*, Budapest, 1967, no. 6.

*Mihály Simai*

SOME CONCLUSIONS

Export performance is influenced by the prices and qualities of the products produced and exported. There are specific administrative regulations still imposed on the exports of the socialist states in many developed western industrial countries. In some cases, the requirements of financing create serious obstacles. Here we want to emphasize only some of the conclusions which can be drawn from the export performance of the CMEA countries, based on studies of trade between 1961 and 1965 in their main export markets.

One of the more general conclusions is the need to increase the interdependence of production processes in promoting export trade within the CMEA.

The share of exports, which is based on production agreements, is still very small in the total exports of the CMEA countries. This is not only a consequence of the limited specialization and co-operation among CMEA members, which has been mentioned previously. It is also a result of the relatively minor role of joint investments, product-sharing systems and technical co-operation. These relations are playing a very important role in the export trade between the developed capitalist countries.

The needs of development of the CMEA countries did not overcome the contradiction between the aim of increasing the international interdependence of output in different countries and the economic policy dictated by the requirements of imports and, on this basis, attempting to maximize the export revenues. This is one of the reasons why the export performance of the CMEA countries in the category of machinery and equipment fluctuated so greatly. There were sporadic examples of co-operation on different levels in the field of raw materials, processing and supplies, especially with the Soviet Union. There are some joint enterprises too. There were many plans to increase bilateral industrial co-operation. These were, however, only small steps forward from the long-term commodity trade agreements which play a positive role from the point of view of individual countries in the expansion of output and exports. The long-term agreements facilitated long-term planning because they secured imported supplies at stable prices and also provided export markets. However, they proved to be insufficient to promote efficiency and the faster transfer of technical progress.

The long-term agreements did not make the CMEA partners interested in achieving greater technical efficiency. The relations between the sellers and the buyers are different from those which exist between united producers mutually interested in the technological development of the new products and in the benefits derived thereby.

A new situation is emerging with the reform of planning and management. The new development strategy requires a much broader view in the most important sectors of the economy. The full-scale introduction of the planned reform measures will create a new framework in the international economy. The present, highly centralized form of international economic co-operation will be replaced by relations among economies with different degrees of centralization in their decision-making processes. The existing forms of international economic relations are necessarily inconsistent with the internal logic of the new relations. New economic incentives are built into the system to speed up technical progress and introduce the necessary measures to achieve the goals.

One more argument must be taken into account in this concluding section. Export performance from the point of view of individual countries means competition. In the framework of this paper, we have not discussed the competitive character of the relations in export markets among the individual socialist countries. No doubt competition is or can be, to a certain extent, an incentive towards general progress. For example, Bulgaria, being less industrialized, can approach or surpass in the volume of her 'specialized' exports the more industrialized countries, and this is beneficial to CMEA. Competition cannot be eliminated completely. There is no absolute division of labour, due to the present level of technology and consumption habits. It cannot however be considered a healthy phenomenon that the country specialised in a product on the basis of CMEA recommendations faces the competition of another CMEA member in the same product, because the partner started producing despite the agreements and even started exporting it. This cannot be eliminated by the present forms and methods of co-operation. Moral discipline itself is not sufficient to create incentives against these practices. In spite of the search for legal sanctions, it would be much better to find the forms of mutual interest among the countries.

Another general conclusion is the need to increase and improve additional services. The reason why export performance is better in the field of raw materials, semi-manufactured goods, foodstuffs and less sophisticated consumer goods, is basically not the consequence of administrative or political obstacles. These products usually do not require additional supplementary services or supply of spare parts. They are considered as traditional elements in the consumption of importing countries. In those cases where the steady increase of exports requires important additional investments in services, the export performance is usually weaker. Those socialist countries exporting machinery and equipment lag behind their competitors more in the supply of additional and necessary services than in standards of qualities, usefulness, etc. While western private enterprise is receiving government subsidies or tax credits for the promotion of exports, in the socialist countries these activities are considered unnecessary; also, in most cases they can be paid only in hard currencies. These investments depreciate in the uncertain export market. The situation is creating a vicious circle in some markets. The small volume of exports provides a slow return on investments, and the small export volume is in many cases due to the lack of this type of investment. The same is true to a certain extent of the commercial propaganda of the socialist countries abroad.

The studies of export performance also support the views of those authors who consider the importance of marketing and especially market research – even among the socialist countries – as vital from the point of view of the expansion of exports.[1] In the socialist countries, market research and marketing are justified by the new status of the plans in some countries and by the unforeseen circumstances, creating discrepancies between the long-term, medium-term and short-term programmes.

Active marketing and market research can also promote the process of socialist integration. Experience has shown that the integration process develops simultaneously along different lines. One is the increasing specialization and co-operation among countries, which creates inter-relations among the economies. The other is the standardization of consumption and output which helps integration by facilitating the immediate replacement of a product produced in one country by a product produced in another, without any problems.

Scientific marketing and market research are not only tools which passively register this process but also provide active help by revealing the possibilities and the facilities for influencing sales, their extent and methods. All this is extremely important in the long-term export policies.

The development of world trade proves that a modern export policy is not only a trade policy but also a long-term development programme for output and consumption structures. The technological development in foreign trade is marked by those goods which satisfy new needs or satisfy existing needs more efficiently. Foreign trade, by transferring these goods, is a very important sphere for inter-relating and promoting the techno-

[1] See, for example, articles in *Külkereskedelem*, 1967, No. 5, *Viata Economica*, 18 August 1967, *Deutsche Aussenpolitik*, 1967, No. 7, *Die Wirtschaft*, 13 January 1968.

logical development of different countries. The international inter-dependence of the consumption patterns of individual countries is bringing about the needs spontaneously and by this means spreading the new products, which thus influence the patterns of output and consumption. Active marketing and market research in socialist and non-socialist relations can accelerate progress and from the point of view of individual economies can make this process more efficient.

# 7. A comparative analysis of the effects of foreign trade on the Hungarian economy

MÁRIA AUGUSTINOVICS

The impact of foreign trade on the volume and sectoral pattern of production, on primary inputs, on foreign trade turnover itself and on various final uses can be investigated by comparing the Hungarian economy with the EEC countries with respect to the discrepancy between the actual economic structure and an assumed autarkic one defined by input–output data.

To characterize the importance of foreign trade and its role in the economy it is usually considered sufficient to express the value of imports and exports as percentages of national income. Economic policy would then concentrate mainly on the balance of trade, which amounts to only a few per cent of total trade. Now it is obvious that if disequilibrium occurred not under the influence of random fluctuations but as a result of a trend, the causes would have to be sought in the pattern of foreign trade and even in the structure of the whole economy. It should be equally obvious that the role of foreign trade in the economy as a whole and the intensity of the interrelations between foreign trade and economic structure are not necessarily proportional to the ratio of the volume of external trade to national income; many facts must be derived in order to obtain a clear picture of the role of foreign trade in a country's economy.

The tools of modern analysis, particularly input–output analysis, enable us to solve this problem step by step. The general use of these methods makes it possible to analyse the Hungarian economy in an international setting. Some results of an analysis carried out along these lines are surveyed in the present article.[1] The reader will kindly notice, that this analysis was carried out some years ago and the facts recorded are ten years old. They will not necessarily hold for the Hungarian economy of the seventies.

[1] The investigations were conducted at the Institute of Economic Planning, National Planning Office. A detailed survey of the results is given in M. Augustinovics, *A külkereskedelem és a népazdaság főbb arányai* [Foreign trade and the major proportions of the economy], Publications of the Institute of Economic Planning, National Planning Office, No. 2, 1967. The model which served as a basis for the investigations has been described in M. Augustinovics, *Input–output Methods in Analysing and Planning Foreign Trade*, presented to the Ad Hoc Group on Import/Export Projections, UN Economic Commission for Europe, Geneva, 1967.

In our analysis, an approximate quantification of the autarky concept plays a central role. Autarky is, of course, neither a workable hypothesis, nor a genuine alternative for most countries; the concept serves only as a yardstick by which to examine the importance of foreign trade in production and consumption. Let us first work out approximately the situation that would prevail under autarky, and relate the actual trade-influenced structure of the economy to this hypothetical situation. The difference between the two situations will characterize the effects of external trade on economic structure.

An autarkic situation in the economy cannot, of course, be quantified with full accuracy, since the input–output tables at our disposal reflect the effects of foreign trade. Under total autarky the input coefficients (reflecting production conditions and technology) would be different – but how different we do not know. For the present analysis autarky is defined as a situation where a country satisfies both final and productive demand from its own production, carried out with the present sectoral input pattern.[1]

The autarkic economic structures, as interpreted here, were compared on the basis of 14-sector input–output tables for Hungary (1961), France, Italy, Belgium, the Netherlands (all 1959) and the Federal Republic of Germany (1960). Then the differences between the autarkic and the actual situations in the various fields of production and consumption – i.e. the intensity of the effects of foreign trade – were examined to see whether they were proportional to the ratio of the volume of foreign trade to national income. The latter, too, was computed from the input–output tables. The data are shown in Table 1, and will serve throughout this paper as a basis of comparison.

A single computation of this type does not necessarily yield conclusive results, relying as it does on the statistically not unobjectionable input–output tables of a few countries pertaining to a single year, but lacking the full quantification of the autarky concept.[2] In order to arrive at reliable results, similar computations will have to be performed on the basis of

[1] A comparison of the actual situation with an autarky thus supposed was first used by W. W. Leontief to characterize the production pattern of countries with different levels of development (W. W. Leontief, 'The Structure of Development', in *Input–Output Economics*, Oxford University Press, New York, 1966). Our analysis differs from his in that we have quantified the level and pattern under autarky not only for total output by industries but also for output for the various final uses, and for primary inputs. (This was possible because import data were available not only in a breakdown by commodity groups but also in a breakdown by users.)

[2] Since then the Statistical Office of the European Economic Community has published a revised version of the input–output tables used; a repetition of our computations on the basis of the new tables could, however, for the time being, not be undertaken.

TABLE I[1]

| | Exports as a percentage of national income | Imports as a percentage of | |
|---|---|---|---|
| | | exports | national income |
| France 1959 | 16.5 | 81.4 | 13.4 |
| Italy 1959 | 15.8 | 100.5 | 15.9 |
| German Fed. Rep. 1960 | 23.9 | 80.8 | 19.3 |
| Hungary 1961[2] | 32.4 | 97.7 | 32.7 |
| Belgium 1959 | 48.4 | 100.5 | 48.6 |
| The Netherlands 1959 | 59.1 | 84.3 | 49.8 |

more accurate tables with various sector breakdowns, covering more years and a greater number of countries.

It will still be worthwhile to study the first approximate results since – if we consider them correct until further verification or refutation – they may provide food for thought on many important problems.

THE VOLUME AND SECTOR PATTERN OF PRODUCTION

The effect of foreign trade on the volume and pattern of production, or more precisely the intensity of this effect, is fundamentally determined by the similarities or differences between the sector pattern of exports and imports.[3]

[1] *EEC data*: imports at c.i.f. prices net of re-exports; exports, imports and national income exclusive of what according to Hungarian methodology are termed 'non-productive' services; net of depreciation. (Net Material Product in UN terminology.) *Hungarian data*: imports at prices conforming to the domestic price level of exports but reflecting the actual relative purchase price proportions; national income corrected accordingly. Since all data relating to the individual countries refer to the year here indicated, the reference will henceforth be omitted.

[2] Control computations based on rather simple methods and at world-market (dollar) prices show Hungarian exports to amount to only about 20–22 per cent of national income. The higher percentage obtained from the computations based on the input–output tables must, therefore, be due to the peculiar proportions of the domestic price system prevailing in 1961. However, this fact could not be accounted for in the complex investigations surveyed here since, in the input–output tables used, the proportions of production and consumption are based on the same domestic price system and are thus commensurable with the 32 per cent export share.

[3] Our computations relate to identical volumes of exports and imports, since only in this manner can they be considered as aggregates of commodities substituting for each other, exchanged for each other and representing each other's inputs and outputs, respectively. (Export surpluses or deficits figure in domestic final demand as items increasing or decreasing the national wealth and in a commodity composition corresponding to the average pattern of exports.) Thus, hereafter our results will really depend only on the structural differences between exports and imports. The differences in volume – the problems of the balance of foreign trade – will not be treated in this paper.

In most countries the products of nearly every industry are both exported and imported. Thus, there is a part of turnover which is balanced within the industries themselves; let us call this the *assortment exchange*, assuming that e.g. machinery exported and machinery imported differ from each other in some aspect of assortment, let us say, quality. Another part of turnover consists of positive or negative sectoral balances; let us call this the *sectoral exchange*.

In the countries examined, trade is divided between two characteristically different parts as shown in Table 2.[1]

TABLE 2

|  | Sectoral exchange | Assortment exchange | Total turnover |
|---|---|---|---|
| France | 41.7 | 58.3 | 100.0 |
| Italy | 38.1 | 61.9 | 100.0 |
| German Fed. Rep. | 52.2 | 47.8 | 100.0 |
| Hungary | 31.4 | 68.6 | 100.0 |
| Belgium | 34.0 | 66.0 | 100.0 |
| The Netherlands | 37.0 | 63.0 | 100.0 |

If the share of sectoral exchange is examined in conjunction with the volume of turnover, the graph shown in Fig. 1 may be drawn.

As can be seen, the share of sectoral exchange does not grow proportionately with the volume of turnover; in fact, in small countries with an

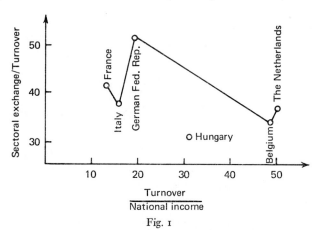

Fig. 1

<hr>

[1] Division of trade into these two parts depends to a greater extent on the sector breakdown applied than do the other indicators treated in this paper. With other methods of aggregation other values would be obtained. It is assumed, however, that this would affect all countries in the same direction, if not to the same extent, and thus their order would not change.

'open' economy this ratio is smaller than in large countries with a 'more closed' economy. It seems that there is a limit to the growth of sectoral exchange – meaning the specialization of individual industries in exports or in imports. Beyond a certain extent the growth of foreign trade must necessarily take the form of an assortment exchange, especially in small countries.

It is, however, conspicuous that the share of sectoral exchange in total turnover is smallest in Hungary, which implies that the differences between the patterns of exports and imports are smallest here. The foreign trade specialization of industries is below the level that could, in comparison with the countries examined, be expected on the basis of the relative volume of foreign trade. As a consequence, the global 'supporting' material requirements of exports and imports (i.e. the materials actually used for exports and the materials which would be used if the imported goods were domestically produced) are nearly equal.

In other words, the multiplier effects of exports and imports on production are identical in Hungary, while in the other countries they differ from each other (see Table 3).

TABLE 3

| | Total output[1] necessary for the domestic production of a unit of | | Exports Imports |
|---|---|---|---|
| | imports | exports | |
| France | 1.640 | 1.808 | 1.103 |
| Italy | 1.983 | 2.012 | 1.015 |
| German Fed. Rep. | 2.005 | 2.016 | 1.005 |
| Hungary | 2.260 | 2.260 | 1.000 |
| Belgium | 2.201 | 2.366 | 1.075 |
| The Netherlands | 2.373 | 2.178 | 0.919 |

Thus the total output 'saved' through imports as compared with the production requirements under autarky is of the same magnitude as the 'additional output' necessary for exports. In the other countries, the two output requirements are different.

As can be seen from Table 4, in Hungary the actual level of output does not differ from that under supposed autarky; in other words, the inter-

---

[1] Total output is computed, as are national income and exports and imports, in accordance with the Hungarian methodology, exclusive of 'non-productive' services (MPS).

TABLE 4

| | Output under autarky | Deduct for imports | 'Self-sufficiency' (1 − 2) | Add for exports | Actual output (3 + 4) | Differ-ence (1 − 5) |
|---|---|---|---|---|---|---|
| | (1) | (2) | (3) | (4) | (5) | (6) |
| France | 100.0 | 11.9 | 88.1 | 13.1 | 101.2 | − 1.2 |
| Italy | 100.0 | 14.7 | 85.3 | 14.9 | 100.2 | − 0.2 |
| German Fed. Rep. | 100.0 | 18.3 | 81.7 | 18.4 | 100.1 | − 0.1 |
| Hungary | 100.0 | 28.7 | 71.3 | 28.7 | 100.0 | . |
| Belgium | 100.0 | 48.5 | 51.5 | 52.1 | 103.6 | − 3.6 |
| The Netherlands | 100.0 | 48.9 | 51.1 | 44.9 | 96.0 | + 4.0 |

national exchange of goods does not modify the level of national output. However, in the other countries under investigation such a modifying effect can be seen. It is present to a smaller extent even in the large countries whose economy is much more 'closed' than the Hungarian, and in the smaller countries with an 'open' economy it amounts to about four per cent of total production.

Of course, the international exchange of commodities influences not only the level but also the sector pattern of production. The sector patterns of exports and imports differ from each other, if only slightly. Their in-direct material requirements, though equal in global terms, are drawn from the output of different industries; in other words, their 'multiplier effect' does not affect the same industries. The modifying effect means therefore that a different volume of output is brought about in other in-dustries than would be the case under autarky. As a consequence of the international exchange of goods a country will produce not only more or less but also to a certain extent different commodities than it would with-out this exchange taking place.

The volume of this production 'diverted' into other industries can also be established. (It represents half the sum of the absolute values of relative discrepancies between the actual and autarkic sectoral outputs). The relation of this volume of output to total turnover shows the intensity of the influence of trade on the sectoral pattern of production; its share in total production, on the other hand, is a comprehensive indicator of the impact of foreign trade on the structure of production. The relevant data are shown in Table 5.

As can be seen, the effect of trade on the sectoral structure of produc-tion is smallest in Hungary. However, the relative volume of trade is greater than in the larger countries. Accordingly, the 'diverted' production

TABLE 5

|  | Volume of output 'diverted' to other industries as a percentage of | |
|  | foreign trade | total production under autarky |
|---|---|---|
| France | 52.4 | 3.8 |
| Italy | 49.5 | 3.6 |
| German Fed. Rep. | 66.3 | 6.0 |
| Hungary | 40.0 | 5.1 |
| Belgium | 47.1 | 10.4 |
| The Netherlands | 46.9 | 9.7 |

still represents a higher share of the total than in France or Italy, but a smaller one than in the Federal Republic of Germany where intensity is rather high – not to mention the 'small' countries. Again, the lag can be most clearly seen in connection with the relative size of trade (see Fig. 2).

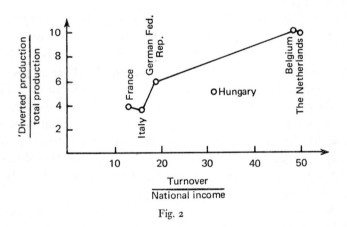

Fig. 2

It may, accordingly, be stated that in Hungary the effect of the international exchange of commodities on the structure of production is considerably weaker than could be expected on the basis of the relative volume of turnover.

If now we want to establish the sectoral differences between the actual and the autarkic situation not only in relation to total production, but also from the point of view of the individual industries themselves, the following simple procedure may be applied.

Let us work out for the individual industries the differences between the actual and autarkic production levels as a percentage of the autarkic level. We shall determine the unweighted mean of these relative differences and call it the *average difference*. Again, let us establish the deviations in individual industries from this mean and call it the *dispersion*. Finally, let us compute the ratio of dispersion to the average difference and call it *relative dispersion*. The numerical results are shown in Table 6.

TABLE 6

|  | Average difference | Dispersion | Relative dispersion |
|---|---|---|---|
| France | 8.4 | 6.7 | 79.8 |
| Italy | 13.4 | 12.4 | 92.5 |
| German Fed. Rep. | 11.9 | 8.3 | 69.7 |
| Hungary | 12.2 | 6.3 | 51.6 |
| Belgium | 20.8 | 16.5 | 79.3 |
| The Netherlands | 23.7 | 17.7 | 74.7 |

Let us take Hungary as an example. Here the average difference from autarky is 12.2 per cent. Since the table does not show it, let us mention for the sake of illustration that the greatest difference can be found in the clothing industry (27.8 per cent) and the smallest in agriculture (4.9 per cent). Thus, the difference in agriculture is 7.3 points smaller and that in the clothing industry 15.6 points greater than the average difference. The figure of 6.3 per cent in column 2 of the table represents the average for all industries.

The average difference illustrates another aspect of a phenomenon which has already been treated, relating as it does to the relative proportions of production 'diverted' to other industries. The indicators of dispersion and relative dispersion, on the other hand, provide new information; they show how the average level of 'diversification' has come about. Is it due to large deviations in a few industries or to small deviations in many? Are there large differences from the levels of output which would prevail under autarky in a few industries or small differences in many industries? Is the modification in the structure of production concentrated in a few industries or spread over many?

According to the data in Table 6, dispersion and relative dispersion are smallest in Hungary. Thus the exchange of goods affects the production level of individual industries more evenly than in the other countries, where it diverts some industries from their own autarkic levels to a great extent while leaving others almost unaffected. The effect of the international exchange of commodities on the sector pattern of production is – beside being relatively weaker – more dispersed in Hungary than in any of the other countries under investigation.[1]

It will be worthwhile to examine the concentration of the effect separately in 'exporting' industries, i.e. those producing more than the autarkic level, and in 'importing' ones, i.e. those which produce less. Instead of listing the data the graph derived is shown in Fig. 3.

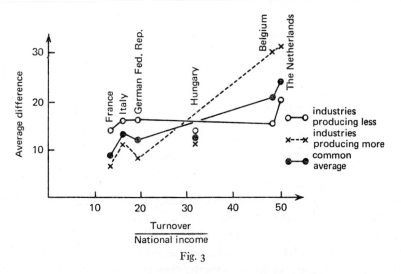

Fig. 3

In the large countries with 'closed' economies the difference between the actual and the autarkic production is greatest in the industries which turn out less than is needed for domestic requirements. In these countries the 'deficit' is concentrated among a few commodities (coal, oil and agricultural products) while there are several industries producing greater or smaller surpluses for export. The share of 'exporting' industries, i.e. of those producing above the autarkic level, is 60 to 70 per cent of total production.

In smaller countries with 'open' economies the situation is reversed. Here, the 'deficit' is dispersed, and there are many industries whose actual level of production is to a certain extent lower than it would be under autarky. On the other hand, the surplus destined for export is produced by one or two industries specialized for the purpose (such as metallurgy, clothing and transportation in Belgium; transportation, almost exclusively, in the Netherlands, where its actual performance is nearly double that

[1] Though posing the problem in a different way and adopting different methods, but relying also on Western European input–output data, T. Szira also arrives at similar conclusions in his article: 'Az impari ágazati koncentráció kerdéséhez' [On the sectoral concentration of industry], *Közgazdasági Szemle*, No. 7–8, 1966.

under autarky). These industries are mostly the smaller ones. In both countries, the 'exporting' industries account for 37 per cent of total production.

It is rather difficult to present a clear picture of the situation in Hungary. Most Hungarian industries are 'importing' ones, i.e. producing less than needed for domestic requirements. Only a few are 'exporting'. Thus, from this point of view, Hungary resembles the small countries. However, the 'importing' industries are small and the 'exporting' industries are the largest, and the difference between the actual and the autarkic levels is therefore greater in the case of the 'importing' industries. The latter produce on average 14.2 per cent less than their own autarkic level, while the 'exporting' industries are turning out 11.5 per cent more on average. From this point of view Hungary therefore resembles the large countries as can be seen from Fig. 3.

Not only the averages, but also the extreme differences lie between narrower limits in Hungary than in most other countries (Table 7).

TABLE 7

| | Industry producing | | | |
|---|---|---|---|---|
| | least | | most | |
| | in comparison to autarkic level; and its output as a percentage of autarkic level | | | |
| France | petroleum | 80.4 | clothing | 116.1 |
| Italy | coal mining | 14.6 | transportation | 125.2 |
| German Fed. Rep. | agriculture | 67.5 | transportation | 120.4 |
| Hungary | woodworking industry | 77.3 | clothing | 127.8 |
| Belgium | agriculture | 67.9 | metallurgy | 167.7 |
| The Netherlands | petroleum | 56.4 | transportation | 194.8 |

It can be seen that only in France are both 'extreme' industries closer to the autarkic level; in all other countries at least one is more extreme than in Hungary, in the smaller countries both are.

Thus, the patterns of both imports and exports contribute to the fact that in this country the modification of the sectoral structure is less concentrated than in other countries. While in a large number of industries less is produced than under autarky, the phenomenon of a few industries with a much lower output than under autarky is absent. On the other hand, a higher level of output than under autarky occurs only in the case of the largest industries; there are thus no industries specializing expressly in exports.

## Mária Augustinovics

It appears that a mere relative growth of foreign trade turnover will not necessarily render the economy 'open' to the same extent. The mutual interrelations between external trade and production structure are less close in the Hungarian economy than could be assumed from the relative volume of turnover.

### PRIMARY INPUTS

All countries engaged in foreign trade use part of their available labour and capital for exports and save a certain amount of labour and capital by importing. The problem of what factors determine the proportions prevailing in this exchange has been a central, unsolved problem of the theory of international trade ever since Ricardo. It was a turning point when – with the aid of input–output tables – the relative capital intensity of foreign trade in some countries could be quantified and the facts mostly contradicted the generally accepted theorems. The results of the first computation of this type are known as the 'Leontief paradox'.[1] This was followed by several similar investigations.[2]

A discussion of the theoretical problem would be beyond the scope of this paper, and only some results of our investigations will be presented here.

The primary–input data of the West European countries (such as the labour force, the value of fixed assets, etc.) were not available in the required sector breakdown. Thus only the ratio of amortization to wages could be used, since this could be established from the input–output tables at our disposal.[3] It may be assumed that within a country, in the comparison of different bills of goods, this ratio sufficiently characterizes the relation between fixed assets and labour inputs, although it cannot be used for comparisons between different countries.[4] The results relating

---

[1] W. W. Leontier, 'Domestic production and foreign trade: the American capital position re-examined', *Proceedings of the American Philosophical Society*, 97, Sept. 1953.

[2] A general survey of the whole problem and a rich bibliography may be found in Part 3 of a series of articles by J. S. Chipman: 'A survey of the theory of international trade', *Econometrica*, Vol. 34, No. 1, Jan. 1966. The countries examined in the present study are dealt with by K. W. Roskamp, 'Factor proportions and foreign trade: the case of West Germany', *Weltwirtschaftliches Archiv*, 1963, Heft 2, and by A. Rácz, 'Magyarország külkereskedelmének jellege a munkaráfordítás és az állóeszköztartalom figyelembevételevel' [The character of Hungarian foreign trade with regard to labour inputs and capital contents], *Közgazdasági Szemle*, No. 2, 1966.

[3] Even the data on wages had to be corrected by estimates based on employment figures, to make them comparable with the Hungarian figures, which comprise the total income from work of the working population including after-tax incomes of self-employed farmers and artisans.

[4] Justification of this assumption under certain conditions was given in a paper (Augustinovics, M., *Methods of international and intertemporal comparison of structure*) presented at the 4th International Conference on Input–Output Techniques. It still needs to be established whether the proportions prevailing in the Common Market countries meet these conditions.

to Hungary have been proved to hold even when checked on the basis of the available manpower and fixed capital data.[1] Still, for the sake of comparability and uniform treatment only the amortization wage ratio is presented in this study. The data are given in Table 8.

TABLE 8

| | Ratio of amortization to wages | | | | Exports/ Imports (2/1) | Actual/ Autarkic produc- tion (4/3) |
|---|---|---|---|---|---|---|
| | | | average for production | | | |
| | in imports | in exports | autarkic | actual | | |
| | (1) | (2) | (3) | (4) | (5) | (6) |
| France | 0.233 | 0.224 | 0.191 | 0.191 | 0.961 | 1.000 |
| Italy | 0.267 | 0.249 | 0.229 | 0.227 | 0.933 | 0.991 |
| German Fed. Rep. | 0.180 | 0.192 | 0.175 | 0.176 | 1.067 | 1.006 |
| Hungary | 0.306 | 0.303 | 0.258 | 0.256 | 0.990 | 0.991 |
| Belgium | 0.210 | 0.233 | 0.207 | 0.218 | 1.110 | 1.053 |
| The Netherlands | 0.186 | 0.228 | 0.188 | 0.206 | 1.219 | 1.096 |

First, the ratio of amortization to wages is in most cases considerably lower for production than for either imports or exports. It seems, therefore, that foreign trade is generally more capital-intensive than production in the participating countries. Summarizing what may be considered as common to all countries we find that the basic reason is the greater share of the capital-intensive sources of energy and raw materials both in exports and in imports than in total production. At the same time, construction, the least capital-intensive industry, does not play any essential role in external trade.

Further, the data show that in France, Italy and Hungary exports are more labour-intensive and contain more labour in comparison to the capital used than imports. With the Federal Republic of Germany, Belgium and the Netherlands, on the other hand, the case is the reverse, their exports being more capital-intensive than their imports.[2]

The question whether or not the situation is paradoxical can be answered only when we have data on the relative supply of capital and labour in the countries concerned. As regards Hungary, capital is a scarcer factor than labour; from this point of view, the pattern of the country's foreign trade

[1] See e.g. A. Rácz, 'Magyarország külkereskedelmének jellege a munkaráfordítás és as állóesz-köztartalom figyelembevételével' (The character of Hungarian foreign trade with regard to labour inputs and capital contents), *Közgazdasági Szemle*, No. 2, 1966.

[2] In the study quoted above, K. W. Roskamp reaches the same conclusion regarding the Federal Republic of Germany.

may be said to be favourable and in conformity with the theorems of the general theory of international trade.

It is, however, conspicuous that the difference between exports and imports is smallest again in Hungary. As a consequence, the difference between actual and autarkic production is also extremely small, since the insignificant difference between exports and imports cannot influence to any considerable extent the average of total production even with a medium

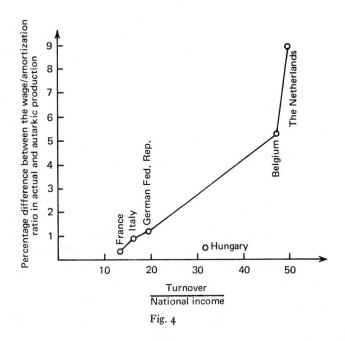

Fig. 4

volume of trade. The effect of foreign trade on the capital-intensity of total production is of the same order of magnitude as in the large countries with the 'most closed' economies; it cannot be considered significant and is well below the 5 to 10 per cent difference appearing in the small countries with open economies (see Fig. 4).

It can thus be established that the international exchange of commodities influences the utilization ratios of primary inputs – that is, the capital intensity of total production – in the Hungarian economy in a favourable direction to only a very small extent considering the volume of trade.

'CUMULATION' IN FOREIGN TRADE

Thus far a brief survey has been given of the effects of foreign trade on production, its volume, sector pattern, capital or labour intensity. Another aspect of the problem is, what consumption purposes does this exchange of commodities serve?

The international exchange of goods provides, first of all, for its own requirements. Obviously, the reason for exporting is to be able to import,[1] but it should be equally obvious that whenever a country uses imported materials in its production, these are used partly in the production of exports. Thus, a definite part of imports will be exported and a definite part of exports consists of imported materials transformed and processed in domestic production.[2] Let us call this part the import content of exports.

In the countries under investigation, the import content of exports, compared with the import content of average final product, was as shown in Table 9.

TABLE 9

| | Import content as a percentage of | | |
| | average final product | exports | Ratio of (2:1) |
|---|---|---|---|
| | (1) | (2) | (3) |
| France | 8.1 | 10.6 | 1.30 |
| Italy | 10.0 | 13.0 | 1.30 |
| German Fed. Rep. | 11.6 | 12.0 | 1.04 |
| Hungary | 17.1 | 20.9 | 1.22 |
| Belgium | 23.5 | 30.6 | 1.30 |
| The Netherlands | 25.4 | 26.3 | 1.03 |

It is striking that the import content of exports is in all countries higher than that of production in general. In other words, this means that of imports used in production a higher proportion goes into exports than into production as a whole. If it has already been established that foreign trade is more capital-intensive, the statement may now be ventured that foreign trade turnover is more 'foreign trade intensive' than the economy.

A closer examination will also reveal that the specific import content of exports is on the whole proportionate to the relative volume of foreign trade (Fig. 5).

If these two statements could be proved to hold for more countries and several periods, it would follow directly that the relative growth of foreign trade – as related to national income – is, in a sense, a self-accelerating

[1] As export surpluses are not dealt with here.
[2] These two parts are identical if – as was done in our computations – the volumes of exports and imports investigated are taken as identical.

process. If the share of imports in domestic production is increasing, total trade is bound to increase at a higher rate, because with a greater volume the share of the 'self-providing' part is also greater; the proportion of imports going into exports, or the import content of export.

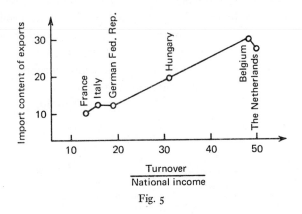

Fig. 5

As regards the structure of the Hungarian economy, the opinion is often voiced that the country's imports 'mainly' serve exports, that 'we import only to export and that the import content of our exports is too high'. In the light of international comparison, these anxieties seem to be unjustified. From the data in Table 9 and Fig. 5 it appears that in Hungary the import content of exports is on the whole proportionate to the relative volume of foreign trade; further, that the difference between the import contents of exports and of total final product cannot be considered excessive.

It is, however, true that of all the interrelations between foreign trade and economic structure this is one of the most critical points which may – particularly with a relatively rapid rate of growth – directly affect the equilibrium of the balance of trade. It is precisely on this account that the relatively reassuring global picture obtained from the static comparisons performed up to now needs to be extended in several directions, partly to account for the changes in proportions which have taken place since 1961 and partly to intensify the analysis of the whole problem, extending it to a thorough investigation of industrial and market situations.

CONSUMPTION AND CAPITAL FORMATION

The remaining part of imports, destined for the domestic market, includes imports for consumption as well as the imported materials used in domestic production for consumption. How then are these imports distributed among the various final uses?

Table 10 shows the import contents of consumption and gross capital formation.

TABLE 10

| | Import content in percentages of | | |
| | consumption | gross capital formation | Ratio of (1:2) |
|---|---|---|---|
| | (1) | (2) | (3) |
| France | 11.2 | 10.3 | 1.09 |
| Italy | 12.1 | 13.4 | 0.90 |
| German Fed. Rep. | 17.0 | 13.3 | 1.28 |
| Hungary | 18.4 | 27.7 | 0.66 |
| Belgium | 28.8 | 33.9 | 0.85 |
| The Netherlands | 30.9 | 41.5 | 0.75 |

As can be seen, the ratio of the import content of consumption to that of capital formation is lowest in Hungary.

In consequence, as compared to the level under autarky, the part 'saved' by imports is smaller and 'self-sufficiency' is greater in total production for consumption purposes than in production for capital formation. In the other countries the situation is either the reverse or prevails only to a lesser extent (Table 11).

TABLE 11

| | 'Saved' by imports as a percentage of total output for | | |
| | consumption | investment | Ratio of (1:2) |
|---|---|---|---|
| | (1) | (2) | (3) |
| France | 10.7 | 10.6 | 1.01 |
| Italy | 12.1 | 14.4 | 0.84 |
| German Fed. Rep. | 17.2 | 14.0 | 1.23 |
| Hungary | 18.9 | 28.2 | 0.67 |
| Belgium | 31.1 | 37.0 | 0.84 |
| The Netherlands | 33.0 | 44.3 | 0.75 |

Thus, it is in Hungary that we find the greatest difference between consumption and capital formation from the point of view of the effects of the international exchange of goods on total production. It is thus in Hungary that production for consumption is most autarkic in character compared with production for capital formation.

*Mária Augustinovics*

A further remarkable difference between the structure of the Hungarian economy and those of the other countries exists in the utilization ratios of primary inputs. It is only in Hungary that capital formation is more capital-intensive than consumption; in all remaining countries examined the case is the reverse. The data – based on the assumption of autarky – are shown in Table 12.

TABLE 12

| | Ratio of amortization to wages in | | Ratio of (2:1) |
| | consumption | investment | |
|---|---|---|---|
| | (1) | (2) | (3) |
| France | 2.01 | 1.62 | 0.63 |
| Italy | 2.35 | 2.16 | 0.92 |
| German Fed. Rep. | 1.84 | 1.54 | 0.84 |
| Hungary | 2.30 | 3.05 | 1.33 |
| Belgium | 2.22 | 1.71 | 0.78 |
| The Netherlands | 2.05 | 1.40 | 0.68 |

The capital intensities of various production-aggregates depend, of course, on the sectoral composition of these aggregates and on the relative capital intensities of the sectors. Even without examining in detail the sectoral patterns of investment and consumption in the individual countries, it is obvious that in the production of consumer goods the role of agriculture is decisive, while in that of investment goods metallurgy, engineering and construction play the dominant part. (It is sufficient to single out these particular sectors, because as regards the relative capital intensities of the rest, i.e. their ranking according to capital intensity, there is no fundamental difference between Hungary and the other countries examined.) The relative capital intensities of the sectors mentioned are characterized by the data in Table 13.[1]

In the western countries examined metallurgy is one and a half times to twice as capital-intensive as agriculture, in Hungary more than eight times. In western countries engineering is about as capital-intensive as agriculture, in Hungary its capital intensity is two and a half times that of

[1] These data are inaccurate from several points of view. In the case of western countries corrected data were used (see footnote 3, p. 142). As regards Hungary, amortization in agriculture figures among the data of the 1961 table presumably with a low value; it should be raised by approximately 25–30 per cent. Moreover, the amortization/wage ratio reflects less than accurately the capital/wage ratio of individual sectors because of the discrepancies between actual amortization rates. However, even considering the widest margins of error, these inaccuracies cannot account for the striking qualitative differences emerging from the figures.

TABLE 13

|  | Ratio of amortization to wages of various industries in relation to agriculture | | |
|  | metallurgy | engineering (agriculture = 1) | construction |
|---|---|---|---|
| France | 2.03 | 0.99 | 0.42 |
| Italy | 1.43 | 1.07 | 0.76 |
| German Fed. Rep. | 1.53 | 0.99 | 0.61 |
| Hungary | 8.38 | 2.52 | 1.13 |
| Belgium | 2.10 | 1.21 | 0.79 |
| The Netherlands | 1.31 | 0.88 | 0.41 |

agriculture. Construction is in western countries less capital-intensive than agriculture; in Hungary it is more capital-intensive.

Thus, in comparison to the most investment-oriented industries, agriculture is much less capitalized in Hungary than in western capitalist countries. This is because in Hungarian agriculture, the amortization/wage ratio is lower, whereas in Hungarian heavy industries it is higher than in the western countries. This qualitative difference explains at any rate the inverse relation of consumption to capital formation from the point of view of relative capital intensity.

The international exchange of commodities diminishes to some extent the difference between the capital intensities of Hungarian consumption and capital formation; however, it does not eliminate it nor does it change the inverse situation in comparison to western countries. In the final analysis, actual production for capital formation is only 1.2 times as capital-intensive as production for consumption, as against the 1.33 coefficient under assumed autarky.

To sum up, it may be stated that Hungarian foreign trade serves consumption to a lesser and capital formation to a greater extent than either Hungarian domestic production or the foreign trade of the western countries examined.

In conclusion it is necessary to call the reader's attention repeatedly to the fact that all statements ventured here rely on highly aggregate input–output tables, imperfect from the statistical point of view and covering but a single year and a few countries.

In spite of these facts, the majority of the conclusions reached seem to accord with commonsense and with what is well known to those familiar with the conditions prevailing in the Hungarian economy. Of course, this is no proof in itself, just as the contrary will not prove the inaccuracy of any statement. All these conclusions await further investigation, as do many other generally accepted theorems.

At the same time, these facts are insufficient for the purpose of forming a comprehensive, qualitative judgment on the role of foreign trade in the Hungarian economy. To differ from or to bear a resemblance to other countries is in itself neither good nor bad – even in the case of richer countries. What is unfavourable from one point of view may be favourable or, at least, necessary from some other. For a comprehensive judgment many qualifications, conditions and factors should be considered which could not be examined in this paper, the factors of economic geography and economic history among them.

If the results of the analysis had to be summed up in a single conclusion, this could be worded as follows. The role, effect and relative importance of foreign trade in an economy are much too complex to lend themselves to characterization by a single indicator such as the ratio of the volume of exports to that of national income. Comprehensive characterization of the effects on the volume and the sectoral pattern of production and on primary inputs will show that this generally applied indicator somewhat exaggerates the role of foreign trade in shaping the structure of the Hungarian economy. The reciprocal effects of international exchange and economic structure are weaker and the Hungarian economy – especially in consumption – is less foreign-trade-oriented than indicated or justified by the given volume of external trade.

# 8. The problem of the central management of foreign trade turnover

## MARTON TARDOS

In Hungary, every branch of the economy is intimately connected with foreign trade. Therefore questions of control over foreign trade cannot be separated from those of the management of the economy as a whole.

Thus, the Hungarian economy is unambiguously a centrally controlled economy, which is looking for the most convenient form of central management, and within this for the best form of central control over foreign trade.

In past years, a system of management through central directives has prevailed. This system of control has been based on a procedure whereby central agencies, headed by the Planning Office, prepared the national plan, using a large number of experts. The plan has been drawn up, in general, on the basis of expert opinion, and with norms for the inputs of material, manpower, investment, etc. The norms have been determined taking account of experience and technological and economic estimates. These estimates have resulted in state directives concerning production and the use of capital, labour and raw materials. Among the directives there appeared export targets; the funds were extended to purchase permitted imports as well.

This system of directives has not been sufficiently efficient, for the following reasons:

(*a*) The conditions for directive control, that is, the flow and the processing of information, as well as the unambiguity of the criteria of decision making, have not been assured;

(*b*) Directives conflicted, and a system of orders which were often only partially enforced left many details unplanned.[1] Directives have generally been made only for product-groups and main sectors in an aggregated manner.

(*c*) Thus, the system of instructions did not determine every detail of the enterprises' activities. Hence, systems of material incentives have been

---

[1] Here we disregard the not infrequent case in which a non-feasible aim has been set by the plan-directive.

introduced, for example, for increased profits which, according to the basic considerations of the system, were intended to supply guidance for activities unregulated in the general instructions. Incentive schemes too were conflicting, as the efforts of one enterprise toward profit maximization were often thwarted by those of another. In the process of decision making, industry frequently disregarded the point of view of commerce, and *vice versa*. This has been possible because industry has been concerned only with the fulfilment of the target figures and has not been encouraged to co-ordinate its activity with those of other sectors.

(*d*) Another contradiction was that the information on production and domestic and foreign markets, which served as a basis for both plan-directives and the system of incentives, frequently became obsolete.

The above mentioned complex of contradictions often rendered the fulfilment of the directives impossible, or else the fulfilment did not lead to the results expected from the plan-calculations. Difficulties have frequently been increased by the lack of stocks – owing to the shortcomings of planning – required for the maintenance of continuous economic activity.

There are, basically, two ways to eliminate the problems of this system. The first one is a further strengthening of the directive method of central control, through the improvement of the flow of information and the introduction of programming. The second possibility lies in the operation of central management through economic regulators.

## THE OPTIMIZATION MODEL OF FOREIGN TRADE TURNOVER

Let us examine first the likely results of an improvement of the flow of information and the introduction of programming for the national economy and for the control of foreign trade.

The foundations for foreign trade decisions can be laid by a linear programming model of the following type:

$$(1) \quad \sum_k x_{jk} + \sum_i (z_{ij} - y_{ij}) - \sum_r \sum_k x_{rk} a_{rnj} = f_j$$

$$(2) \quad 0 \leqslant x_{jk} \leqslant G_{jk}$$

$$(3) \quad 0 \leqslant y_{ij} \leqslant P_{ij}$$

$$(4) \quad 0 \leqslant z_{ij} \leqslant E_{ij}$$

$$(5) \quad \sum_j \sum_k x_{jk} c_{jkl} \leqslant C_l$$

$$(6) \quad b'_i \leqslant \sum_j (Y_{ij} P_{ij} - z_{ij} q_{ij}) \leqslant b''_i$$

$$1 \leqslant i \leqslant m$$
$$1 \leqslant j \leqslant n$$
$$1 \leqslant r \leqslant n$$
$$1 \leqslant k \leqslant k'$$
$$1 \leqslant l \leqslant l'$$

We are looking for the optimum solution under conditions (1)–(6) which can be expressed alternatively by the following objective functions:

$$\text{maximize} \sum_{j=1}^{n} f_j \alpha_j;$$

$$\text{maximize} \sum_{i=1}^{m} \sum_{j=1}^{n} (y_{ij} p_{ij} - z_{ij} q_{ij}) \pi_i;$$

$$\text{maximize} \sum_{j=1}^{m} \sum_{k=1}^{k'} \sum_{l=1}^{l'} x_{jk} c_{jkl} \pi_l.$$

where

$x_{jk}$ = production of product $j$ by technique $k$.

$x_{rk}$ = production of product $r$ by technique $k$.

$y_{ij}$ = export of product $j$ to market $i$.

$z_{ij}$ = import of product $j$ from market $i$.

$a_{rkj}$ = input of product $j$ to product $r$ which is made by technique $k$.

$c_{jkl}$ = input of resource $l$ to product $j$ made by technique $k$.

$p_{ij}$ = export price of $j$ in market $i$.

$q_{ij}$ = import price of $j$ in market $i$.

$f_j$ = domestic demand for $j$ external to model.

$g_{jk}$ = maximum production of $j$ by technique $k$.

$P_{ij}$ = export constraint on $j$ in market $i$.

$E_{ij}$ = import constraint on $j$ in market $i$.

$C_l$ = constraint on disposal of limited resource $l$ by central authority.

$b_i' b_i''$ = minimum and maximum permitted values of balance of trade in market $i$.

Parameters of economic policy:

$\alpha_j$ = vector of final excess demand outside the model;

$\pi_i$ = value of currency (exchange rate) of country $i$;

$\pi_l$ = price for central resource $l$.

The system of constraints of the model comprises equations of 6 types:

The first equation expresses the commodity balance of product $j$. We subtract exports from the sum total of production and imports, and arrive at domestic consumption. The latter consists of two parts: the quantity required as inputs in other sectors and the demand external to the model.

The second equation is an expression for capacity-constraints imposed on the production of product $j$ by technique $k$.

The third equation denotes the constraints imposed on export sales of product $j$ in market $i$.

The fourth equation denotes constraints on import purchase of product $j$ in market $i$.

The fifth equation expresses the constraints for central resources, such as manpower, investment, etc.

The sixth equation, finally, contains the upper and lower bounds for the balance of trade in each market.

The model has, as usual, three alternative objective functions, or, possibly, some combination of these.

The first objective function is an expression of the maximization of domestic supply outside the model, according to certain weights. The second is a temporary aim, but one of great significance in many centrally planned economies: that of the improvement of the balance of payments.

The economic content of the third objective function is, essentially, a minimization of costs at a given price structure of the limited resources.

With the aid of the above programming model, we arrive at the optimal activities. Thus, it is possible to state that the application of programming methods and the formulation of their results as directives essentially corresponds to the idea developed by Barone that 'a collective state' is able to guide its economy rationally, if it is assured of a solution to the problems expressed in thousands of equations.[1]

At the time of Barone all this was only a dream; is it possible now, in the age of electronics?

Experience has taught us that we have come closer to the solution, but that it is still impossible, for the following two reasons:

First of all, there is not sufficient information at our disposal, and what we have is not exact. Hence, the relationships to be built into the model are not exact and frequently obsolete.

The second problem arises because the capacity limitations of electronic machines often compel us to simplify even the well observed interrelations. This is demonstrated, for example, by the fact that we have been obliged to linearize interdependencies, to calculate with product groups instead of products, etc.

Were we aiming at a plan based on the results of programming, we could expect similar conflicts in economic life as have arisen under directive management which does not make use of programming results. Most of the conflicts arise from the differences between the assumptions of the model and reality. There would be only one improvement in comparison to the system of plan-directives working along traditional lines: the plans

[1] Barone, E., 'The ministry of production in the collectivist state', F. A. Hayek (ed.), *Collectivist Economic Planning*. London, Routledge, 1935.

themselves would be based on abundant and more detailed information, as well as on a consistent estimation of the factors which were taken into consideration.

ECONOMIC REGULATORS SERVING CENTRAL MANAGEMENT

Another solution of the problem of central economic management is guidance making use of economic regulators. The recent reform of the mechanism of economic management in Hungary makes a very decisive step in this direction. The main postulates of the reform were the following:

— Enterprises are independent economic units determining the structure of their production and sales. Central agencies give directives to the enterprises only in exceptional cases. Central agencies for the management of the economy influence economic processes through economic regulators.

— Enterprises determine their own structure on the basis of their own system of preferences.

— Under the new system of management, the enterprises, freed from rigid directives, are able to adjust their activities easily to external market conditions.

— Central agencies are able to establish economic regulators which make the enterprises interested in the fulfilment of the national plan.

Our system can be formalized by stating that its basic element is the production enterprise. Every production enterprise is autonomous, choosing its own best production and sales structure. Thus, we are dealing with a programming model, with a system of constraints considered linear for the sake of easier handling, and with an objective function which is either linear or hyperbolic.

When describing the model, we denote its variables by $x$, $y$, $z$ and $w$. By $x$ we denote production, by $y$ export-sales and by $z$ sales on the domestic market. We use $w$ to denote competitive import purchases in supplementary computations. Technical coefficients characterizing the objective economic situation of the enterprise are denoted by minuscules of the alphabet, whereas the constraints are denoted by capital letters. Rent- and price-type economic regulators expressing decisions of central agencies are marked by minuscules of the greek alphabet, quantitative regulators by capital letters of the latter.

The first type of the equations is a commodity balance: expressing that production minus sales is equal to the change in stocks.

$$x_h - \sum_{w=i} y_{hi} - z_h = R_h \quad (h = 1 \ldots m; \, i = 1 \ldots n), \qquad (1)$$

where

$x_h$ = production of $h$.

$y_{hi}$ = export of $h$ to market $i$. In general, there are two export variables.

$z_h$ = home sale of product $h$.

$R_h$ = change in stocks of product $h$.

The second type of equation characterizes the bottlenecks of the enterprises, the utilization of capacities.

$$\sum_{h=1}^{m} x_h g_{ht} \leqslant G_t \quad (h = 1 \ldots m; t = 1 \ldots \text{T}), \tag{2}$$

where

$g_{ht}$ = claim of production $x_h$ from capacity $t$.

$G_t$ = capacity constraint $t$. (Under capacities we understand real equipment as well as other limited resources, like labour, or some kind of skilled labour, etc.)

The third type of equations describes the foreign demand, both in the socialist and non-socialist markets. If sales might be increased by reducing prices, we include several variables for each market for a product.

$$y_{hi} \leqslant P_{hi} \quad (h = 1 \ldots m; i = 1 \ldots n), \tag{3}$$

where $P_{hi}$ = demand for product $h$ in market $i$.

The fourth type of equations described the upper bounds of home demand. If sales might be increased here, as it was mentioned before, by reducing prices, we include several variables for each product, too.

Home demand for product $h$ consists of two elements: on one hand, the demand of enterprises included in the computation and, on the other hand, the demand of the outside world. In the course of the enterprise level computations, the demand for commodity $h$ of the given enterprise $j$ by the other enterprises included in the model is taken into account considering the latest information.

$$z_h \leqslant D_h^x + \sum_{\substack{r=1 \\ r \neq j}}^{n} \sum_{\substack{k=1 \\ k \neq h}}^{m} \bar{x}_{rk} d_{rkh} = D_h \quad (h = 1 \ldots k \ldots m; j = 1 \ldots r \ldots n), \tag{4}$$

where

$D_h$ = home demand for product $h$.

$D_h^x$ = demand for product $h$ from outside the model.

$d_{rkh}$ = the input of $h$ for the production of $x_{rk}$.

$x_{rk}$ = production of commodity $k$ in enterprise $r$ according to latest information.

If product $h$ is also available from imports and imports are free, a supplementary investigation is required. Sales of the home product are only possible if they are cheaper than the imported commodity, hence

if
$$p_{jh} \geqslant \bar{q}_{hi}\,(\lambda_i + \mu_{hi})\;(h = 1 \ldots m;\, i = 1 \ldots n), \qquad (5)$$

then
$$w_{hi} \leqslant E_{hi}$$

and
$$z_h + \sum_i w_{hi} \leqslant D_h$$

where

$p_{jh}$ = home price of product $h$.
$q_{hi}$ = import price of product $h$ in market $i$.
$\lambda_i$ = exchange multiplier (exchange rate) in market $i$.
$\mu_{hi}$ = the import duty on product $h$ in market $i$.
$w_{hi}$ = the import of product $h$ from market $i$.
$E_{hi}$ = the import supply of product $h$ from market $i$.

$P_{hi}$ and $D_h$ treated in general as upper bounds, determining the export and home demand, might be obligatory home or export sales prescribed by the central agencies ($Z_{hi}$ or $H_i$). In these cases, instead of inequalities, equalities are figuring in the model.

If exports are to be licensed and the foreign demand is larger than the licensed quantity ($\Delta_{hi}$), the upper bound of the enterprise model is the licensed quantity.

In the course of supplementary computations, if the competitive import demand exceeds the licensed quantity of imports ($E_{hi}$), the latter will be taken as an upper bound.

The most general form of the enterprise preference function is the vector of profits. Its elements consist of the difference between returns and expenditure.

$$\sum_{h=1}^{m} \sum_{i=1}^{n} y_{hi}\,q_{hi}\,(\lambda_i + v_j) + \sum_{k=1}^{m} z_h\,p_{jh} - \sum_{h=1}^{m} x_h\,\theta_h - \Theta_j \pm N_j \to \max \qquad (6)$$

where

$q_{hi}$ = export price for product $h$ on market $i$.
$\lambda_i$ = exchange multiplier (exchange rate) in market $i$.
$v_j$ = government compensation (export subsidy) for exports of enterprise $j$.
$p_{jh}$ = home price for product $h$.
$\theta_h$ = variable costs of product $h$.

*Marton Tardos*

$\Theta_j$ = constant costs of enterprise $j$.[1]

$N_j$ = production tax $(-)$, price-equalization $(+)$, subsidy $(+)$, for enterprise $j$.

According to the existing rules, stimulation of employees and workers to increase profits is indirect, through the increase of the profit-sharing fund, more precisely, through the ratio of the latter to the total amount of wages and salaries. The profit-sharing fund is calculated by a complicated formula, consisting of the profit and the wages salaries themselves, as well as four supplementary items:

— the capital/labour ratio corrected, in order to equalize the incomes, by a coefficient (wage-multiplier) varying by industrial branches;

— the graded progressive taxation of the profit-sharing fund: $f(\alpha,\beta,\gamma)$;

— the special regulation of the enterprise average wage; as the increase of the average wage – which has to come from the profit-sharing fund – is taxed identically with the latter.[2]

— and the regulation affecting the distribution of the profit-sharing fund among the three categories of workers and employees. The latter are centrally divided into three categories; for each category the maximum profit-sharing/wage ratio and, in the same way, the distribution of the fund itself is determined.

For the sake of simplifying the already too sophisticated formula, we introduce a new production-sale variable: $x'_{hi}$ expressing the production and the sales of product $h$ on market $i$. Among the markets here the home market is also included.

Thereafter we formulate the alternate objective function of the enterprise:

$$\frac{\alpha\beta}{\tau\beta+M} \cdot f(\alpha,\beta,\gamma) \cdot \frac{1}{Y+\sum_{h=1}^{m} x_h l_h v_h} = \max, \qquad (7)$$

where the first fraction is the taxed profit-sharing fund and the second is the reciprocal of the corrected wage bill, and the symbols are defined as follows:

$\alpha$ = accountable profit $\sum_{h=i}^{m}\sum_{i=1} x'_{hi} l_{hi} - \Theta \pm N + \Xi$.

$\beta$ = actual staff multiplied by the fixed average wage $(L + \sum x'_h l_h)\sigma$.

[1] The major part of costs are centrally fixed prices for inputs, taxes and interest rates. Therefore, they are treated in the model as economic regulators.

[2] An additional regulation temporarily excludes a rise of the average wage exceeding 4 per cent.

[3] Since 1968 the formula has been modified three times to a limited degree.

$\gamma$ = system of graded progressive taxation.

N = production tax ($-$), price equalization ($+$), subsidy ($+$) for enterprise $j$.

$\Theta$ = constant cost of enterprise.

$\Xi$ = constant costs due to average wage increase.

$\sigma$ = fixed average wage.

L = constant manpower demand.

$l_h$ = variable manpower demand of product $h$.

$\tau$ = wage coefficient.

M = stock of fixed and working assets.

Y = constant wage costs corrected by maximum of profit-sharing fund each category.

$v_h$ = variable wage cost of product $h$ corrected by maximum of profit-sharing fund each category.

The model of the whole economy consists of all the enterprise models, characterized above, as well as of the system of central constraints.

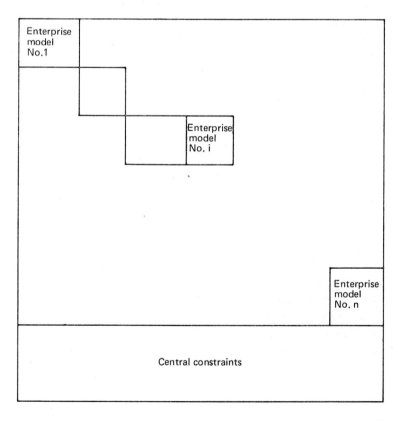

*Marton Tardos*

There are two important questions in such a model for the centre. First, to what degree do the enterprises draw upon central resources and secondly, to what degree do the enterprises supply their products to the economy among others exports.

For this purpose the central economic plan is drawn up. It consists of two parts: on the one hand it determines the available resources, and on the other hand, it weighs up what quantity of goods has to be exported. In the framework of the new mechanism, this is not done by the central authorities. Instead, they introduce economic regulators in the expectation that under their impact the plan – which in that case may be called central economic expectation – will be fulfilled.

The central expectations of the model are as follows:
certain items of domestic supply;
balance, and certain items, of trade turnover;
balance of state budget;
all personal incomes;
justified enterprise applications for short-term and long-term credits;
sum total of enterprise development funds;
sum total of enterprise reserve funds.

In order to stimulate the fulfilment of central economic expectations, the centre uses two kinds of regulators: prices and quantitative restrictions.

The system of the regulators of enterprise activities is the following:

Price regulators:
taxes and dues on wages, social security;
charge for use of funds; interest on working assets;
production tax on enterprises; government aid to enterprises (price equalization or subsidy);
price-multiplier which works as exchange rate;
government compensation for exports;
customs duty on products;
wage-multiplier of enterprises;
gradually progressive taxation of profit from profit-sharing fund;
basic average wage of enterprises;
maximum price for products;
tax on development fund;
share of enterprise amortization fund resting with enterprise;
share of enterprise profit which has to be put into the reserve fund;
value for correction of amortization given to enterprise by state budget, or reserved centrally;

accountable profit of enterprise;
basic wage payable by enterprise;
system of taxation.

Quantitative restrictions or instructions as regulators:

export licences;
import licences;
obligatory supply quota for domestic market;
obligatory export targets.

## SOME PROPERTIES OF THE FORMALIZED MODEL OF THE NEW ECONOMIC MECHANISM

The economic model outlined briefly here is a specific model. The reader familiar with programming will easily recognize that it is very similar to a programming model divided into enterprise-units. If we disregard the system of central regulators, then this model and the linear alternative of the competitive equilibrium model simplified by Dorfman, Samuelson and Solow are essentially the same.

The competitive equilibrium model is a model consisting of partial units (enterprises), which is proved to have a solution, under certain conditions, which is optimal from the point of view of both the enterprises and the national economy.[1] This optimum solution is accompanied by prices leading automatically to the equilibrium of supply and demand. In all partial models these prices are uniform and are equal to the marginal costs of the products, and to the marginal productivity of resources.[2]

The differences between the abstract model of competititive equilibrium and that of the new mechanism are demonstrated primarily by four factors:
— First, while the prices for central resources are uniform for all sectors in the competitive equilibrium model, they frequently differ, especially for foreign currency, for different enterprises in the model of the new economic mechanism.
— Secondly, the uniform prices for products in the competitive equilibrium model ensure that every producer arrives at a profit at these prices, whereas the model of the new system of economic management is only able to achieve this by subsidies, or by a redistribution of the profits among enterprises.
— Thirdly, the centre regulates production and consumption not only by means of prices.

[1] By optimum here we understand a Pareto-optimum.
[2] Dorfman, Samuelson and Solow, *Programming and Economic Analysis*, McGraw-Hill, 1958.

— The fourth, and perhaps the most important difference, lies in the objective function of the enterprise itself. In the competitive equilibrium models the objective of the enterprise is either minimization of costs or maximization of returns, or maximization of profit. In the model of our economic mechanism, the maximization of the profit-sharing fund of the wage-earners represents a system of preferences at least equal to that of profit, or, taking into consideration its impact, an even stronger one. At the same time, account has to be taken of the fact that in every case where a part of the income of wage-earners has been made dependent on the profits of the enterprise, the increase of the profit-sharing fund becomes an objective of the enterprise. In this case, as mentioned before, the enterprise objective function is a rational fraction, with variables of the second degree both in the numerator and the denominator and expressing a gradually progressive system of taxation.

So what is the difference from the economic point of view between the abstract model of the new economic mechanism and that of competitive equilibrium?

The first difference is that the mechanism does not value the resources of the national economy in a uniform way for all enterprises in this model. Moreover, even a given enterprise passes different judgments on the resources in connection with different business transactions. If, for example, in the abstract model of our mechanism, the foreign currency multiplier is 60 Ft per dollar and there is a possibility of producing one dollar by the input of 61 Ft, then enterprises not receiving state compensation will ignore it, whereas others will accept it gladly, as state compensation makes such a transaction profitable for them.

If an enterprise is receiving state compensation and it has the choice whether to increase its production by export activities or by those of import-substitution, it will choose the export transaction, even if its economic efficiency is worse in this respect.

The second set of differences is that an efficient enterprise is not sufficiently stimulated to expand production, compared to producers with worse results. Both sets of differences disturb rational decision making and the formation of an optimal structure of production and distribution.

The third set of differences arises because there are direct quantitative regulators, apart from prices. The conservation of quantitative regulators in certain spheres does not seem unjustified on the basis of empirical evidence. Without them it is impossible to fulfil the central expectations.

In so far as we insist upon the central determination of the parameters of productive activities, we require, even in a competitive equilibrium model, regulators other than prices. All this justifies only the use of direct regulators, not the actual degree of their use in the economy.

Finally, we have arrived at the fourth set of differences between the two models; the impact of the maximization of the profit-sharing fund, which is a specific enterprise objective function. First, every such system of management which determines the participation fund on the basis of the wages paid and the profit realized, has the common feature that it cannot assure the uniformity of the marginal productivity of the resources in sectors or enterprises. Were the profit-sharing fund calculated exclusively on the basis of the profit/wage ratio, we would have to face the following problem: we should have to evaluate the activities of the enterprise, which, though useful from the point of view of the national economy and even increasing enterprise profit, are unfavourable from the point of view of the participation fund in every case where the ratio of marginal profit and wages starts to decline.

Secondly, another specific problem arises in that other funds are playing a part in the calculation of the profit-sharing fund. Thirdly, the profit-sharing fund may be used to regulate average wages. In that case, the marginal productivity of the central resources will differ from enterprise to enterprise, owing to differences in the wage funds ratio. This means that, because of the enterprise objective function, the model will not converge towards an equilibrium solution. This will lead to a situation in which, depending on the wage fund/profit ratio, certain enterprises will refuse even profitable transactions, while others are gladly accepting trade which makes a loss. A further feature of this situation is that the same business offer will be taken up by one enterprise and rejected by another.

There are, in general, three ways to stimulate the enterprises:

(1) Not to connect the incomes of the wage earners of the enterprise directly with the results of the latter. In this case, the enterprise objective function will not influence the convergence of the model. A similar situation arises if only the incomes of the managers depend to some extent on profits.

(2) To make the enterprise profit-sharing fund depend on the funds and wages.

(3) To do the same as in (2) with the difference that the profit-sharing fund is used as a general regulating tool of incomes as is done in Hungary.

We have already discussed the shortcomings of the second and third solutions. Against the first solution, we can only say that here the material incentives for the people employed by the enterprise are not directly dependent on the achievement of that enterprise. This system can only be efficient if the results of the enterprise have a social significance or moral value and if the state agencies have sound judgment and sufficient standing to be able to allot bonuses from profits to the employees of the enterprise without stipulations, thus fostering the interests of the national economy.

Were it possible to fulfil these conditions, another problem is raised which we have not yet discussed. The activities of the management are usually aimed at laying the foundations for the future of the enterprise. Hence, it is not right to make their incomes dependent only on the results achieved at the present, for this may interfere with the long-term aims of development.

Beside these four main differences, there is another basic difference between the two models. The set of objective functions of the profit-maximizing competitive equilibrium system is easy to survey. But the complicated objective function of the model of the new economic mechanism itself limits its predictive value. This complicated objective function means that the managers of the enterprise are in a difficult position, if they want to choose between various development possibilities.

We have also to recognize another difference in that the ideal world of competitive equilibrium exists only in abstractions. In reality, the economy is much more complex than in the model where competitive equilibrium prevails. There is no market economy where optima occur in the manner described above, nor where equilibrium prices come into being in the way we have outlined. The conditions of the competitive equilibrium model which are alien to reality are as follows:
— the principle of diminishing returns;
— the divisibility of resources;
— the unambiguous character of enterprise preferences.

Further, it is well known that in the linear model of competitive equilibrium the price system does not determine the optimal activities in a unique way but that there are alternative optima.

Therefore, we would certainly be justified in diverging from a system of regulations which is in accordance with the competitive equilibrium model if we thereby eliminated the shortcomings of the latter. But it seems that certain specific features of our system of regulations do not eliminate factors disturbing equilibrium.

After examining the abstract model of the Hungarian economic mechanism, economists must start now, following the introduction of the system of regulations, to investigate the differences between model and reality.

The new system of central management in Hungary starts out from three important assumptions: first, it assumes that enterprise activities are determined in an unambiguous and uncontradictory manner by the maximization of both profits and the profit-sharing fund. Secondly, it assumes that the centre is in possession of correct technological and economic information. Finally, it assumes that the regulators are indeed able to influence economic activity in the desired way.

Future economic research has, as an important task, to control these assumptions, and to reveal the causes of the divergence between assumed and actual economic activities.

## 9. Conceptual changes in the Hungarian external payments system within the new economic mechanism

KÁROLY KÖVER

As about forty per cent of Hungary's national income is exchanged through trade, the authorities are concerned with trends in foreign trade; more specifically, with how the terms of trade and the structure and geographical distribution of trade affect economic growth, technical progress and structural change. Given the basis of state ownership of the means of production, the central plan remains valid, but it is implemented not through a system of directives, but through one of incentives. So the major policy decisions are taken centrally, and the incentives to management are geared to these decisions. Thus, within limits, the enterprises can act on their own responsibility.

### THE FIRST MODEL OF THE HUNGARIAN MONETARY SYSTEM BETWEEN 1950 AND 1967

Foreign trade is usually carried on by the exchange of currencies. The exporter sells commodities abroad, and the currency received is exchanged at a home bank. The importer purchases goods abroad while at home he purchases foreign exchange to pay for the imports. This exchange can be carried on both in an exchange system that is exempt from any direct restriction, and in an exchange control system. The rate of exchange has a direct influence on the amount of imports and exports.

Up to 1968 the foreign exchange policy operated through direct instructions. The theoretical starting point of the monetary system prevailing in the years between 1950 and 1967 was that as foreign currency could not be regarded as a commodity, it was not exchanged on the market.

When goods were exported, the foreign exchange was handed over to the central bank; when goods were imported, the required foreign exchange was distributed among the various enterprises, as set out in the import plan.

The second starting point was that if foreign exchange is not a commodity it cannot have an economically formed price; its rate of exchange is not an active factor, only an accounting unit.

166

The third thesis was that the rate of exchange of foreign currency under socialism does not influence the development of foreign trade, and because of this it is not a factor in the formation of the balance of payments. The rate of exchange does not connect the structure of prices within the country with those on the world market in key currencies, and therefore it does not have a significant effect on the volume, structure and geographical distribution of trade.

Because of this, the rate of exchange was eliminated from the foreign trade management system. But, as even under socialism products take the form of commodities, the effect of the rate of exchange was not eliminated automatically; rather it had to be neutralized in a suitable way. This was effected by the introduction of a buffer mechanism. The buffer mechanism had to operate so that the divergencies and their probable effects did not contravene the central plan or export and import plans. On the one hand the interests of the enterprise were not affected by them, and on the other hand the prices of imported commodities did not influence the internal price structure fixed by the authorities.

The buffer mechanism functioned in our country through a significantly raised rate of exchange for the forint. This mechanism balanced the differences between home and foreign prices in both export and import. Clearly, if the given level of the rate of exchange did not directly influence the above mentioned aspects of foreign trade then it had to work through the buffer mechanism. The more over-valued the home currency was in relation to the export turnover, the larger the amount that streamed out of the buffer stock in more or less direct proportion to the size of the over-valuation.

The neutralization of the role of the rate of exchange of currencies was the consequence of the theoretical standpoint which denied the effectiveness and the advantages of comparative costs in the Hungarian situation, or rather it meant that the doctrine of comparative costs was taken to be the theoretical justification for the preservation of a semi-colonial economic structure. However, the static theory of comparative advantage was not completed by any dynamic dialectical conception. For Hungary in the forties and fifties the free application of the static theory of comparative costs would have meant the preservation of a backward economic structure. Because the industrialization of the country occurred in an economically more advanced environment than ours it demanded that newly created industry should not feel the suffocating effect of comparative disadvantage. Eliminating the effect of the rate of exchange created the possibility of eliminating the influence of static comparative costs in economic development. But this did not mean that it was replaced by a dynamic conception of comparative advantages. On account of this the introduction of the buffer mechanism represented a significantly realistic step. The principle of value, effective on the market, had a positive influence not on the enterprises' interests and economy but on the buffer mechanism. As a result both the producing and trading enterprises became insensitive to market influences. For the sake of the higher profits to be gained through foreign trade, they cut inputs and raised prices as high as possible. The material interest of foreign trade enterprises was not to increase their profit through realistic calculation, but at the beginning to maximize the volume of exports, and later to meet the targets of the given gross exchange earning plan. The interdependence between exchange earnings and input costs receded into the background in the system of material interests. The producing enterprises and foreign trade companies were not interested in the structure of foreign trade. The production and export of uneconomical goods was not associated with any disadvantage compared with that of more economical ones. Better business was not rewarded by proportionally higher profits.

As a result of the policy of industrialization a radical transformation had taken place in the country's economic structure. The national income had grown in comparison to the pre-war level and industry's contribution to the national income had become overwhelming. A large number of new enterprises had come into existence whose economical operation, and through this the optimization of the contribution of foreign trade to growth, had become matters of the greatest importance for the development of the national economy. Conditions had to be created under which the producing and marketing units would be interested not in gross results generally, but in growth.

In order to reform foreign exchange policy, a reform had first to be made in the price system which ought to provide information to both producer and consumer about the costs of production of goods. Further, a realistic rate of exchange had to be determined. The rate of exchange had to indicate the balance of the comparative cost structure. There should also be a proper system of incentives fundamentally based on profit; in this sense the rate of exchange must create a reasonable connection between the home and foreign rate of exchange. It must connect the home and foreign price structures; thus the share of economically produced goods in our exports should increase and uneconomical exports should definitely diminish. For this reason both producing enterprises and foreign trade companies must become interested in increasing their profits through export. Foreign trade must actively influence the development of the national economy. Branches of the economy that most increase their sales in foreign markets must be encouraged.

Economically, the rate of exchange and the price system must fulfil the following tasks:

(1) They should enable the forint to be realistically compared with the rouble and the dollar. This has two important parts. First: the rate of exchange must approximately express that ratio of values that is really represented by the various currencies. Secondly, the rate of exchange must facilitate the continuation of home monetary, credit and foreign exchange policies on both national and enterprise levels.

(2) The rate of exchange must make the composition of exports and imports economic on national and enterprise scales, and increase their efficiency. It must provide an indicator for the national economy of when the structure of exports and imports is favourable or unfavourable and it should encourage the operation of the country's international trade and monetary relations on the basis of comparative advantage.

(3) The rate of exchange should promote the movement of assets between countries (mixed enterprises) to rationalize the international division of labour.

(4) It should contribute to the rational development of foreign trade in proper relation with the country's economic and political interests.

(5) The rate of exchange must, last but not least, ensure that the balance of payments of the country is in equilibrium over, say, five or six years.

It is clear from this list of targets that, according to our conception, there should be a single rate of exchange for any foreign trade business deal. This means that forint costs serve as the basis of calculation for every foreign transaction. The application of multiple rates of exchange conflicts with the idea of the national economy as a single unit, makes impossible the unified application of comparative inputs, destroys the unified money and exchange policies and creates uncertainty, which brings subjectivism into economic life.

Concerning the determination of the level of the rate of exchange, there are three concepts to consider:

(1) the rate of exchange which links the price level of the home currency and the key currency dominating the world market;

(2) the average rate of exchange ruling for exports;

(3) the marginal rate of exchange for exports.

According to the first concept of the basis of the establishment of the rate of exchange, purchasing power parity of the given currency against the key currency is accepted. It can be corrected according to the condition of the balance of payments.

*Károly Köver*

As the domestic value of the currency is determined by the general price level prevailing in the country, the currency parity is a link between the domestic price level and that prevailing on the world market.[1]

This means that the currency parity is established according to its domestic value on the basis of an average value of a quantity of goods as if exchanged for gold, or a currency that embodies gold and plays an important role in the world market. This, of course, does not mean that the national and international labour inputs of exports and imports must coincide. It only implies that the average price level of the country should be brought into harmony by establishing parity between the currency's gold content and its purchasing power.

If the currency parity is established at a level higher than is merited by its purchasing power, the domestic price level expressed in gold will be higher than the international price level. This will be demonstrated by exports, since the home prices or domestic cost of exported goods will be higher than the price on the world market, and the opposite for imports.

If parity is calculated on the basis of the price level and it has officially been accepted, then the direct conversion of the prices of goods and their comparison with world market prices offer a basis by which to calculate whether it is worth exporting or importing certain commodities. If the currency parity expresses the average price level, commodities of which the home price is lower than the world price will be exported. The lower the home price compared to the world market price the more economical is the production and export of the given article, and *vice versa*. Apart from the selling and purchasing prices, the transportation and storing costs must also be considered.

Of course, currency parity is not the only factor determining trade policy, but nevertheless it is a factor. Consequently production of goods for export and home consumption should be increased when the home price shows a favourable picture compared to the market price or when it seems that within a reasonable time limit the price of commodities might fall below the average price level.

It follows that, based on a realistic parity, the economic nature of foreign trade can be better measured, both on foreign trade company and national

[1] In our press one encounters statements which imply that the starting point for establishing the rate of exchange is not the reciprocal relations between the rates of exchange, but the currency's 'exchange value'. But the exchange value is a ratio with two values, one in the denominator, the other in the numerator. The value of paper money is represented by its representative value in circulation, namely, the value that is represented in circulation by the unit quantity of money. The comparison of the values of representation gives in the case of unexchangeable currencies their 'exchange value'. This – in myopinion – can be obtained by comparing the price levels.

economy levels, than by the official parity that is unrelated to purchasing power.

It also follows that the socialist currency parity is expressed by the gold content, but the gold content also depends on the relative price level of the given currency.

When determining the currency parity, it is not so much the relation between the price of the respective goods and the gold price that is important, but the ratio between the price levels in the various countries and the quantitative relation between the various currencies which is expressed by the gold content.

At present the gold standard is not functioning, and gold is not a medium of circulation, so it is not the gold content that determines prices and the currency purchasing power. So it is not the currency gold content that determines the prices of commodities but it is the average level of the prices of commodities that determines the representative or nominal gold content of the currency. However, the establishment of the gold content meets the requirements for expressing the price relations. Price relations between currencies must be able to be expressed in the same way in every currency. It is the purchasing power of the currency that should determine the currency's gold content, taking into consideration the purchasing power and gold content of other currencies.

An improperly established currency parity could have a negative effect in two fields:

1. It disallows the measurement of the profitability of foreign trade companies; it hinders the realization of economic foreign trade, and necessitates the introduction of manipulations (foreign exchange factors, premium or discount on exchange, etc.).

2. It also affects the invisible trade turnover, mainly foreign tourism.

Not even a socialist state can deliberately establish its currency's value and gold content so that they express existing economic relations. The establishment of the home price level is within the scope of the socialist state, but having established prices the currency parity must be determined on the basis of price levels that exist externally.

The unity of national enterprise interests concerning foreign trade also makes it important to establish the parity in a relatively realistic way. If the parity is properly established then a harmony between the interest of the enterprise and those of the national economy is more easily established.

It is worthwhile to establish parity on the basis of purchasing power as far as foreign countries are concerned. The accusation of dumping has frequently been levelled against socialist countries by Western countries.

*Károly Köver*

Establishing currency parity in harmony with the purchasing power will prevent the application of discriminatory measures of trade policy against socialist countries on the grounds that they export considerably below the home price.

EXPORT–OUTPUT AVERAGE RATE OF EXCHANGE

The average export–output ratio or 'key' indicates how many forints of home input are needed at the producer's price level on average in order to acquire through commodity export the foreign currency unit that serves as a basis.

This average output key might serve as the starting point in foreign trade when selling or purchasing foreign currencies.

The use of the average output key as a rate of exchange requires that some commodities can be exported from the country at more favourable prices than the average.

No particular problem emerges here as the value of the foreign currency received 'includes' all the home inputs; moreover some profit remains as well. But there is a difficulty since half of the exports are produced by a home input less favourable than the average. For these goods the value of the foreign currency received does not cover the cost of the home inputs, and hence it becomes uneconomical to export. In this case, in order to prevent the cessation of exports which are necessary for the national interest, the health of the national economy and the equilibrium of the balance of payments require that a subsidy be applied. The subsidy must be fixed and paid by the respective state authorities to the exporting producer. The subsidy must cover the difference between the whole input and the foreign exchange earning and it must secure some profit for the producing enterprise. To encourage the enterprises to amend their export structure and input proportions the subsidy must gradually diminish.

Customs duties are closely related to the rate of exchange from the point of view of comparative advantages. When determining the import structure national interest might come into the picture outweighing economic criteria. Such interests include the protection of certain branches of the economy, securing a home market for the branches of industry to be developed and maintaining the level of employment. For such purposes customs levels should be fixed so that with a given rate of exchange the imported goods cannot compete with those produced at home.

An important economic interdependence follows: the higher we fix the rate of exchange of the home currency in comparison with its price level (the higher its normal gold content is) the higher the customs level and the wider the sphere of protected commodities should be, and *vice versa*.

## MARGINAL RATE OF EXCHANGE

The theory of the marginal rate of exchange was stated in the Hungarian economic literature in the following way: 'marginal rate of exchange is not the export–output cost of the worst single deal, but *that average rate of exchange of the worst band of export deals that can be held economically motivated* – in given circumstances – to keep the equilibrium of balance of payments'. The lowest fifth or tenth part of exports arranged according to the criteria of efficiency represents that basket of goods whose average rate of exchange can be regarded as a 'reasonable' marginal rate of exchange.

The marginal rate of exchange should have the following functions: in foreign trade management the rate of exchange should be directed towards economic decisions in four respects:

(1) For export producers and exporters cost margins must be such as to determine the level of output which is in the best interest of the economy as a whole.

(2) In the case of imports there must be an indication of the cost level above which *in general* it is worth importing rather than producing at home.

(3) For the producers of import substituting products it must be noted up to what level it is worth saving exchange.

(4) Those who use exchanges must be informed about the consequences of increasing or diminishing the use of foreign exchanges.

So according to the marginal rate of exchange the increase of exports is reasonable until the import articles to be purchased with this foreign exchange at that marginal rate of exchange are no longer more economical than home production. This is an export–import marginal rate of exchange.

Only this marginal rate of foreign exchange is able to inform the economic units up to what cost level it is economical for the national economy to increase exports, and where the expansion of import-substituting production becomes unprofitable.[1]

One can well discern from the concept of the marginal rate of exchange as explained above that this theory places the effectuation of comparative advantages at the centre of foreign trade and of any economic activity which connects with it and works towards its realization.

The marginal rate of exchange must also be linked with a suitable system of incentives: the maximization of the yield must be central to the material interests.

The marginal rate of exchange theory opposes the average output theory

---

[1] Sándor Balázsi, 'Producers' prices, foreign exchange prices, price levelling', *Közgazdasági Szemle*, pp. 1065–6, 1964.

and considers the latter less suitable for co-ordinating the individual interests with those of the national economy in the field of foreign trade. The biggest deficiency of the application of an average rate of exchange is that on this basis favourable and unfavourable exports and imports are not differentiated at the national economy level, but exports are divided into two parts, one of which is more favourable than the average, and the other of which is less. But an export which is less favourable than the average at an economy-wide level can still be comparatively advantageous. Since the average output rate of exchange excludes the less favourable part of exports, it requires that an extraordinarily wide range of goods should be subsidized, and the system of incentives becomes clumsy and breaks the principle of unified rates of exchange since, due to the subsidies, a differentiated *de facto* rate of exchange is created. In contrast, with a marginal rate of exchange, subsidies have to be allotted for only a comparatively narrow range of export products.

Comparing the respective types of rates of exchange we can make the following statement:

(1) If we start from the export trade, from the commodity structure and its price level, and suppose that exports are composed of commodities more favourable than those in the average input proportion, then it is not the average output but the marginal rate of exchange that is more acceptable economically. In this case it almost coincides with the average rate of exchange which would be received on the basis of the gross national product.

(2) But if the composition of exports is such that the export commodities have not been properly selected and their input proportions do not differ from the average of the gross national product, then the average output key rather than the marginal rate of exchange must be applied.

It can therefore be supposed that in our situation it is better to apply the average output key to find an initial value of the rate of exchange than to look for the marginal rate of exchange.

THE CHANGE IN THE METHOD OF FINANCING TRADE

The commodity character of money, and the application of the rate of exchange as an economic category in the home financing of foreign trade, demand a unification of external and domestic financing. Under the old economic mechanism, the export producer received the home prices of the commodities when they were handed over to the exporting foreign trade company. The price of commodities was paid independently of the date at which the value of the exchange was received from abroad, of whether the goods were sold there for cash or on credit, and of the quantitative relationship between home price and the market price abroad. The case of imports is the opposite: the enterprises importing commodities from abroad paid for the import when the foreign trade company delivered the goods irrespective of the extent to which the foreign currency payment preceded the home delivery of the commodities. In import there was no direct connection between the purchase price in external exchange and the domestic delivery price, and between both and the input which the country had to use to earn the exchange needed for import. In this case imports were more favoured than exports. As a result, there was a steady pressure on the currency authorities from the importers, who demanded more and more foreign exchange. As the Hungarian economy is highly import-sensitive, the balance of payments was adversely affected, while efforts to export were hindered.

The new method of financing foreign trade has removed this disparity. In the case of exports the exporting company receives the value of the commodities in forints only when the commodities have been sold abroad, and when the exchange value of the export has been transferred into the country from abroad. The export earnings of the exporting company, and thereby its profits, are in direct relation to the selling price abroad. The export subsidy is not general but particular; it is not given for commodities but to the whole company, and its size must gradually diminish. This system – it is supposed – will force the companies towards the most profitable composition of exports and will induce them to cut inputs. This they will have to do on account of the predetermined and gradually diminishing size of the export subsidy. In order to promote exports, payment documents of good security are discounted by the National Bank. Such documents might be: credits opened by a first class bank, first class bills and other credit documents guaranteed by a bank. This means that the exporting companies are free to give short term foreign credits. But at the same time they must reckon with the risks of giving credit. The risk of giving credit is a factor in the credit insurance costs introduced recently. When opening export credits longer than a year the companies in question remain under direct control. To carry on such an activity they require a permit from the central bank. Possessing this, and other guarantees demanded by the bank, the credit documents can be discounted. This does not mean that the bank purchasing the documents has underwritten the crediting risks as well. Even after discounting the bank retains rights of claim against the company.

Parity between the forint and foreign exchange financing has also been created for imports. The delivery price of import goods is determined by multiplying the purchasing price in foreign currency by the valid rate of exchange. The customs duties, the value of various import services and the costs of financing must be added to the above price. To control imports there is an obligatory deposit of some multiple of the value of the import in the authorized bank.

To be able to purchase commodities abroad, a company must fulfil two conditions. The first is that it should acquire an import permit from the foreign trade authorities. Secondly, to buy the foreign exchange necessary for the import and to cover expenses, the company must possess the required quantity of forints. The costs involved in purchasing foreign exchange can be covered from two sources:

(1) The company's own floating balances. If it possesses an import permit the company has the right to decide how to use the commodities, that is, the bank is obliged to sell the necessary exchange to the company.

(2) The credits given by the bank: the bank forms its credit policy according to the central plan. The credit policy is an important economic control for influencing imports territorially and structurally and bringing the balance of payments into equilibrium. The bank is not obliged by the existence of an import licence to grant the import credit. The bank gives a credit only if it is in accordance with its credit policy: for example, if the import will in the future have a favourable effect on the balance of payments, and will not unnecessarily increase stocks, etc.

The national and international price structure became interdependent through trade. The relation between the inner and outer price structures exercises a significant influence on the composition of trade, on its size and geographical arrangement. At the same time the new monetary system creates the possibility for foreign price proportions to influence home prices, and through this consumption. Accordingly there is a tendency for price ratios to be equalized. The aspects of this equalizing tendency which are regarded as unfavourable from the point of view of the development of the national economy are to be limited by the system of customs duties and subsidies. As a matter of fact, the result is that the competition between the importing and home producing areas is limited, and the external purchasing areas can select among relatively wider assortments of goods for home consumption.

Customs duties have become a major part of domestic input and so they have emerged as price forming factors. Under the old economic mechanism customs duties did not play this part so directly. But there was a significant difference between the external purchasing price and that fixed by the authorities, which was settled among the budget items. Though there was a parallel customs system that had no influence on domestic price formation, the difference between the import price and the authorized domestic price accrued to the budget as an indirect tax. As a result it was not the customs duties that determined the domestic prices of import commodities but the difference between the authorized home price and the purchasing price which decided the size of the tax. Under the old system therefore, tariff returns did not have an export-increasing effect.

Under the new economic management system the customs return is used as an export incentive. Exports are not burdened with the customs duties that are used to reduce imports, but the high import ratio built into our exports is, and the ever accumulating customs duties would represent unfavourable competition for Hungarian commodities as compared to those of other countries.

That is the reason why the importer, as soon as he certifies that the imported goods, in some way or other, represent a certain part of export goods, receives from the state the amount of the customs duties paid on that part of the import.

The principle of organization of the Hungarian monetary economy will remain the monetary monopoly. This means that foreign exchange obtained from exports must be sold to the National Bank by exporters, which is the only source of the necessary foreign currencies for importers.

But the respective tasks of the monetary monopoly have undergone a radical change. In past years one of the most important tasks of this monopoly was that it should eliminate the effect of external price structures in domestic commodity and money relations. In the new economic system it should create an active link between foreign and domestic prices. Besides, the monetary monopoly must formulate and put into effect the exchange policy rules and principles necessary to stimulate economic efficiency and give proper protection to the country's economy. It is another task of the monetary monopoly to take part in currency collaboration on an international level, considering mutual interests and partner countries' monetary policies. Having noted these basic principles it seems proper to emphasize that the monetary monopoly as an institution of the socialist state should not be identified with some particular system of international settlements. Monetary monopoly is not tied to bilateral or multilateral settlement or to convertibility. The various kinds of settlement are formed and applied by the monetary monopoly according to its basic policies.

# 10. The terms of trade in the foreign trade of Hungary 1957–1967

ADAM MARTON

## 1. INTRODUCTION

Foreign trade plays an important role in the Hungarian economy. The large volume of imports has been determined primarily by two factors: a scarcity of raw materials and the economic structure of the country. In many sectors of the economy, most of the raw material supplies as well as an important part of the energy necessary for the country have to be provided through foreign trade. Imports of investment goods have also been considerable.

Exports have made rapid progress during recent years and in 1967 they were two and a half times greater than in 1958, considerably exceeding the 125 per cent increase in industrial production. Imports have increased at an even faster rate than exports and in 1967 their volume was almost three times larger than in 1958.

As a result of the relatively large foreign trade turnover[1] the various factors affecting exports and imports have had a very strong effect on the economic life of the country; this paper deals with one factor which is more or less independent of our country and is influenced by the world-market: i.e. with the development of import and export prices.

The statistical examination of external trade prices was started in Hungary in 1957; the organization both from the methodological and practical point of view has been set going with the responsible participation of the author.

In view of the fact that external trade prices suffered considerable changes during 1958, it was fortunate that the first year of price observation was 1957, since it has thus been possible to investigate three consecutive periods of paramount importance in the course of the past ten years.

From 1957 to 1967, a general tendency of decreasing prices in external trade could be observed though the rate of decrease varied from one year to the other.

[1] Exports, in 1967, amounted to about 30% of the GNP. (In Hungary, as in the other socialist countries, the method of GNP computation differs slightly from the practice adopted by the Western countries; using the latter, the share of exports would become somewhat less).

178

Imports from socialist countries showed in 1958 a price decrease of 4%, and in the following years, 1965 inclusive, a consistent though less important decreasing trend from year to year. 1966–67 is remarkable again for a larger decrease so that, in 1967, the price level had decreased by about 13% in ten years.

Export prices have shown an overall decrease of roughly 7% during the period; thus there was an improvement of the terms of trade of about 6%.

As for trade with non-socialist countries, import prices showed an even larger decrease during the period while export prices have varied very little from the prices of exports to socialist countries. However, there have been short-term but sharp price increases in respect of certain commodities on the markets of non-socialist countries (of, e.g., raw hides, copper, sugar, beef). These have influenced price indices to a disproportionate extent, so that there has been considerable price fluctuation. The terms of trade index shows an improvement of about 10%.

Before beginning the detailed analysis of price changes it seems reasonable to give a brief history of the period 1957–67 on the two world-markets.

## 2. THE DEVELOPMENT OF PRICES ON THE WORLD MARKET

Because of the special price policy followed by the socialist countries in their trade among themselves, price changes on the capitalist world market have only an indirect effect.

Though they are not independent of the prices existing on the capitalist world market, socialist foreign trade prices very often do not change for years.

Post-war trade among the socialist countries was transacted until 1948–9 at world-market prices. At that time, the share of the capitalist world in the external trade of these countries was 50–70 per cent, and consequently there would have been no reason to fix different prices. Even accounts were kept in dollars, accounting in roubles being introduced only in 1950. Prices were fixed for the first time in 1951, on the basis of those prevailing in the third quarter of 1950. The purpose of this measure was to eliminate the impact of the price rises caused by the Korean war.

At that time the growth of foreign trade among the socialist countries was extremely rapid. During the late fifties, the share of the socialist countries in Hungarian foreign trade reached about 70% and since then it has hardly changed. However, it soon became evident that prices set in that way became considerably detached from the world market prices. The first price adjustment on the socialist world market took place in 1956, when the prices of some of the most important raw materials (coal and coke) were brought into line with those prevailing on the capitalist world market.

After these preliminaries, the problem of price policy was discussed at the Bucharest session of the CMEA in 1958. The starting point was that, on the basis of the principle of mutual advantage, prices have to assure economic development, the expansion of trade, etc. Prices must still remain stable but in justified cases and without giving an outlet for the fluctuations caused by capitalist market phenomena, price corrections have to be made according to long-standing and economically well established tendencies.

Thus the principle of a price-stop had not been invalidated, although slight modifications of its content had been made possible. In spite of the price corrections carried out after the 1958 Bucharest session, leading to a considerable fall in the prices of raw materials in 1958 compared to 1957, by the beginning of the year 1960, prices had again become considerably detached from the prices prevailing on the world market. Therefore, from 1 January 1966 onwards new prices were adopted. The new prices were set after consideration of the capitalist world market prices. Price changes were based on bilateral and multilateral negotiations. Prices in the future will still not reflect short-term fluctuations on the capitalist world market but corrections for economic and technical reasons will probably be more frequent.

The price level prevailing in the trade of Hungary with non-socialist countries is influenced by changes of the relevant prices on the capitalist world market. Since 1957 the main features of the world raw materials prices, which were important from the point of view of Hungarian foreign trade, could be summarized as follows:

There was a decrease in the prices of almost all commodities in 1958 as against 1957. The fall in the price level continued in 1959, though there were some commodities, like raw hides, the prices of which increased.

During 1960, the general decrease of raw material prices ceased, and in many cases price increases could even be observed. This phenomenon has been reflected by the Reuter price index which, in 1960, was 5 points above its level in 1950, though between January and December 1960 a continuous fall in this index could be observed. The price increases affected mainly steel products and non-ferrous metals, but crude rubber, cellulose, wool and certain chemical products also became more expensive. On the other hand, there was a decrease in the prices of coal, crude oil and of certain varieties of cotton. The world price level fell in 1961; this may be accounted for by the fact that commodities such as steel, lead, copper, tin, wool and raw hides experienced price falls in 1961, whereas they had experienced rises in 1960.

In the course of the following year, prices generally came to a standstill; some slighter decreases have occurred. Within the general price stability of 1962, one could observe opposing tendencies in the price development of industrial and agricultural products. Raw material prices continued to decrease, though at a slower rate. But there were price increases in many important agricultural products (e.g., wheat, barley, sugar, butter, lard).

In 1963 the prices of minerals hardly changed, while the prices of agricultural produce rose considerably. As a result the general price level of raw materials was the highest for six years.

In 1964, the slow increase in the price level continued. There were two factors: first was the rise in the prices of non-ferrous metals. Prices had been held at a low level as there had been over-production of non-ferrous metals. In order to counterbalance this, production and market controlling measures were enforced. As a result, supply fell behind the slowly increasing demand and prices suddenly rose.

The second factor was the considerable increase in food and fodder prices, mainly at the beginning of the year. As an effect of the hard winter 1962–3, yields were unfavourable all over Europe and, as a result, there was a large rise in agricultural prices at the end of 1963 and the beginning of 1964.

In 1965 the world market price level of raw materials decreased considerably. Prices as a whole were determined by the low level of those for industrial materials, mainly steel, crude oil and rubber, and by a decrease of the prices of agricultural products.

Prices on the non-socialist world market changed little during 1966. Though in the first half of the year raw materials registered a general increase, due to orders placed by the United States for military purposes, the second half of the year again showed a decreasing price tendency. This decrease was partly caused by the slackening of the rate of industrial production in some of the leading capitalist countries. Of the more important commodities, steel, coal, rubber, cotton, tin and lead experienced price falls, copper being the only major commodity whose price continued to rise in 1966.

The decreasing tendency persisted and the index reached a record low during 1967. Non-ferrous metals and industrial raw materials of agricultural origin reached a low level in the first half of the year and the price decrease of foodstuffs and raw materials for the food industry occurred in the second half.

The above-mentioned features are reflected in the Reuter raw materials price index.

*Development of Reuter's raw material price index* (18 Sept. 1931 = 100)

| Year | | Year | | Year | |
|------|-------|------|-------|------|-------|
| 1957 | 459.6 | 1961 | 414.9 | 1965 | 452.8 |
| 1958 | 414.5 | 1962 | 412.7 | 1966 | 446.9 |
| 1959 | 417.3 | 1963 | 464.3 | 1967 | 431.2 |
| 1960 | 422.1 | 1964 | 473.8 | | |

3. CHANGES IN HUNGARIAN EXTERNAL TRADE PRICES IN 1958[1]

In 1958, there occurred important price changes in our external trade with both socialist and non-socialist countries.

Compared with the previous year, prices in 1958 developed in an advantageous way. While import prices fell by almost 5%, export prices fell by only 1%, so that the terms of trade improved by almost 4%. (See Table 1.)

TABLE 1. *External trade price indices 1958* (1957 = 100)

| | Import | | | Export | | |
|---|---|---|---|---|---|---|
| | socialist | non-socialist countries | average | socialist | non-socialist countries | average |
| Industrial products* | 100.0 | 97.5 | 99.5 | 99.2 | 102.8 | 100.1 |
| Raw materials and semi-finished goods | 95.0 | 92.2 | 94.2 | 102.0 | 95.4 | 99.7 |
| Food industry raw materials and foodstuffs | 94.1 | 93.0 | 93.6 | 95.2 | 96.4 | 95.8 |
| Average | 96.1 | 93.0 | 95.2 | 99.0 | 99.0 | 99.0 |

* Machines and machinery equipment and industrial consumption goods (cf. commodity classification in Appendix 1).

The improvement in the terms of trade is due to the fact that price indices of raw materials – as a result of the divergences in the commodity pattern of trade – had decreased more in respect of imports than of exports.[2]

[1] The data referring to the export–import price indices for the years 1957–8 are much affected by considerable uncertainties originating from the first experimental survey; they have to be handled with more caution than those of the following years.
[2] The importance of the indices of the different relations, country groups and/or main commodity groups is determined by their specific weight in the turnover.
  In appendix 4 the relations and commodity pattern of external trade turnover during the period 1957–67 is shown.

In 1958, changes in import prices (in the case of trade with socialist countries) were the result of the adoption of new prices (cf. Table 2). Also price changes in our trade with the non-socialist countries were, in the case of some important raw materials, by no means negligible.

TABLE 2. *Import prices of selected commodities in 1958* (Index: 1957 = 100)

|  | Socialist | Non-socialist countries |
|---|---|---|
| Coal | 79.9 | — |
| Iron-ore | 122.1 | 94.9 |
| Pig-iron | 113.3 | — |
| Blast-furnace coke | 95.7 | — |
| Copper sulphate | 133.2 | 71.8 |
| Crude sulphate | 109.8 | 102.6 |
| Soft sawn wood | 97.9 | 97.8 |
| Raw hides | — | 95.5 |
| Raw cotton | 81.8 | 87.1 |
| Worsted wool | — | 79.2 |
| Coffee | 99.8 | 83.0 |
| Lemon | — | 96.5 |

In exports the fall in the prices of raw materials, semi-finished goods and foodstuffs was less than the fall in prices of the important products. Among these were products whose prices on the world market had been stable (Table 3).

TABLE 3. *Export prices of selected commodities in 1958* (Index: 1957 = 100)

|  | Socialist | Non-socialist countries |
|---|---|---|
| Bauxite | 99.7 | — |
| Aluminium | 99.5 | — |
| Fuel oil | 92.8 | 83.5 |
| Aluminium sheets | 108.8 | 111.9 |
| Bitumen | 98.1 | 106.2 |
| Pigs for slaughter | 93.4 | 94.0 |
| Pork | 94.2 | — |
| Slaughtered poultry | 91.4 | 100.5 |
| Eggs (fresh) | 100.4 | 110.4 |

4. HUNGARIAN EXTERNAL TRADE PRICES DURING THE PERIOD 1958–65

In 1965, Hungarian import and export prices did not show any great variations compared with 1958. In 1965 import prices were about 3% less, while export prices were about 1% less than in 1958. As a result, the terms of trade were more favourable by about 3% than in 1958. The prices of imports from socialist countries were about 2% lower, while those from non-socialist countries were about 4% lower than in 1958. The prices of goods exported to socialist countries were roughly the same as they had been seven years before. The prices of exports to non-socialist countries were lower by about 1.5% (cf. Table 4).

TABLE 4. *External trade price indices*

| | 1958 | 1959 | 1960 | 1961 | 1962 | 1963 | 1964 | 1965 |
|---|---|---|---|---|---|---|---|---|
| | | | | Import (A) | | | | |
| Socialist | 100.0 | 99.5 | 98.2 | 97.8 | 98.0 | 96.5 | 97.1 | 97.6 |
| Non-socialist countries | 100.0 | 99.1 | 102.7 | 95.8 | 92.6 | 91.7 | 94.4 | 95.9 |
| Total | 100.0 | 99.4 | 99.3 | 97.1 | 96.3 | 95.0 | 96.3 | 97.1 |
| | | | | Export (B) | | | | |
| Socialist | 100.0 | 98.5 | 98.3 | 98.9 | 98.8 | 99.2 | 98.8 | 99.7 |
| Non-socialist countries | 100.0 | 95.1 | 95.6 | 95.8 | 93.0 | 99.0 | 99.9 | 98.4 |
| Total | 100.0 | 97.6 | 97.6 | 98.1 | 97.4 | 99.2 | 99.3 | 99.5 |
| | | | | Terms of trade (B/A) | | | | |
| Socialist | 100.0 | 99.0 | 100.1 | 101.1 | 100.8 | 102.8 | 101.8 | 102.2 |
| Non-socialist countries | 100.0 | 96.0 | 93.1 | 100.0 | 100.4 | 108.0 | 105.8 | 102.6 |
| Total | 100.0 | 98.2 | 98.3 | 101.0 | 101.1 | 104.4 | 103.1 | 102.5 |

(*a*) Price movements in trade with socialist countries

In our trade with socialist countries, prices did not show great fluctuations even in respect of commodity groups: some exceptions are due to the fact that these years cover the period between two general price corrections. The slight divergences of price indices from one year to the next are due mainly to the changes in the commodity pattern of the relations between countries with different price levels. Besides, each year there were some commodities the prices of which had been lowered during the period.

The prices of foodstuffs and of raw materials for the food industry decreased; first of all as a result of a reduction in the prices of cereals. The reason for the 6% decrease in 1959 compared to 1958 was the lower price of wheat when purchased in bulk. In 1960, the fall in maize and wheat prices resulted in the price level falling by 7% compared with the previous year. After that period there occurred some increases and decreases until 1965, but the price level was about the same as in 1960.

As for the export of foodstuffs, a fall in prices was registered during the period but as a consequence of the existing commodity pattern its results were insignificant (cf. the price indices of the main commodity groups in Appendixes 2 and 3).

(*b*) Price movements in trade with non-socialist countries

THE TRENDS IN IMPORT PRICES

As for imports from non-socialist countries, there was a general price fall in each commodity group compared with 1958. Price movements have been determined by trade in raw materials and foodstuffs which amount to almost 80 per cent of the total turnover. These fluctuations came about as a result of changes in world-market prices (cf. Table 5).

TABLE 5. *Price indices of trade with non-socialist countries, main commodity groups* (*Imports*) (1958 = 100)

| Year | Total | Machines and machinery equipment | Industrial consumption goods | Raw materials and semi-products | Food industry raw materials and foodstuffs |
|---|---|---|---|---|---|
| 1959 | 99.1 | 94.6 | 81.6 | 103.0 | 85.8 |
| 1960 | 102.7 | 93.3 | 81.6 | 109.0 | 84.4 |
| 1961 | 95.8 | 93.3 | 78.3 | 99.1 | 83.0 |
| 1962 | 92.6 | 94.3 | 78.6 | 93.6 | 83.1 |
| 1963 | 91.7 | 93.5 | 78.5 | 90.6 | 88.4 |
| 1964 | 94.4 | 84.8 | 81.0 | 95.4 | 96.1 |
| 1965 | 95.9 | 85.6 | 81.9 | 99.2 | 88.2 |

In 1965, the prices of imported raw materials were at about the same level as in 1958, but in some years there occurred important fluctuations. In 1960 prices were about 10 per cent higher than in 1958, while in 1963 they were 10 per cent lower. The prices of certain commodities played a particularly important role in the development of the general price level (see tables 6 and 7).

The prices of raw materials imported from non-socialist countries rose by about 3 per cent in 1959 compared with 1958, this being mainly due to the 80% rise in raw hide prices. Price fluctuations of raw hide on the world market were considerable; in mid-1959, the price was double the average 1958 price, but by the end of the year it had started to fall.

In 1960, the price increase of 5–6% was firstly a result of the rise in world market prices of heavy industrial raw materials, which accounted for a large proportion of our imports. There occurred a rise in the prices of

TABLE 6. *Price development of some important raw materials imported from non-socialist countries* (Index: 1958 = 100)

| Commodity | 1959 | 1960 | 1961 | 1962 | 1963 | 1964 | 1965 |
|---|---|---|---|---|---|---|---|
| Iron-ore | 109 | 111 | 80 | 69 | 46 | 65 | 64 |
| Hot-rolled steel | 95 | 109 | 90 | 87 | 89 | 90 | 92 |
| Copper | 116 | 125 | 116 | 129 | 130 | 151 | 180 |
| Lead | 103 | 109 | 116 | 122 | 118 | 155 | 192 |
| Crude rubber | 122 | 149 | 114 | 105 | 102 | 95 | 95 |
| Cellulose | 90 | 102 | 107 | 97 | 102 | 114 | 113 |
| Raw cotton | 93 | 98 | 92 | 88 | 83 | 87 | 86 |
| Washed fine wool | 75 | 72 | 69 | 68 | 78 | 89 | 83 |
| Raw hides | 179 | 179 | 146 | 138 | 105 | 102 | 138 |

steel products (beton steel, steel-wire, different sheets and plates, etc.), of non-ferrous metals and steel tempering metals (copper, lead, tin, zinc, cadmium, etc.) and – mainly as a consequence of an increase in the cost of sea transport – of the refined iron-ore imported from India. Given the adverse changes in the price level, a role must be attributed to the price level of raw hide imports remaining constant, despite the considerable overall price decrease on the world market amounting to about 25%.

While import prices decreased in general by about 9 per cent in 1961, the price of iron-ore decreased by about 30% and that of rolled steel products by about 17%. Among non-ferrous metals, the import price of tin and copper was about 10% lower in 1961 than in 1960. In respect of raw hides and crude rubber, the price decrease was much more important: the purchasing prices in 1961 were respectively about 18 and 25% lower than in the previous year. On the other hand the purchases of smelting lead and cadmium were more expensive.

During 1962 prices continued to fall by about 6 per cent, a fact which was reflected in almost each commodity of importance in our imports: rolled steel products (3%), crude rubber (8%), raw cotton (4%), raw hides (8%). But there were some rises, as in the case of copper (11%) and pine-wood (6%). According to the tendencies prevailing on the world market, prices in 1963 were falling again: among others the prices of iron-ore, pig-iron, crude rubber and raw hide. On the other hand, in the case of some commodities, as for example cellulose and wool, there was a rise in prices.

During 1964, raw material prices increased by about 5% and the trend of falling prices, which had lasted for years, came to an end. Prices of non-ferrous metals, of iron-ore, of some chemical products and of a number of industrial raw materials of agricultural origin (cotton, wool, oxhide, etc.)

rose. In 1965 raw material prices exceeded the previous year's prices by about 5% and approximated the 1958 level. The price increase was due, among other things, to rises in the prices of copper, lead, raw hides etc.

Recently, the prices of foodstuffs imported from non-socialist markets were considerably below the 1958 level. A minimum was reached in 1961–2 when prices were about 17% lower than in 1958. By 1964, prices were about 10% above the 1962 level, but in 1965 we could register a new decrease (cf. Table 7).

TABLE 7. *Prices of selected foodstuffs imported from non-socialist countries* (Index: 1958 = 100)

| Commodities | 1959 | 1960 | 1961 | 1962 | 1963 | 1964 | 1965 |
|---|---|---|---|---|---|---|---|
| Wheat | — | 100* | 113 | 110 | 109 | 128 | 107 |
| Barley | — | — | 100† | 120 | 118 | 124 | 120 |
| Beef | — | 100* | 89 | 82 | 73 | 108 | 102 |
| Pork | — | 100* | 98 | 94 | 116 | 137 | 113 |
| Coffee | 75 | 77 | 78 | 75 | 74 | 98 | 81 |
| Cacao-beans | 83 | 66 | 54 | 56 | 54 | 60 | 48 |
| Suet | 95 | 80 | 85 | 71 | 63 | 73 | 91 |
| Raw bacon for lard | — | 100* | 129 | 104 | 125 | 137 | 102 |
| Vegetable oil and shortening | 97 | 103 | 104 | 99 | 90 | 95 | 91 |
| Lemons | 70 | 88 | 85 | 77 | 138 | 71 | 82 |
| Oranges | 94 | 93 | 95 | 95 | 102 | 94 | 92 |

\* Index: 1960 = 100.  † Index: 1961 = 100.

The prices of foodstuffs in 1959 were about 15 per cent lower than in the preceding year. This was due to a fall in the prices of several commodities which make up a great share of our trade, such as cacao-beans, coffee, lemons and oranges. In the following two years the price level fell, though only slightly. In 1962 the prices of foodstuffs did not change. Mainly as a result of wheat imports, the commodity pattern of our trade underwent a drastic change. With the general stability of prices, rises were less frequent (only in the cases of barley, cacao-beans, cocoa-powder, wheat flour) than price cuts. In 1963 prices increased by about 6%. There had been an increase, for instance, in the price of maize, lemon, oranges, pork and lard, and a decrease in the price of coffee, cacao-beans and beef. The price of wheat imported from capitalist countries did not change in comparison to the previous year, though there was a rise in wheat prices on the world market during the last months of 1963, because the wheat imported that year had been contracted earlier. In 1964, prices increased by about 9 per cent, due mainly to the rise in the prices of foodstuffs imported from capitalist countries. Wheat and beef prices increased for instance by 17% and 50% respectively. Besides, there was an increase in the level of prices of beer, coffee and cacao-beans imported from less developed countries. During 1965, the prices of foodstuffs imported from non-socialist countries fell by about 8%, as a result of the cut in the prices of flour, beef, coffee and cacao-beans.

THE TRENDS IN EXPORT PRICES

TABLE 8. *Price indices of trade with non-socialist countries, main commodity groups* (*Exports*) (Index: 1958 = 100)

| Year | Total | Machines and machinery equipment | Industrial consumption goods | Raw materials and semi-products | Food industry raw materials and foodstuffs |
|---|---|---|---|---|---|
| 1959 | 95.1 | 103.3 | 89.1 | 92.2 | 98.8 |
| 1960 | 95.6 | 105.7 | 90.0 | 95.2 | 97.1 |
| 1961 | 95.8 | 107.8 | 89.4 | 95.5 | 96.8 |
| 1962 | 93.0 | 105.8 | 83.5 | 91.3 | 97.4 |
| 1963 | 99.0 | 105.4 | 81.7 | 90.0 | 116.8 |
| 1964 | 99.9 | 106.9 | 82.2 | 89.2 | 118.9 |
| 1965 | 98.4 | 105.7 | 81.2 | 91.2 | 113.4 |

Despite the fact that the average level of export prices in 1965 was the same as that in 1958, important fluctuations could be observed in each year and in each commodity group (cf. Table 8). The volume of exports of consumer goods and their share in trade tended to increase while their prices declined considerably. Thus it seems plausible that an increase in their export was linked to accepting falling prices.

Prices of consumer goods fell by 10% in 1959. The price fall was due to the fact that several important goods, such as cotton textiles, leather shoes and bulbs, suffered a 5–10 per cent price decrease. In the same year, there occurred a large fall in the prices of pharmaceutical basic materials which are classified by the CMEA in that group. In the following two years prices did not change, while in 1962, mainly as a result of the price decrease in piece-goods and clothes, prices decreased again by about 7%. On account of the further decrease of prices of the same goods in 1963, the average price level decreased by another 2–3%. During 1964 and 1965, prices remained practically at the same level.

Raw material prices declined during the period under question – this commodity group accounts for about 30 per cent of total exports. The trend was determined by the 8% cut in prices during 1959. The same year, among the most important commodities, the price of sulphuric acid was about 1% lower, bauxite 6% lower, and aluminium, fuel oil and bitumen more than 10% lower, than in 1958. In 1960 prices increased by approximately 3%, mainly as a result of an increase in the prices of bauxite and aluminium by about 6%, of steel tubes by 20% and of rolled steel products by 18%. In the course of 1961 prices changed but in 1962 they declined by 5%.

During this period, a decrease in the price of rolled steel products by 20% and in the price of steel tubes by more than 10% came about as a result of increasing competition and reduced demand in the capitalist market. Parallel to the further decrease in world prices, in 1963 prices fell by about 2%, mainly as a result of the cut in the prices of steel and aluminium, which were exported in large quantities. In 1964, the decrease in prices continued and it was only in 1965 that a smaller increase took place (cf. Table 9).

TABLE 9. *Prices of some important raw materials exported to non-socialist countries* (Index: 1958 = 100)

| Commodity | 1959 | 1960 | 1961 | 1962 | 1963 | 1964 | 1965 |
|---|---|---|---|---|---|---|---|
| Bauxite | 94 | 100 | 66 | 73 | 74 | 62 | 54 |
| Aluminium | 86 | 91 | 95 | 92 | 86 | 91 | 91 |
| Rolled steel | 99 | 117 | 100 | 97 | 94 | 91 | 99 |
| Steel tubes | 96 | 122 | 115 | 109 | 102 | 109 | 109 |
| Aluminium sheets | 78 | 77 | 90 | 70 | 71 | 73 | 76 |
| Fuel oil | 85 | 90 | 87 | 94 | 100 | 71 | 67 |
| Bitumen | 88 | 91 | 89 | 80 | 78 | 70 | 69 |

In the 1958–65 period the most diversified picture was shown by the prices of foodstuffs. During the first three years prices declined somewhat while in 1962 there was a slight increase and a more important one during 1963–4 (about 20%). In 1965 a decrease of about 6% was registered (cf. Table 10).

Within an average price fall of 2 per cent, in 1959 the prices of beef cattle, pigs for slaughter and butter increased, while those of eggs, goose-liver etc., decreased. The further decrease in export prices of foodstuffs in 1960 was brought about by the fall in the prices of sunflower-oil, pigs for slaughter, eggs, beef, cooking oil, wine and dairy products. Price increases were not observed among the most important commodities. In 1961–2 there were practically no price changes. Prices of foodstuffs increased considerably, by about 20% in the course of 1963. The most advantageous change was the increase in sugar prices which almost tripled on the world

TABLE 10. *Prices of the most important foodstuffs exported to non-socialist countries* (Index: 1958 = 100)

| Commodity | 1959 | 1960 | 1961 | 1962 | 1963 | 1964 | 1965 |
|---|---|---|---|---|---|---|---|
| Beef-cattle | 103 | 101 | 98 | 100 | 106 | 135 | 141 |
| Pigs for slaughter | 106 | 103 | 100 | 103 | 109 | 117 | 104 |
| Beef | 112 | 99 | 69 | 70 | 100 | 124 | 122 |
| Pork | — | — | — | 100 | 108 | 123 | 113 |
| Bacon | 98 | 96 | 89 | 79 | 85 | 82 | 74 |
| Salami | 102 | 103 | 107 | 108 | 108 | 113 | 114 |
| Slaughtered poultry | 95 | 95 | 91 | 95 | 96 | 94 | 93 |
| Eggs | 88 | 79 | 94 | 74 | 99 | 61 | 66 |
| Onions | 98 | 90 | 93 | 106 | 124 | 121 | 104 |
| Ground red paprika | 98 | 108 | 189 | 200 | 186 | 208 | 214 |
| Apples | 98 | 97 | 104 | 79 | 65 | 78 | 103 |

market while effective export prices were more than three times the previous year's level. It was also of great importance that the prices of our traditional exports increased in conformity with world market prices.

In 1964, prices continued to rise slightly. They were greatly influenced by the considerable recession in sugar prices resulting from an increased supply. The average 1964 price was about 30% lower than a year before. On the other hand, there was a further increase in 1964 in the world market prices of animals for slaughter and animal products, these amounting to almost 60 per cent of our exports to developed capitalist countries. In 1965, the export prices of foodstuffs decreased by about 6%, because of the decrease in the prices of sugar, pigs for slaughter, meat, butter, bacon, etc.

5. PRICES IN HUNGARIAN EXTERNAL TRADE IN 1966–7

During this period a considerable change in prices was registered. Import prices showed a gradual fall of about 3% p.a. compared with the previous year and were in 1967 about 8% lower than in 1958. In export prices the decrease was somewhat less conspicuous, amounting to about 5.4% during the two years. In this period, terms of trade showed a further small improvement and were, as a result of earlier price changes, more favourable by about 3% than in 1958 (cf. Table 11).

(a) The trends in import prices

The foremost feature of the period in question was, as stated earlier, the introduction of new contractual prices between the CMEA countries having an important share in Hungary's external trade. As a consequence, import prices registered a decline of almost 4% in 1966, and of more than

TABLE 11. *External trade price indices + (1958 = 100)*

| | Imports (A) | | | Exports (B) | | | Terms of trade (B/A) | | |
|---|---|---|---|---|---|---|---|---|---|
| | 1965 | 1966 | 1967 | 1965 | 1966 | 1967 | 1965 | 1966 | 1967 |
| Socialist | 97.6 | 93.7 | 91.4 | 99.7 | 96.7 | 94.3 | 102.2 | 103.2 | 103.2 |
| Non-socialist countries | 95.9 | 96.9 | 92.0 | 98.4 | 95.8 | 94.2 | 102.6 | 98.9 | 102.4 |
| Total | 97.1 | 94.7 | 91.6 | 99.5 | 96.6 | 94.5 | 102.5 | 102.0 | 103.2 |

2% in 1967, bringing about a total fall of 8.6% compared with 1958. The rate of decrease differed between the main commodity groups.

The prices of commodities purchased from non-socialist countries rose by 1% in 1966 and decreased by about 5% in 1967 compared with the previous year: the total decrease as compared to 1958 prices was about 8%.[1]

TABLE 12. *Price indices of import turnover according to main commodity groups (1958 = 100)*

| Year | Total | Machines and machinery equipment | Industrial consumption goods | Raw materials and semi-manufactured products | Food industry raw materials and foodstuffs |
|---|---|---|---|---|---|
| | | Socialist countries | | | |
| 1965 | 97.6 | 98.2 | 101.8 | 97.8 | 85.8 |
| 1966 | 93.7 | 98.1 | 94.6 | 92.1 | 81.0 |
| 1967 | 91.4 | 99.3 | 94.6 | 87.1 | 80.1 |
| | | Non-socialist countries | | | |
| 1965 | 95.9 | 85.6 | 81.9 | 99.9 | 88.2 |
| 1966 | 96.9 | 80.9 | 81.5 | 103.4 | 88.9 |
| 1967 | 92.0 | 80.9 | 77.7 | 95.0 | 88.6 |

The prices of machinery and machinery equipment showed very little change during the period in question. Consumer goods registered a decrease consistent with the trends outlined. The prices of raw materials and semi-manufactured products (this group accounting to about half of the total imports) were lower in 1967 by about 10% in trade with socialist countries, and by about 5% in trade with non-socialist countries, as compared with 1965 (see Table 12). As to the commodity pattern of socialist imports, price adjustments caused a significant decrease in the prices of coal, briquets, crude oil, iron-ore, foundry cokes, cellulose, etc.,

[1] In the period 1966–7, about 67% of the external trade was transacted with the socialist, and the remaining 33% with non-socialist countries.

while an increase was noted in the import prices of copper, zinc, round pine timber, etc. In 1966 the price indices of imports from non-socialist countries were decisively shaped by the record high level of copper and raw hide prices on the world market: the general decrease of raw material prices in the subsequent year, however, proved beneficial so far as purchase prices of almost all important import commodities were concerned.

(*b*) The trends in export prices

Export prices in our trade with socialist countries showed an overall decrease of 3 % in 1966, and of about 2 % in 1967 compared with the previous year, so that by 1967 an overall decrease of export prices by about 6%, compared with 1958, was registered. Also in trade with non-socialist countries, our exports netted less during the period in question: however, as the decrease of import prices was more significant in 1967, a slight improvement in the terms of trade was ultimately recorded (see Table 13).

TABLE 13. *Price indices of export turnover according to main commodity groups* (1958 = 100)

| Year | Total | Machines and machinery equipment | Industrial consumption goods | Raw materials and semi-manufactured products | Food industry raw materials and foodstuffs |
|---|---|---|---|---|---|
| | | Socialist countries | | | |
| 1965 | 99.7 | 101.2 | 96.8 | 101.9 | 97.4 |
| 1966 | 96.7 | 100.3 | 89.8 | 96.4 | 97.5 |
| 1967 | 94.3 | 99.4 | 85.9 | 92.2 | 95.7 |
| | | Non-socialist countries | | | |
| 1965 | 98.4 | 105.7 | 81.2 | 91.2 | 113.4 |
| 1966 | 95.8 | 103.9 | 79.7 | 87.9 | 110.3 |
| 1967 | 94.2 | 104.4 | 78.7 | 88.4 | 105.8 |

Machinery exports directed to socialist countries and amounting to 42 % of total turnover were not affected by the price adjustment during the period since price increases and decreases cancelled each other. The price of consumer goods, however, decreased during the period by about 10%, i.e. exceeding somewhat the rate of the decrease in import prices. Export prices of, e.g. television and wireless sets, textiles and clothing were significantly reduced. The 10% fall in the prices of raw materials and semi-manufactured products was brought about mainly by the following commodities: bauxite, aluminium oxide, rolled articles, basic pharmaceutical products, petrol, etc. The fact that the prices of exported foodstuffs showed no significant changes in the first year of the period is due to the specific character of the commodity pattern: even in 1967 only a 2% decrease was registered. It may be remarked that the prices of animal products (sold in great quantities to Western markets) have generally risen, while the prices of canned goods and vegetable products have fallen.

As for our exports to non-socialist countries, a considerable part, about 36%, consisted of raw materials. The prices of Hungarian raw materials exported to the capitalist countries were determined, in 1966, primarily by the price decrease registered for rolled steel, which made up the bulk of the exports as well as for steel tubes, fuel-oil and nitrogen fertilizers. During 1967 export prices did not follow the general decreasing trend on the world market, but showed a small increase compared with the previous year. Though rolled steel, basic pharmaceutical products and nitrogen fertilizers still netted less, there was an increase of about 4–5% in the prices of petrol, fuel-oil and bitumen and of as much as 12% in the price of diesel oil compared with 1966.

Foodstuffs, accounting for about 35% of the total exports to non-socialist countries, were represented primarily by beef-cattle and raw meat (amounting to about half of the total figure). Among these, beef-cattle, one of our most important export items, realized its highest prices in 1966, when a slow decreasing trend set in as a result of the disadvantageous levy imposed by the Common Market countries. There has also been a smaller decrease in raw meat prices, for seasonal reasons: on the other hand, hogs and raw pig flesh made some price advances. In 1967, Western European markets were less accessible to Hungarian beef-cattle exports owing to increased production in the Common Market countries, and a further increase of the levy introduced in the previous year: a notable exception from this phenomenon was Italy where purchases of Hungarian cattle were increased. The prices of hogs for slaughter were about 7% lower in developed capitalist countries in 1967 than in the previous year. Marked decreases were shown in the prices of poultry (slaughtered), butter, eggs, cheese, etc.

6. SUMMARY

Price changes in the external trade of Hungary between 1957 and 1967 may be briefly summarized as follows:

A general decrease in prices in the trade with both socialist and non-socialist countries has been noticeable. Annual trade indices have, however, been considerably influenced by the fact that in the mutual trade of socialist countries prices are not exposed to the transient, short-term but sometimes violent price fluctuations of capitalist markets but follow the basic tendencies of those markets with a certain time-lag. The small price decreases are, therefore, a result of the considerable price fluctuations on non-socialist markets. It will be noticed that the general price decrease in external trade was accompanied by a decisive increase in domestic prices in both socialist and non-socialist countries, the latter including both Western Europe and the United States.

Summarizing the price development in the four main groups of commodities, the following may be ascertained:

(*a*) *Machinery and equipment* prices were steady during the period and there were also some signs of price increases in machinery on Western European markets. This is a consequence of rapid technical progress which necessarily involves ever shortening lives for new types of machinery in international trade. If new types of machinery enter the international market, older machinery quickly becomes almost unsaleable. Investment policy looks everywhere for larger capacities and up-to-date performance, almost irrespective of prices. It is a general phenomenon that a certain type of machinery or equipment fetches almost similar prices as long as it appears on the market; if a newer type appears (with relatively higher or lower prices), it will not be comparable with the earlier one, so that the indirect change in price (which may, in fact, be an increase) will not be represented in the price index. Price indices of machinery and equipment will also have to be judged from this point of view. (The comparison of the prices of similar machines is a difficult task and can be carried out in specific cases only.)

(*b*) The prices of *industrial consumption* goods have shown a marked tendency to decrease during the period. The prices of a number of articles, representing a large share of Hungarian exports, e.g., of television and wireless sets, bicycles, etc., are falling notably owing to a saturation of the international market (signs of which even start to appear on the internal market, generating difficulties of sale). As regards clothing commodities, the enormous increase in the production of both traditional and up-to-date synthetic materials has given rise to ever sharpening competition entailing the falling-off of these prices.

(*c*) The prices of *raw materials and semi-manufactured products* show, despite some transitory increases, decreases during the period. Even in the mutual trade of socialist countries, a long term effect of the price changes on the capitalist market is felt and may cause a decrease in prices. On the other hand, however, demand on the socialist world market is larger than the supply, indicating that the price decrease has not been brought about by a larger supply but by the impact of the capitalist market. Hungary is in particular need of raw materials, some of which, though vital for the country's economy, cannot be bought from socialist countries; significant amounts have to be purchased, therefore, from the capitalist markets, a fact which entails rather serious problems connected with the country's balance of payments. The effect of decreasing prices, if not associated with an increased supply of these commodities, may not simply be considered an advantage, quite apart from the uncertainty as to whether such a favourable effect on the balance of trade is linked with countries with which we need to improve our financial position.

(*d*) The most dynamic changes have been observed in the prices of foodstuffs where, as a consequence of the commodity pattern of Hungarian external trade, the relative price decrease was smallest. Animal food products have shown a marked price increase during the period (poultry excepted). Sales on Western European markets have been rendered more difficult because of discrimination on the part of some Common Market countries, so that recently signs of marked price decreases have been registered. Prices of foodstuffs of vegetable origin, including canned food, exported mainly to the socialist countries, have shown a price decrease during the period.

APPENDIX I. NOTES ON METHODOLOGY

The uniform CMEA foreign trade commodity classification comprises 9 main groups, within which there are two digit groups and three digit subgroups. In this report the 9 main groups of the classification appear in 4 reduced main groups:

MACHINERY AND EQUIPMENT (the first main group of the classification)

It covers machines, machinery equipment and their parts. Here can be found plant, energy and electrical equipment, agricultural machinery, transport equipment, instruments etc.

CONSUMER GOODS (the ninth main group of the classification)

This group covers industrial products serving consumption purposes. Here belong the light industrial products, like textile products, clothes, shoes, furniture as well as household machinery and durable goods such as radio and television sets, bicycles and pharmaceutical commodities.

RAW MATERIALS AND SEMI-MANUFACTURED PRODUCTS (the 2nd–5th main groups of the classification)

This covers all the raw materials and semi-manufactured products (except those of the food industry) e.g., fuels, non-metallic raw materials, metals, rolled products, metallic manufactures, wires and cables, as well as organic and non-organic chemical products, fertilizers, crude rubber and rubber products, building materials, etc.

FOODSTUFFS AND FOOD-INDUSTRY MATERIALS (the 6th–8th main groups of the classification)

All the raw materials for the food industry are grouped under this heading, like cereals, meat and meat products, animals, spices, products of the milling, dairy and confectionery industries, vegetables, fruits, canned products, etc.

APPENDIX 2. *Hungarian external trade price indices* (1958 = 100)

| | Import price index (A) | | | Export price index (B) | | | Terms of trade (B/A) | | |
|---|---|---|---|---|---|---|---|---|---|
| Year | Total | socialist | non-socialist countries | Total | socialist | non-socialist countries | Total | socialist | non-socialist countries |
| 1957 | 105.0 | 104.1 | 107.5 | 101.0 | 101.0 | 101.0 | 96.2 | 97.0 | 94.0 |
| 1958 | 100.0 | 100.0 | 100.0 | 100.0 | 100.0 | 100.0 | 100.0 | 100.0 | 100.0 |
| 1959 | 99.4 | 99.5 | 99.1 | 97.6 | 98.5 | 95.1 | 98.2 | 99.0 | 96.0 |
| 1960 | 99.3 | 98.2 | 102.7 | 97.6 | 98.3 | 95.6 | 98.3 | 100.1 | 93.1 |
| 1961 | 97.1 | 97.8 | 95.8 | 98.1 | 98.9 | 95.8 | 101.0 | 101.1 | 100.0 |
| 1962 | 96.3 | 98.0 | 92.6 | 97.4 | 98.8 | 93.0 | 101.1 | 100.8 | 100.4 |
| 1963 | 95.0 | 96.5 | 91.7 | 99.2 | 99.2 | 99.0 | 104.4 | 102.8 | 108.0 |
| 1964 | 96.3 | 97.1 | 94.4 | 99.3 | 98.8 | 99.9 | 103.1 | 101.8 | 105.8 |
| 1965 | 97.1 | 97.6 | 95.9 | 99.5 | 99.7 | 98.4 | 102.5 | 102.2 | 102.6 |
| 1966 | 94.7 | 93.7 | 96.9 | 96.6 | 96.7 | 95.8 | 102.0 | 103.2 | 98.9 |
| 1967 | 91.6 | 91.4 | 92.0 | 94.5 | 94.3 | 94.2 | 103.2 | 103.2 | 102.4 |

APPENDIX 3. *A. Hungarian external trade price indices by main commodity groups* (1958 = 100)

| Year | Total | Machines and machinery equipment | Industrial consumption goods | Raw materials and semi-manufactured products | Food industry raw materials and foodstuffs |
|---|---|---|---|---|---|
| Imports | | | | | |
| 1957 | 105.0 | 100.5 | | 106.2 | 106.8 |
| 1958 | 100.0 | 100.0 | 100.0 | 100.0 | 100.0 |
| 1959 | 99.4 | 98.4 | 96.5 | 100.8 | 91.0 |
| 1960 | 99.3 | 95.8 | 93.1 | 102.9 | 85.5 |
| 1961 | 97.1 | 95.7 | 93.8 | 98.6 | 88.8 |
| 1962 | 96.3 | 96.0 | 91.6 | 97.3 | 88.0 |
| 1963 | 95.0 | 97.1 | 92.8 | 94.1 | 89.1 |
| 1964 | 96.3 | 95.5 | 96.1 | 96.0 | 95.8 |
| 1965 | 97.1 | 95.8 | 96.7 | 98.1 | 89.1 |
| 1966 | 94.7 | 94.6 | 91.2 | 95.3 | 87.7 |
| 1967 | 91.6 | 95.4 | 90.2 | 89.3 | 87.4 |
| Exports | | | | | |
| 1957 | 101.0 | 99.9 | | 100.3 | 104.4 |
| 1958 | 100.0 | 100.0 | 100.0 | 100.0 | 100.0 |
| 1959 | 97.6 | 99.5 | 93.6 | 97.5 | 98.1 |
| 1960 | 97.6 | 99.7 | 92.8 | 98.5 | 97.6 |
| 1961 | 98.1 | 100.5 | 92.7 | 98.8 | 98.1 |
| 1962 | 97.4 | 100.0 | 91.5 | 98.4 | 97.6 |
| 1963 | 99.2 | 101.0 | 91.0 | 97.1 | 107.5 |
| 1964 | 99.3 | 100.8 | 91.0 | 97.1 | 107.5 |
| 1965 | 99.5 | 101.4 | 92.0 | 98.0 | 105.4 |
| 1966 | 96.6 | 100.5 | 86.8 | 93.4 | 104.0 |
| 1967 | 94.5 | 99.7 | 83.8 | 91.2 | 101.0 |

APPENDIX 3 (cont.). *B. Hungarian external trade price indices with socialist countries by main commodity groups* (1958 = 100)

| Year | Total | Machines and machinery equipment | Industrial consumption goods | Raw materials and semi-manu-factured products | Food industry raw materials and foodstuffs |
|---|---|---|---|---|---|
| | | *Imports* | | | |
| 1957 | 104.1 | 100.0 | | 105.3 | 106.3 |
| 1958 | 100.0 | 100.0 | 100.0 | 100.0 | 100.0 |
| 1959 | 99.5 | 99.4 | 101.6 | 99.9 | 93.8 |
| 1960 | 98.2 | 96.6 | 97.4 | 100.5 | 86.4 |
| 1961 | 97.8 | 96.5 | 99.3 | 98.7 | 92.4 |
| 1962 | 98.0 | 96.6 | 96.3 | 99.5 | 91.8 |
| 1963 | 96.5 | 98.0 | 97.8 | 96.2 | 85.9 |
| 1964 | 97.1 | 98.1 | 101.4 | 96.7 | 89.5 |
| 1965 | 97.6 | 98.2 | 101.8 | 97.8 | 85.8 |
| 1966 | 93.7 | 98.1 | 94.6 | 92.1 | 81.0 |
| 1967 | 91.4 | 99.3 | 94.6 | 87.1 | 80.1 |
| | | *Exports* | | | |
| 1957 | 101.0 | 100.8 | | 98.0 | 105.0 |
| 1958 | 100.0 | 100.0 | 100.0 | 100.0 | 100.0 |
| 1959 | 98.5 | 99.2 | 95.8 | 100.5 | 97.5 |
| 1960 | 98.3 | 99.3 | 94.2 | 100.5 | 98.2 |
| 1961 | 98.9 | 99.9 | 94.5 | 100.8 | 99.5 |
| 1962 | 98.8 | 99.5 | 95.1 | 102.4 | 98.0 |
| 1963 | 99.2 | 100.6 | 95.0 | 101.2 | 99.0 |
| 1964 | 98.8 | 100.4 | 94.8 | 101.7 | 96.9 |
| 1965 | 99.7 | 101.2 | 96.8 | 101.9 | 97.4 |
| 1966 | 96.7 | 100.3 | 89.8 | 96.4 | 97.5 |
| 1967 | 94.3 | 99.4 | 85.9 | 92.2 | 95.7 |

APPENDIX 3 (cont.). *C. Hungarian external trade price indices with non-socialist countries by main commodity groups* (1958 = 100)

| Year | Total | Machines and machinery equipment | Industrial consumption goods | Raw materials and semi-manufactured products | Food industry raw materials and foodstuffs |
|---|---|---|---|---|---|
| | | Imports | | | |
| 1957 | 107.5 | 102.4 | | 108.4 | 107.5 |
| 1958 | 100.0 | 100.0 | 100.0 | 100.0 | 100.0 |
| 1959 | 99.1 | 94.6 | 81.6 | 103.0 | 85.8 |
| 1960 | 102.7 | 93.3 | 81.6 | 109.0 | 84.4 |
| 1961 | 95.8 | 93.3 | 78.3 | 99.1 | 83.0 |
| 1962 | 92.6 | 94.3 | 78.6 | 93.6 | 83.1 |
| 1963 | 91.7 | 93.5 | 78.5 | 90.6 | 88.4 |
| 1964 | 94.4 | 84.8 | 81.0 | 95.4 | 96.1 |
| 1965 | 95.9 | 85.6 | 81.9 | 99.9 | 88.2 |
| 1966 | 96.9 | 80.9 | 81.5 | 103.4 | 88.9 |
| 1967 | 92.0 | 80.9 | 77.7 | 95.0 | 88.6 |
| | | Exports | | | |
| 1957 | 101.0 | 97.3 | | 104.6 | 103.7 |
| 1958 | 100.0 | 100.0 | 100.0 | 100.0 | 100.0 |
| 1959 | 95.1 | 103.3 | 89.1 | 92.2 | 98.8 |
| 1960 | 95.6 | 105.7 | 90.0 | 95.2 | 97.1 |
| 1961 | 95.8 | 107.8 | 89.4 | 95.5 | 96.8 |
| 1962 | 93.0 | 105.8 | 83.5 | 91.3 | 97.4 |
| 1963 | 99.0 | 105.4 | 81.7 | 90.0 | 116.8 |
| 1964 | 99.9 | 106.9 | 82.2 | 89.2 | 118.9 |
| 1965 | 98.4 | 105.7 | 81.2 | 91.2 | 113.4 |
| 1966 | 95.8 | 103.9 | 79.7 | 87.9 | 110.3 |
| 1967 | 94.2 | 104.4 | 78.7 | 88.4 | 105.8 |

APPENDIX 4. *A. Pattern of Hungarian external trade with socialist and non-socialist countries*

| | Imports | | | Exports | | |
|---|---|---|---|---|---|---|
| Year | Total | socialist | non-socialist countries | Total | socialist | non-socialist countries |
| | | (%) | (%) | | (%) | (%) |
| 1957 | 100.0 | 72.8 | 27.2 | 100.0 | 67.7 | 32.3 |
| 1958 | 100.0 | 71.4 | 28.6 | 100.0 | 71.9 | 28.1 |
| 1959 | 100.0 | 71.9 | 28.1 | 100.0 | 70.2 | 29.8 |
| 1960 | 100.0 | 70.4 | 29.6 | 100.0 | 71.3 | 28.7 |
| 1961 | 100.0 | 68.7 | 31.3 | 100.0 | 73.5 | 26.5 |
| 1962 | 100.0 | 71.4 | 28.6 | 100.0 | 73.7 | 26.3 |
| 1963 | 100.0 | 69.0 | 31.0 | 100.0 | 70.4 | 29.6 |
| 1964 | 100.0 | 66.6 | 33.4 | 100.0 | 71.2 | 28.8 |
| 1965 | 100.0 | 67.0 | 33.0 | 100.0 | 70.1 | 29.9 |
| 1966 | 100.0 | 64.9 | 35.1 | 100.0 | 68.3 | 31.7 |
| 1967 | 100.0 | 66.6 | 33.4 | 100.0 | 68.6 | 31.4 |

APPENDIX 4 (cont.). *B. Pattern of Hungarian external trade with socialist countries*

| Year | Total | Machines and machinery equipment | Industrial consumption goods | Raw materials and semi-manufactured products | Food industry raw materials and foodstuffs |
|---|---|---|---|---|---|
| | | Imports | | | |
| 1957 | 100.0 | 13.6 | 7.2 | 68.6 | 10.6 |
| 1958 | 100.0 | 18.5 | 4.5 | 69.3 | 7.7 |
| 1959 | 100.0 | 29.3 | 5.3 | 56.7 | 8.7 |
| 1960 | 100.0 | 32.9 | 6.0 | 53.7 | 7.4 |
| 1961 | 100.0 | 31.1 | 5.6 | 55.3 | 8.0 |
| 1962 | 100.0 | 35.5 | 5.2 | 53.1 | 6.2 |
| 1963 | 100.0 | 36.5 | 6.3 | 52.5 | 4.7 |
| 1964 | 100.0 | 35.9 | 6.0 | 55.5 | 2.6 |
| 1965 | 100.0 | 34.0 | 6.1 | 54.5 | 5.4 |
| 1966 | 100.0 | 34.3 | 6.7 | 55.5 | 3.5 |
| 1967 | 100.0 | 37.8 | 7.1 | 49.0 | 6.1 |
| | | Exports | | | |
| 1957 | 100.0 | 51.9 | 9.6 | 19.7 | 18.8 |
| 1958 | 100.0 | 46.4 | 16.6 | 20.9 | 16.1 |
| 1959 | 100.0 | 45.9 | 19.1 | 19.4 | 15.6 |
| 1960 | 100.0 | 49.4 | 16.8 | 19.8 | 14.0 |
| 1961 | 100.0 | 46.8 | 20.6 | 19.1 | 13.5 |
| 1962 | 100.0 | 45.1 | 22.1 | 19.4 | 13.4 |
| 1963 | 100.0 | 45.2 | 20.3 | 19.7 | 14.8 |
| 1964 | 100.0 | 44.7 | 19.1 | 21.0 | 15.2 |
| 1965 | 100.0 | 43.1 | 21.4 | 19.6 | 15.9 |
| 1966 | 100.0 | 42.1 | 23.2 | 19.5 | 15.2 |
| 1967 | 100.0 | 42.3 | 23.5 | 18.4 | 15.8 |

APPENDIX 4 (cont.). *C. Pattern of Hungarian external trade with non-socialist*

| Year | Total | Machines and machinery equipment | Industrial consumption goods | Raw materials and semi-manufactured products | Food industry raw materials and foodstuffs |
|---|---|---|---|---|---|
| | | Imports | | | |
| 1957 | 100.0 | 8.8 | 4.3 | 65.9 | 21.0 |
| 1958 | 100.0 | 12.7 | 4.7 | 72.0 | 10.6 |
| 1959 | 100.0 | 15.6 | 3.0 | 71.6 | 9.8 |
| 1960 | 100.0 | 15.8 | 2.7 | 71.2 | 10.3 |
| 1961 | 100.0 | 13.3 | 3.1 | 67.4 | 16.2 |
| 1962 | 100.0 | 16.3 | 3.4 | 61.9 | 18.4 |
| 1963 | 100.0 | 16.3 | 2.9 | 59.6 | 21.2 |
| 1964 | 100.0 | 16.1 | 3.5 | 60.0 | 20.4 |
| 1965 | 100.0 | 16.1 | 3.7 | 61.9 | 18.3 |
| 1966 | 100.0 | 17.7 | 4.0 | 61.5 | 16.8 |
| 1967 | 100.0 | 21.6 | 5.0 | 60.2 | 13.4 |
| | | Exports | | | |
| 1957 | 100.0 | 11.6 | 22.3 | 24.5 | 41.6 |
| 1958 | 100.0 | 8.8 | 21.4 | 30.0 | 39.8 |
| 1959 | 100.0 | 7.7 | 18.1 | 34.7 | 39.5 |
| 1960 | 100 0 | 9.8 | 20.4 | 32.8 | 37.0 |
| 1961 | 100.0 | 10.7 | 20.5 | 31.6 | 37.2 |
| 1962 | 100.0 | 11.1 | 21.0 | 30.5 | 37.4 |
| 1963 | 100.0 | 7.6 | 19.6 | 29.7 | 43.1 |
| 1964 | 100.0 | 7.0 | 22.7 | 34.7 | 35.6 |
| 1965 | 100.0 | 8.3 | 21.1 | 33.9 | 36.7 |
| 1966 | 100.0 | 7.9 | 21.1 | 35.5 | 35.5 |
| 1967 | 100.0 | 6.8 | 22.2 | 35.9 | 35.1 |

# 11. Tentative outlines of a new world economic concept

JÓZSEF BOGNÁR

Just occasionally it is worthwhile making an approach to such a fundamental human activity as the economy from the most simple angle. By
most simple we mean the definition of this activity and the objectives and
meaning of the processes which accompany it. Hundreds of millions of
people take part in this activity, but their participation takes place within
a certain framework and through different institutions and organizations.
Without such a framework and such organizations its fundamental objectives could clearly not be achieved. The experience of history has shown
that these structures and institutions – at once the expression and the
vehicle of certain human interests and endeavours, whether collective or
particular – follow their own dynamic laws, and as a result directly pursue
particular objectives; objectives which are not completely consonant with
the fundamental objectives of the economy, or, indeed, may even contradict
them. The conflict between the fundamental human objectives and the
particular institutional objectives tends to become acute

(*a*) the less elastic and the more bureaucratic the institution in question,
and

(*b*) the greater the change taking place in society, in international life,
and in the economy itself (for instance, the technological revolution).

In the world of rational political and economic activities, only to appre-
hend it is not sufficient; in order to achieve the fundamental objectives,
the framework, the institutions, the mechanism of the economy must also
change, even though this meets with opposition from the institutions concerned. The only purpose of the economy, i.e. the world economy in the
full sense of the term, is to meet the needs of humanity on a rising standard
of living, and thereby encourage the full development of human faculties.

If the world economy is viewed from this angle, we must reach the conclusion that the means of production which are utilized and the capacities
which are available are still not sufficient to meet the demands of the
world's population. And since the population of the world has grown
faster than production – particularly agricultural production in the last ten
years – per capita consumption has fallen.

Since the world economy works through the framework and within the

limits of different national economies, it follows that its inadequate operation does not affect the whole population on the globe equally, since in one
part of the world, where capital and scientific knowledge are plentiful, an
ever-decreasing number of people are able to produce the goods needed
to meet the high demands of the population, while in the other the scarcity
of both make it impossible to expand economic growth. This growing
contrast has become particularly dangerous in the present age, when the
political history of mankind is beginning to develop along the same lines,
communications are developing at a tremendous rate and the demographic
explosion daily widens the gulf between the distribution of modern means
of production throughout the world and the distribution of its population.
Another factor to be taken into account is the rapid growth in the number
of nations, i.e. in national economies: of the one hundred and twenty independent nations in existence more than one hundred have a population
below fifteen million.

It is therefore quite natural that mankind is again compelled to adjust
the framework and economic institutions which embody the economy, in
order to meet its fundamental objectives.

International economic relations designed to promote the maximum
growth of the world economy as a whole – and the single national economies within it – have passed through three characteristic phases of development in this century.

It was essentially the system of free trade that was dominant in the first
phase up to the time of the world crisis in 1929, a phase in which the
structure of the economy invariably subserved the stronger partner. During
the twenty or thirty years following the crisis, the second phase developed,
when the war and acute international tensions prompted the national
economies to depend far more on the domestic market, and consequently
on a policy of bilateral agreements and protection. This policy was not only
dominant in the socialist countries, where the dynamic conception of
protection for nascent industries had been adopted, but in the advanced
capitalist countries as well, since most (about 70 per cent) of the imports of raw
materials and agricultural products were subject to customs duty, to quotas,
and high taxes. (The duties levied on raw materials exported from the developing countries – with the exception of crude oil – amounted to $800 million
a year at that time, whereas taxes reached the sum of $2,200 million.)

In the third stage of development the outline of new forms of international economic co-operation began to emerge, such as attempts to achieve
regional blocs, and experiments in association, and the new forms have
quite clearly produced considerable results.

*József Bognár*

Generally speaking, the countries taking part in some form of association have evolved certain economic and trade rules for

(*a*) the development of economic ties between the member states,

(*b*) the promotion of the rapid growth of the national economies,

(*c*) the stake one nation has in the economic advancement of the others.

Regionally uniform trading techniques clearly meant not only preferences for the member states, but also disadvantages for trading partners outside the association. As a result the internal increase of trade within the association reached a point where it became an obstacle to the expansion of trade with countries outside it.

But all the various systems have so far proved unable to solve the four basic problems of the world economy today. They are as follows:

(1) The reduction and gradual liquidation of the gulf between the economically underdeveloped countries and the other parts of the world.

(2) The ideological confrontation and economic competition resulting from the coexistence of the capitalist and socialist systems.

(3) The growing economic polarization among the advanced capitalist countries, in particular between the United States on the one hand and Western Europe on the other – as a consequence of which the West-European economy is being downgraded and is acquiring a reproducing character.

(4) Owing to the rapid growth in the number of national economies, the world economic mechanism built on principles of international competition and private enterprise is becoming increasingly unsuitable as a means of securing a comparatively balanced development of the world economy and of promoting the rational utilization of the means of production and productive capacities.

It is worth analysing these four problems in greater detail.

(1) No less than 89 per cent of the world's income, 88 per cent of the gold and currency reserves, and 94 per cent of steel production are concentrated in thirty countries representing 29 per cent of the world population at the present time, a figure that will have dropped to 19 per cent in the year A.D. 2000.

60.6 per cent of the cereal production of the world, including rice and maize, 68.6 per cent of its meat production and 79.3 per cent of its protein production, are concentrated in the same thirty countries.

There is an even wider divergence in the long-range factors of economic growth, since no less than about 95 per cent of the world's scientific research capacity is to be found in the advanced countries.

It is therefore quite evident that with such a distribution of intellectual and material resources, i.e. the factors affecting economic growth, the difference between the industrially advanced and the economically under-developed countries has not diminished but increased during the last ten years.

Per capita national income in the developing countries has fallen since 1958. Their share in world exports and imports has been substantially reduced. The developing countries have found it necessary to increase imports of agricultural staple products. The terms of trade have also taken an unfavourable turn for the developing countries (a deterioration of 28 per cent between 1950 and 1962).

After comparing import needs and export possibilities, on the assumption of a population growth of 2.3 per cent a year, the Geneva World Trade Conference came to the conclusion that in 1970 the annual deficit in the balance of payments of the developing countries will amount to as much as $20,000 million.

When assessing the various developments to be anticipated it becomes fairly evident that the long-range trends of economic growth are making for polarization, and the present forms of international trade – the actual world market mechanism – only go to increase the differences. The mere process of exchange, i.e. the exchange of goods on the basis of mutual advantages and equality, is insufficient to correct the uneven distribution of the production factors. One reason is that the process of exchange is the result of other processes which precede it. The other reason is that not only the commodities themselves are meeting in competition on the market, but the economic powers as well, whose influence inside and outside the market obviously has a great effect upon the modalities of the exchange. In recent decades the advanced capitalist world has seen the development of precisely those economic super-powers which have been able to turn the processes affecting the conditions of exchange to their own advantage.

The widening gulf between the industrialized and the economically underdeveloped countries must consequently be bridged by such econ-omico-political measures as make it possible

(*a*) to transfer a part of the world income to the developing countries,

(*b*) to achieve the industrial division of labour in terms of an overall comprehensive plan,

(*c*) to undertake and co-ordinate the solution of certain basic economic problems (for instance, the food and agricultural problems of the economic-ally underdeveloped countries, mainly Asia) through action on a world scale.

These comprehensive economico-political measures could be carried out partly through the market mechanism, by correcting it in a definite direc-tion, and partly by other means.

*József Bognár*

A part of the national incomes could be redistributed, for instance, by adjusting the prices of raw materials. It is common knowledge that the principle of demand and supply results in low incomes for the producers of primary products. According to the economico-political practice adopted today in the advanced countries, the proceeds from the centres of growth are transferred to agriculture by taking steps to see that the income of the producers should not differ essentially from the income of workers in the growth industries. The chief agency of the transfer mechanism is the *price policy*. Prices – of raw materials as well – ought to be high enough to effect such a transfer without allowing excessive high prices to lead to over-production (barter agreements) or to the substitution of synthetic for raw materials.

Adjustment of the prices of raw materials is not in itself enough, since the factors of growth still remain scarce. The major part of the transfer of income must therefore be carried out in some other manner.

A new division of labour carried out as part of a comprehensive design would demand the transfer of certain industrial activities to the economically underdeveloped countries. The governments of the advanced countries would have to commit themselves to the purchase of a certain amount of industrial goods. These agreements could be negotiated through the market if the market is understood, as at present, to mean the short- and long-term agreements of legally independent but economically interrelated and interdependent enterprises.

A settlement of the food problem demands a whole series of planned, co-ordinated and interdependent agreements. This type of activity should be planned and co-ordinated by international organizations, such as the UN, FAO and UNCTAD, but in order to increase the complex possibilities of giving aid and assistance they will have to accept all offers that can be converted into aid in some form or other.

(2) The simultaneous existence of capitalist and socialist systems in the world involves both ideological confrontation and economic competition. In the course of this confrontation each system exerts every effort to convince the world of its superiority, i.e. of its capacity to solve the problems which have developed in the course of historical development, in a more efficient, more equitable and more modern manner. The functional capacity of a social-economic system cannot be separated from the results it achieves in the economic field, i.e. from its rising productivity, technological development, the growth rate of the national income and an equitable system of distribution. Socialism – the newer social-economic system – makes every effort to demonstrate that it is capable of meeting the high-

level needs of the population without the oppression or economic exploitation of other peoples in the course of its rapid economic advancement. This economic competition, however, shows itself in the first place in an intensified drive in the domestic economy, but does not necessarily extend to the field of international trade.

Some of the socialist countries of Europe have reached the state where the increase of exports takes precedence in the economy over the substitution of imports through the development of domestic production. Western sources usually describe it as a 'shortcoming' of the planned economies that their policy of planned priorities in development acts as an obstacle to imports.

This 'shortcoming' is connected in the first place not with the volume but with the type of import. Since the socialist countries of Europe are very anxious to import specialized plant and equipment, this 'shortcoming' – as far as the Western desire to export is concerned – is in fact an advantage. The planned economy does not set out to create an indiscriminate export industry in conflict with the economic efforts of other countries, and which would compel their own governments to market them abroad at any price. Obviously, once the new economic mechanism has been introduced, the socialist countries will be anxious to create favourable conditions for export and import with a due regard to such factors as prices, costs and trade structure. It must be taken for granted that after the introduction of the new economic mechanism, increased efforts will be made to encourage the co-ordination of East–West trading procedures and techniques, efforts that began in 1959 with the European Economic Council and have continued since 1963 with the *Ad Hoc* Group.

There is not much point in discussing earlier East–West problems, since an entirely new situation has developed in both international politics and world trade, though I cannot refrain from pointing out that Mr Gunnar Alder-Karlsson (Stockholm) gave a remarkable lecture on this question at the 5th Conference of ESTO (*Institut für Europäische Studien*) that is still well worth reading. What I want to stress is that East–West economic co-operation is part of larger world processes, and its significance and future prospects cannot be adequately assessed without the analysis of these processes. I shall consequently examine the question of East–West co-operation only after describing the other factors which determine the character of the world economy today.

(3) A growing number of economic and scientific developments show that Western Europe can no longer keep pace with the United States in four of their growth industries, each of them with multiplying effects in

terms of technology. These are the machine industry, the chemical industry, electronics and spacecraft development. With regard to the machine industry, the manufacture of automatic machinery and equipment has lately made great advances in the United States; European enterprises buy most of their computers from the United States, and the annual addition to the number of digital computers in the States is larger than the whole stock of digital computers in the three economically strongest countries of Western Europe.

There is a concentration of European enterprises in the chemical industry and important results have been achieved. On the other hand new investment in America is largely centred in the chemical industry.

The strongest sector of the American chemical industry is to be found in the sector dealing with the 'revolution in materials' connected with space research. This revolution in materials not only involves the introduction of new synthetic materials (the first, *corfam*, is expected to lead to substantial changes), but extends to other fields as well. Some believe that polymers are due to become the 'fundamental structural material' of our civilization. In pharmacology, for instance, there is the manufacture of drugs based on molecular biological processes. Here American industry has made an excellent start, which it is exploiting with growing success by assigning large material and intellectual resources to scientific research in this field.

In the electronics industry American superiority is undisputed; in 1964 the United States manufactured 81.9 per cent of the electronic equipment of the world. (The rest is distributed as follows: Great Britain 6 per cent, France 5.1 per cent, the German Federal Republic 4.2 per cent, and Japan 2.8 per cent.)

American superiority is in fact even greater than these figures suggest, since a large part of the electronic equipment manufactured in the West-European countries is produced by American-affiliated firms.

The economic and technical importance of space research can be seen in the multiplication and proliferation of its effects. The demands of space research have created industries for the manufacture of specific equipment. New lines of specialization, new services and instrumentation have given an impetus to the revolution in materials and produced new plant and new complex systems of scientific research. Space research underlies the telecommunication systems based on artificial satellites, which foreshadow the age of 'global telecommunication'.

The cost of the space industry and space research is known to be so high that no country can afford it except the Soviet Union. (In Western Europe

France has been the only country to build a satellite of her own and the carrier rocket which launched it. The latest French satellite has been launched with an American-made rocket.)

But the differences in the four strongest growth industries only reflect the present relative economic strength. The gap in scientific-technological research indicates that the disparity between Western Europe and the United States will steadily increase. It is recognized that the scientific-technological revolution of our days is the most decisive factor in economic progress and rapid technological development. A very close interaction exists between scientific research and economic power, since an economically stronger country can allocate greater intellectual and material resources to scientific research, while the speedy application of scientific inventions yields a greater profit for the economic enterprises.

According to reliable figures per capita scientific expenditure in the U.S.A. is about $96–98; in the countries of the Common Market it scarcely amounts to $17. True, the very low figure in Italy is the main cause of this low average; the average in France is $27, in West Germany $21. Great Britain is superior to the countries of the Six in this respect; per capita scientific expenditure in the United Kingdom is $33. The per capita average, however, does not give us the full picture: the size of the absolute sums invested exerts its own influence. The United States, for instance, spends fourteen times more on scientific research than France, whose population is a quarter of that of the United States. European research, moreover, is not so productive as American research. A number of reasons have been adduced; some say that European science has not been able effectively to weld together inductive (Baconian) and deductive (Cartesian) ways of scientific thinking; others, again, say that in Europe the scientific centres – for traditional reasons – are located at some distance from the economic centres. Expenditure on the development of discoveries consequently takes a larger share in U.S. research expenditure as a whole – 75 per cent – than the sum spent directly on technical development in Europe. (In France, for instance, this figure is 60 per cent.)

In considering the contrary directions American and West-European scientific developments are taking, the brain drain must also be taken into account. There is some alarm that it may turn into intellectual suicide, like the anti-Semitism of Hitler Germany.

According to reliable data, the past ten years have seen the emigration of some 85 thousand highly qualified research workers, young scientists or technological experts from Western Europe to the United States.

Western Europe is already aware of the danger threatening the economy, and society in general, through the backwardness of scientific research, and various plans have been put forward to improve the situation. The idea of a scientific Marshall Plan and the establishment of a West European Technical Development Community have been suggested by leading Italian and British politicians. The United States, working in a parallel direction, has been evolving plans to perpetuate American technical and scientific supremacy. Late in 1966 Professor Kindleberger spoke in Paris of schemes by which research and economic centres would develop new products, to be exported in large quantities, in the first place; their manufacture would at a later stage be turned over to the 'reproducing countries', and the products then imported, while the country with the original research and economic centres would continue to invent and manufacture newer and even more modern products and repeat the pattern.

I shall return to the disparity between the United States and Western Europe later.

(4) The world market mechanism based on competition between nations and enterprises is becoming increasingly incapable of solving basic questions of the world economy. The present world market mechanism influences the distribution of incomes and means of production to the benefit of the economically stronger partner. Owing to the rapidly growing number of national economies, the correct decisions made on the macro-economic level may not always make complete sense on the continental or world level. It is clear that for a long time to come national economies will constitute the framework and foundation of the economic activities of mankind. The last hundred and fifty years have clearly demonstrated that a people will reject the most advanced economic system if it is imposed at the price of its independence, or by outraging its national feelings. Economic integration, or the international planning and co-ordination of certain basic questions, would seem to be in contradiction to the existence and continuation of national economies. It would, however, be a mistake to solve this contradiction with the statement that the new conditions and requirements are the only needs to be considered, and that the interests, aims and emotions of the people as such, of the national entities, can be ignored. Neither human societies nor the world economy can be pro-grammed in abstraction, and the interests, conditions and relationships expressed by national economies are certainly no less real than those now in the making and coming to maturity as a consequence of the scientific-technical revolution and the demographic explosion.

From the mechanism of free competition it logically follows that leading enterprises vie for priority, and concentrate all their efforts on outdistancing the others. As a result they encourage scientific research, allocate large sums of money for technical development, make large capital investments, make a more various and concentrated use of raw materials, press forward with new inventions, modernize their sales departments, etc. This competition between enterprises takes place in a world economy full of striking contradictions in the distribution of the means of production, and as a result it makes the rich richer and the poor poorer. Such a market mechanism may become particularly dangerous in a period when all reasonable human, political and economic considerations require the differences between the rich and the poor to be reduced.

I shall now try to outline the international economic policy and world market mechanism which might best solve these basic problems of the world economy or – to be more correct – bring them closer to solution. It is no accident that I refer to international economic policy in the first place and the world market mechanism only in the second place. What I mean here by economic policy is that highly *conscious* decisions are essential if we want to change the present situation. In theory conscious decisions can be made *irrespective* of the present market mechanism, yet experience has shown that economic policy is ineffective unless rational decisions are backed by a mechanism which expresses the interests and reflects the internal movements of the economy. If politics and this mechanism are kept separate, the decision-making centres may become alienated from the economy, and this leads to bureaucracy. The comparative co-ordination of politics and the market mechanism, on the other hand, not only prevents the development of powerful centres of bureaucracy but also encourages enterprises directly concerned to carry out their own purposes to promote indirectly general economico-political purposes. The economic mechanism required in the present situation should stimulate the economically weaker countries to higher productivity and the advanced ones to a more equitable distribution of wealth. Otherwise it is impossible to conceive a more realistic distribution of the means of production, one more in keeping with the distribution of the population. In the present situation, nevertheless, the mechanism cannot be corrected without the consent of all the participants. The point is that on the international level there are no political or economic centres capable of introducing and operating a new mechanism. Hence the solution of economic problems cannot be separated from the fact that the majority of the national economies operate under conditions of capitalist ownership and follow a distribution system based on these conditions.

In order to reduce the tremendous disparity in the distribution of the means of production and accelerate the growth of the underdeveloped economies, it is consequently necessary to make use of a system which combines more than one method, that is, new tendencies must be encouraged partly by improving the existing mechanism, and partly independently of it. The redistribution of part of the national income might, for instance, be also brought about by raising the price of raw materials, i.e. by a price policy. While negotiations on co-ordinated activities by the international organizations could clear the ground for the new industrial division of labour, the goods themselves can only be exchanged through normal market transactions.

Only international organizations, with the consent of all concerned, are in a position to direct advanced countries to transfer a share of their national income, determined by certain criteria, to the underdeveloped countries. Such criteria might be, for instance, the volume of national income, its per capita value, or the strength of economic ties with the developing countries.

Large-scale activities, as, for instance, increased agricultural production in the Asian countries, can only be planned, organized and co-ordinated on an international basis, i.e. irrespective of the world market mechanism. I consider that the problems of Asia are of primary and decisive importance in this connection, since it holds more than half of the world's population (53 per cent today), its cultivable areas are overpopulated, and yields can no longer be improved by increasing human labour. The monocultures that have developed to maintain the dense population (rice, for instance) have, as everyone knows, exhausted the soil, and the number of work days employed in cultivating one hectare is extremely high.

The great international organizations, therefore, must play a decisive part in assisting the underdeveloped countries. The international organizations of today are undoubtedly far from satisfying requirements. It may, however, be hoped that a reasonable evaluation of the new conditions and requirements, and the impetus provided by the difficulties and contradictions encountered, will gradually lead to the recognition that the world, interdependent and interconnected as it is, wants strong and efficient international organizations.

If we want to prevent the growing polarization between Western Europe and the United States of America, co-operation between the countries of Europe must be based and developed on new foundations. Western Europe and East Europe enjoy different social systems, but the co-operation between these countries and their economic organizations is not an ideological problem but a question of common interests. Some of these common interests spring from natural or historical causes, others derive from the fact that the countries of Western Europe do not want to fall behind the U.S.A., and the socialist countries are anxious to draw level with it. The division of Europe which has resulted in a series of wars over the past hundred years, and came to an unhappy climax in the Cold War, has greatly contributed to weaken the economic, political, scientific and demo_graphic position of the continent.

The common interests which link these countries may create a foundation for economic co-operation, but cannot substitute for it. The shortage of capital in Europe (as compared with the U.S.A.) could be reduced and eased by a co-ordinated, complementary investment policy. A complementary system of industrial development would result in considerable capital savings for both parties, and the capital thus saved could be usefully invested in other fields. Scientific shortages could not only be lessened but even eliminated by common East–West research and co-operation. According to reliable figures the number of scientists in the Soviet Union is around 700 thousand. (In the U.S.A. the figure is about 800 thousand.) Many state-financed and well organized scientific institutions exist in the other socialist countries of Europe. Research in the socialist countries of Europe shares, of course, the general weakness of European science as compared with American, that is, too much theoretical research and relatively few practical results. In other words, the productivity of science is lower than in the United States. But serious efforts are being made to improve the situation, and the new economic mechanism encourages a direct interest in the practical application of theoretical scientific achievements.

The Soviet Prime Minister, Mr Kosygin, made a series of suggestions to Great Britain concerning the expansion of scientific co-operation among the countries of Europe. France and the Soviet Union are beginning a scientific co-operation from which – to quote the official French view – 'France benefits from the achievements of Soviet research (space research, telecommunication, physics of high-power particles), and the Soviet Union directly profits from certain achievements of the western world.' 'The Soviet Union', writes *Le Progrès Scientifique*, the official review of French research institutions 'can thus play a part in the western economic system, particularly in the leading technological industries which are of such great significance for the future'.

In addition to the policy of developing industries which complement one another, co-operation between industrial enterprises could help to promote the expansion of European markets. In most socialist countries the economic reform gives industrial enterprises authority to enter into agreements with foreign enterprises. By industrial co-operation I mean a systematic technical and economic association and connections between two production units before or after the finished production of the goods, as, for instance, the joint production and the marketing of products, co-operation on third markets, the sale and purchase of patents, the exchange of information, business on commission, the provision of the spare parts needed in domestic manufacture in exchange for goods of a similar nature, etc. Industrial co-operation is moreover the best way of maintaining the balance of payments and is also a reliable means of improving the export structure.

A common basis of understanding is necessary between capitalist firms and socialist enterprises, the latter enjoying great independence as a result of the economic reform, if co-operation between them is to increase.

East–West economic co-operation is likely to reveal many opportunities of increasing the capacity of the advanced world to give aid and assistance to the developing countries. This capacity cannot of course be equated with either the amount of surplus or available capital or the general characteristics of an advanced economy. Co-operation on a multilateral and wide-scale basis will enable the capital-absorbing capacity of the developing world to be increased through regular and complex measures.

When considering likely developments and the future of the world economy, the economic problems of the United States must be carefully studied. The U.S.A. possesses huge economic resources and is developing technologically at a tremendous pace. In this respect we face a new situation: technological development is reaching the point where the needs of the population can be supplied by the work of far fewer people than formerly. This fact may lead to great social and racial tensions if governments are unable to improve the system of the internal distribution of wealth. (The distribution principle of the capitalist system is based on private property and marginal productivity; if 'too many' people consequently wish to participate in the work, the margin of productivity is reduced to zero, i.e. the need to introduce new principles of distribution arises.) If the internal system of distribution fails to improve, then an expansive, or in a certain sense, an aggressive, international economic and trade policy develops. The present situation is, naturally, different from what it was in the nineteenth century; overt colonization is not possible. Yet the extensive export of capital, and interests all over the world, result in an aggressive international policy, because these American capital investments need protection. And this protection is preventive in character, supporting and helping to power governments which, on account of their political views, can be relied upon to secure the safety of American interests. When these governments come into conflict with the masses, i.e. with various progressive movements, they promptly turn to the U.S. government for help, thus involving them in unaccountable complications.

There is no need to go further into these processes and all their consequences, I only wish to stress the grave dangers which already exist and are increasingly impending, as a result of these accelerated developments in technology.

Economic power can undoubtedly be employed in very different ways, as the past and the present have shown; to start wars, to threaten the economic independence of other nations, or destroy it. (We have only to recall super-enterprises to be seen in some of the economically underdeveloped African countries emerging from the tribal stage of development.)

The economic resources of mankind are today still insufficient to meet all needs of the world population. It follows that the world urgently needs the tremendous economic and scientific resources of the United States of America. These huge energies must be so directed as to promote economic development on an international scale, the independence of the nations of the world, and co-operation between partners with equal rights.

I should like to emphasize that both East–West co-operation and the giving of aid and assistance to the developing countries offer vast opportunities to the American economy. American society, and in particular the progressive forces, willing to be objective, and following the fighting traditions of freedom in American history, must, however, face a new situation. If in addition to increasing their productivity they are incapable of making the system of distribution more effective, and capital continues to expand by present-day methods, then the world – and the United States in it – will have to face very serious dangers. They stem from economic facts, but their consequences will make themselves felt beyond the economic field, in political and even in strategic planning. If a very rich country is incapable of uniting the high productivity of labour with an efficient system of distribution, then peace, the economically less developed countries, and nations fighting for their rights, are all seriously threatened.

The ideas I have been outlining are rational in character. But is mankind today capable of acting rationally amidst so many different interests and aims? 'Rational' of course is to be understood in the widest possible sense of the word, since millions of examples daily prove that enterprises and national economies are indeed capable of acting rationally *from their own point of view*. But what we want to know, what we are discussing, is whether or not these activities – which in their own spheres of the micro- and the macroeconomy are rational – are to be regarded as rational from the point of view of mankind or the world economy as a whole.

One might sum up the answer by saying that these activities may well come to be rational, within certain limits, if the world market mechanism is improved in conformity with changed requirements, and with due regard to the interests deriving from them; if by well-considered economico-political provisions those who make up the world market come to be interested in one another's economic development, and if we are able to set up international centres of action (not, for the time being, political or economic centres) to plan, organize and co-ordinate activities of basic importance for mankind.

The endorsement of a rational concept of the world economy by all participants requires the power capable of such action, and presupposes partners contributing to them through intellectual conviction. Only through the alliance of these two elements can the forces which oppose the changes on grounds of personal interests be overcome.

The struggle for a new world economic concept, therefore, must be fought not only economically but also politically. The great bulk of economic power is concentrated in the hands of those who oppose change, and only a minority of them is convinced of its inevitability.

Political forces, on the other hand, are more satisfactorily divided; those standing for progress constitute the majority. Political activities of course cannot be divorced from the existing economic situation, but they can precede it by a few steps.

Only the unity of the progressive political forces therefore, and their activities – always taking the position of powers in the world into account – can bring a new world economic concept into operation. If the new ideas fail to strike root and the present world economic mechanism stiffens into rigidity, then human civilization is menaced with disaster in the coming years.

# Index

agreements, clearing, 68
  on economic co-operation, 11, 12, 17, 22, 24
  specialization and co-operation, 117, 126
agriculture, 35, 39, 73, 115, 139, 148–9
  Common market in, 36
  exports of produce, 51, 112, 121, 123, 125–7, 140, 141
  history of, 3, 4, 5, 8, 19, 20
  machines, 23
  prices, 181, 183
Albania, 8, 12
aluminium, 11, 22, 183, 189, 192
Argentina, 55
Asia, 118, 212
'assortment exchange', 135–6
Austria, 2, 3, 4, 5, 6, 8, 52, 84, 121
autarky, 42, 66, 90, 111, 133–50
  consequences of, 20–2, 57
  history of, 4, 5–6, 8, 14, 17–18, 19, 25
'average difference', 139
'average output key', 172–4

balance of payments, clearing, 24
  equilibrium, 45–60, 108, 167–9, 175, 195
balance of trade, 48–9, 132
balances, compensation of, 63–4
Balassa, B., 32
Balkan countries, 3, 5, 10, 11
Bank, Common, of CMEA, 25
Bank, Hungarian General Credit, 9
Bank for International Economic Co-operation, 65, 75–6, 89, 95–6, 97
barley, 187
basic manufactures, 50, 53
bauxite, 11, 183, 189, 192
beef and beef cattle, 179, 187–90 *passim*, 193
beer, 188
Belgium, 3, 30, 133–50
beverages and tobacco, 50, 53
bilateral agreements, 17, 22, 23, 24, 28
  effects of, 49–50
bilateral clearing systems, 66–74, 107
bilateral system of trading and payments, 61–101, 105
  effects of, 62–6
bitumen, 189, 193
Bohemia, 2, 5
'brain drain', 209
'buffer mechanism' in Hungary, 167–8

bulbs, 188
Bulgaria, foreign trade of, 114–31
  history of, 8–24 *passim*
butter, 190, 193

cacao beans, 187, 188
Canada, 30
capital, flow of, 62
  formation of, 146–9, 213
  intensity, 142–4, 148–9
  transfer of, 35
capitalist, economic theory, viii–ix
  market prices, 185–90, 191, 192, 193–4, 198–201
  society, 35, 38–9, 58, 204, 206
cartel policy, 36
cellulose, 180, 186, 191
cereals, 184, 187, 188
change, technical, 45–60
cheese, 193
chemicals, exports of, 22, 24, 50, 52, 114, 122, 123, 125–7
  imports of, 53
  prices of, 180, 183
  processing of, 7, 208–10
China, 119
class-conflict, 29
clearing, bilateral, 67–74
  central, 24, 63–4
clothing industry, 52, 139, 140, 141, 188, 192, 194
CMEA, *see* Council of Mutual Economic Aid
coal and coke, 18–19, 24, 140, 180, 181, 183, 191
coal mining, 141
coffee, 183, 187, 188
cold war, 9, 15, 31
collaboration, economic, 34, 42, 61, 107, 108, 203–4
  history, 11–24
Comecon, *see* Council of Mutual Economic Aid
commerce, 11
Committee, Polish–Czechoslovak Economic, 11
commodity balance equation, 155
commodity pattern of exports, 52, 102, 105, 122–7
commodity relations in socialist countries, 61, 98

# Index

218

# Index

multilateral agreements, 24, 28
  clearing, 107
  system of trading and payments, 61–101
multiplier effects of trade on production, 136
Myrdal, Professor Gunnar, 31,

National Bank of Hungary, 175, 177
national income, 20, 37, 102, 104, 114, 133–4,
  168, 206
  of Hungary, 8
nationalism, 1, 2, 43
NATO, 31
Netherlands, 52, 133–50
nitrogen fertilizers, 193

Office, Central Planning, of CMEA, 25
Office, Planning, of Hungary, 151
oil, prices, 180, 181, 183, 189, 191, 192, 193
  supplies, 23, 24–5, 140
oils, animal and vegetable, 50, 53, 187
optimization, of trade, 152–5, 161
oranges, 187
output, total, 136–7

paper industry, 23
parity, of purchasing power, 169–70
payments system, of CMEA countries, 61–100
petroleum, 141
pharmaceuticals, 52, 188, 192, 193
Pinder John, 34, 36
plans, economic, ix, x, xi, 13, 18–22, 25–6
  in Common Market, 39–40
  co-ordination of, 22, 31, 32
  export, 113–31
  in foreign trade, 61, 71, 73, 77–101 *passim*
  joint, between Czechoslovakia and Poland,
    11
  problems of, 151–2
  reform of, 129
  results of, 47, 51
plastics industry, 35
Poland, export performance of, 114–31
  history of, 4–25 *passim*
policy, international economic, 211
population of world, 202–3
pork, 187, 189, 190
poultry, 189, 190, 193
price, agreements, 81–2, 91
  domestic, 70, 71, 78, 90, 101
  in foreign trade, 68, 73–7 *passim*, 78, 90,
    101–12, 128, 167–77, 178–201
  'own price basis', 101, 104
  regulators of, 160–1
'priority', in economic planning, 51–2, 56, 57
production, integration, 35, 36, 42
  pattern in Hungary, 51, 99, 138
  relations in socialist countries, 61
profits, equation for, 157

motive, 70, 72, 152, 168
  sharing, 158–9, 162–3
programming, in economic planning, 152–5
  limitations of, 154–5
projection, comparative, of development, 113
protectionism, 2–3, 33, 46–7, 66, 90, 203

quota systems, 68–73 *passim*, 78–81, 88, 91

railway rolling stock, 23
rate of exchange, 71, 77, 78, 89, 90, 92, 166–72
  *passim*
  marginal, 173–4
rate of interest, 54
raw hides, 179–92 *passim*
raw materials and semi-finished goods, classification of, 195
  history of, 18, 20, 21, 23, 24
  prices of, 178–95 *passim*, 197–201, 206
  supplies of, 51, 52, 73, 80, 85–6, 91, 97, 112,
    114–15, 116, 123, 124, 125–7
redistribution of national resources, 37, 38–9,
  42, 206
reform of Hungarian economy (1968), xi,
  45–60, 155
regulators, economic, 155–61
restrictions, quantitative, 161
Reuter price index, 180, 182
Rome, Treaty of, 30, 36n, 39
rubber, 180, 181, 186
Rueff, Professor, 46
Rumania, economic performance of, 114–31
  history of, 7, 8, 10, 12, 18, 19, 22

saving, 8, 10, 18, 19–20
Scandinavian countries, 10
scientific research and technology, 209–10,
  213, 214–16
sector pattern of production, 134–42
sectoral exchange, 135–6
servicing of exports, 129–30
socialist economic theory, viii–ix
socialist states, 10, 35, 38–9, 58, 204, 206
  trade of Hungary with, 184–5, 191, 192,
    193–4, 198–201
'soft' currencies, 64–5
sovereignty, economic, 34
  political, 1, 34, 37, 38–9, 40
  *see also* monocentrism
Soviet Union, 70, 76n, 90–2, 93–4, 213
  export performance of, 114–31
  foreign trade in, ix–x
  history of, 4, 9, 10, 16, 17, 19, 24, 25
  planning in, ix, x
spacecraft, 208–9
specialization of production, 23, 62
stability of prices, 46
Stalin J. xi, 14, 15